PENGUIN BOO

THE FIFTH DO

T0005683

Richard A. Clarke served as a key advisor on intelligence and counter-terrorism in the administrations of presidents Ronald Reagan, George H. W. Bush, and Bill Clinton. In 1998, President Clinton appointed him as the National Coordinator for Security, Infrastructure Protection, and Counter-terrorism for the U.S. National Security Council. Since leaving the public sector in 2003, Clarke has taught at the John F. Kennedy School of Government at Harvard University and consulted for ABC News on political and security issues. He now chairs the board of governors of the Middle East Institute. He is the author of seven books, both fiction and nonfiction, including the #1 *New York Times* bestseller *Against All Enemies: Inside America's War on Terror.*

Robert K. Knake is a senior fellow at the Council on Foreign Relations, a senior research scientist at Northeastern University, and an adviser to start-ups, investment firms, and Fortune 500 companies. Knake served from 2011–2015 in the Obama White House as director for cybersecurity policy at the National Security Council. He is the coauthor (with Clarke) of the *New York Times* bestseller *Cyber War.*

⠿⠿⠿ THE ⠿⠿⠿
FIFTH
DOMAIN

Defending Our Country,

Our Companies, and Ourselves

in the Age of Cyber Threats

RICHARD A. CLARKE
and ROBERT K. KNAKE

Penguin Books

PENGUIN BOOKS
An imprint of Penguin Random House LLC
penguinrandomhouse.com

First published in the United States of America by Penguin Press, an imprint of
Penguin Random House LLC, 2019
Published in Penguin Books 2020

ISBN 9780525561989 (paperback)

THE LIBRARY OF CONGRESS HAS CATALOGED THE HARDCOVER EDITION AS FOLLOWS:
Names: Clarke, Richard A. (Richard Alan), 1951– author. |
    Knake, Robert K., author.
Title: The Fifth Domain: Defending Our Country, Our Companies, and Ourselves
    in the Age of Cyber Threats / Richard A. Clarke and Robert K. Knake.
Description: New York: Penguin Press, 2019. | Includes bibliographical
    references and index.
Identifiers: LCCN 2019012065 (print) | LCCN 2019016384 (ebook) |
    ISBN 9780525561972 (ebook) | ISBN 9780525561965 (hardcover)
Subjects: LCSH: Cyberterrorism—United States. | Computer security—
    United States. | Computer networks—Security measures—United States. |
    Corporations—Security measures—United States. | National security—
    United States.
Classification: LCC HV6773.2 (ebook) | LCC HV6773.2 .C585 2019 (print) |
    DDC 363.325—dc23
LC record available at https://lccn.loc.gov/2019012065

Printed in the United States of America

Book design by Daniel Lagin

To the late Michael A. Sheehan:
Soldier, Diplomat, Patriot, Iconoclast, Friend

—RICHARD A. CLARKE

To my son, William, whose deep interest in the causes of war
is driven by his even deeper desire for peace.

—ROBERT K. KNAKE

Contents

....

:::::::::::::::: **PART I** ::::::::::::::::

THE TWENTY-YEAR WAR

Chapter 1

....

THE BACK OF THE BEAST

The future is already here; it's just not very evenly distributed.

—WILLIAM GIBSON

Sitting in the back of the Beast, the armored vehicle custom made for the President of the United States, Bill Clinton wanted to talk about his cousin from Hope, Arkansas. He didn't want to talk about the major speech he was about to give at the National Academy of Sciences. It was January 1999, and Clinton had just proposed budget initiatives to combat emerging threats, including those in the cyber domain. Few people then saw cyber threats as a major problem. But he did. Dick Clarke sat next to him with a PowerPoint deck and an annotated version of the speech, but the President was channeling his Bubba persona, telling a story about Arkansas, and not to be stopped.

When the Beast pulled into the underground parking at the academy, Clinton finally turned to the business at hand. "I read the speech. It's okay." That meant it wasn't.

"But really, isn't what we want to say something like this: Throughout history there is a competition between offensive and defensive technologies and a gap between their development. A guy in a cave carves a rock and attaches it to a stick and creates a spear, and then someone needs to defend against that, so they get some animal hides and make a shield. Later on, people defend towns with walls and then some guy invents battering rams and catapults. But there is time between when an offensive weapon is created and when the defensive counter to it comes along." A Secret Service agent standing next to the vehicle opened the heavy door of the Beast. You cannot really open it from inside.

The President kept going, warming to his theme. "And right now, the problem is that the new offensive technologies have taken to the field and they now have the advantage over the things that we have to defend against them. So, what we have to do is invest in new technologies that will give the defense the advantage again, or at least even out the playing field. Have I got it right?"

Clarke looked at the President, bemused, reminded again about the preternatural ability he had to make the complex comprehensible. Clarke put away his copy of the draft speech and the PowerPoint deck, sighed, and said, "Yeah, Mr. President, you should say that today." And he did.

Nineteen years and three months later, Clinton said the same thing verbatim in answering a question about his cyber-oriented novel while sitting on stage in Washington's Warner Theatre. It was still true. In the intervening twenty years, hundreds of billions of dollars in public and private investment in cybersecurity research, development, and deployment had not fundamentally changed the advantage. It remains a case of what military theorists call offensive advantage or offensive preference.

Offensive Preference in Cyberspace

Any scenario between adversaries is a balance between offense and defense. When the offense has the advantage because of some combination of technological superiority or cost, military theorists write, there will be conflict. When the reverse is true, when it costs more to attack, or when the chances of an attack defeating the defenses is low, greater stability will prevail. We think these generalities apply now to the ongoing hostilities between hackers and corporations, to the current covert espionage done by nation-states, and to the potential for a future nation-state-on-nation-state cyber war. Today, as for the last twenty-five years, the conventional wisdom in the fields of computer science, information technology, and networking is that there is an enormous offensive preference. That might not have been a big deal to most people, except that in the last twenty-five years, we have also made almost everything dependent upon computer networks. In fact, because the offense is thought to have the advantage right now, in a crisis situation of possible conventional warfare, there is likely to be an inclination to go first with a cyberattack.

This book is about how the balance between offense and defense is changing and how the rate of change can be increased to set us on the path to stability. We think it is possible to reduce the risks posed by offensive cyber technologies and actors, and to increase peacetime stability for corporations and crisis stability for nations.

As we write this in 2019, we see a pattern of malicious activity in cyberspace that suggests we are already engaged in a low-grade, simmering cyber conflict with Russia, China, and Iran. We also are beginning to turn a corner on this problem. Estimates put worldwide cybersecurity spending at $114 billion in 2018. Venture capital investment in cybersecurity technology is up, topping $5 billion in 2018 alone. More than three thousand new technology firms have sprung up, backed by ample venture capital, to develop new solutions. Cyber insurance was long a fringe product. Today, the market is (finally) growing and thriving, with almost $2 billion in premiums written in 2017.

Long-standing problems created by government, such as barriers to information sharing, have been solved and companies are actually beginning to organize communities not only to share information, but also to provide mutual aid during crises. One chief information security officer (CISO) at a major bank we spoke with thinks that in five years his bank will largely be immune to cyberattacks as it upgrades from legacy systems that are inherently insecure to systems that are secure by design. Many leaders in Silicon Valley, where optimism is never in short supply, would tend to agree.

Today, if you are a small-business owner, you can conduct most of your work online and do so with the support of cloud service providers that have dedicated thousands of people and billions of dollars to protecting your data. Automation and artificial intelligence have the potential to erase much of the attacker's advantage. Yet, at the same time, attackers are looking at how they can use these tools as well. Quantum computing could provide both impossible-to-break protection for data and the ability to crack all current forms of encryption. Blockchain, which many technologists think could lead to fundamentally more secure protection of data, has for the time being found its biggest use in cryptocurrency, a technology that is decidedly giving an advantage to attackers by allowing criminals to move their ill-gotten gains around anonymously. These technology trends could shift the balance in either direction. It is up to us to determine which way the scales will tip.

The Pentagon has long identified four primary domains of conflict: land, sea, air, and space. In recent years, cyberspace has come to be known as the "fifth domain." Unlike the others, cyberspace is man-made. It can therefore be changed by man. It is a positive attribute of cyberspace that once a weapon has been used and discovered it can be blocked. That is the equivalent of changing the atmosphere so that bombs can no longer fall.

We have been working together on the cyber problem for fifteen years. We both consult for major corporations, cybersecurity companies, and venture-capital and private-equity firms. We have both been adjunct faculty members teaching graduate students about cybersecurity. And, for our sins, we have both spent time in government agencies, Dick Clarke in the Defense Department and State Department, Rob Knake in Homeland Security. The best parts of our government experiences, however, were in the White House, on the National Security Council staff. Dick served on the George H. W. Bush (41), Bill Clinton (42), and George W. Bush (43) staffs. Rob served on the Obama staff (44).

While in the White House, we both had the opportunity to author decision documents (executive orders, presidential directives) on cybersecurity. Dick also drafted the first national strategy on cybersecurity that any nation ever published. So, yes, you can blame us in part for some of the mess, but we think we also have some unique perspectives. Between us we have spent more than four decades closely following the evolution of the cyber threat and the government and corporate response. Ten years ago, when we wrote the book *Cyber War: The Next Threat to National Security and What to Do About It*, our goal was to raise the alarm. We knew the seriousness with which cyber threats were taken in Washington, but didn't see the same level of concern in the private sector. Unfortunately, much of what we wrote about cyber threats turned out to be right, but things have also changed a lot since then, including our prescriptions.

When we wrote *Cyber War*, Silicon Valley, still stuck in its "Don't Be Evil" phase, wouldn't accept that its inventions had the potential to cause real harm. Our intention was to scare government and corporate leaders into addressing the threat before the prospect of cyber war turned into a real cyber war. In the intervening decade, far too little has happened to respond to the threat, while many of our predictions on the emergence of war in cyberspace have regrettably come to be true. Yet cybersecurity remains a solvable problem, one far less difficult to address than a host of others, like climate change, that we face today.

We have full faith that, in time, we will find workable solutions to the problems that plague cyberspace today through an ugly and disruptive process of trial and error. Eventually, businesses will come around to recognizing the value they get from being globally connected and will start investing appropriately to secure that value. Eventually, governments will figure out their roles and begin to help the private sector help itself.

But unless we are smart and proactive, we will solve the challenges we face in cyberspace only after multiple crises. After cyberattacks cause blackouts in the United States, we will make the necessary investments to prevent them. After train derailments, ship collisions, or airplane crashes caused by malicious actors operating in cyberspace kill people, we will build systems that have near-zero tolerance for failures caused by hackers.

The danger is that, after events like these, we won't just do the hard work of making our systems resilient to cyberattacks. Blood will need to be answered with blood. We think it safe to conclude that the next major war the United States enters will be provoked by a cyberattack. That provocation may be accidental. It may be intentional. But the United States does not have a good record of turning the other cheek. And so as we think about what needs to be done to improve cybersecurity, our fundamental goal is to achieve cyber peace so that we do not end up embroiled in more devastating and costly wars in the real world.

Our collective understanding of these problems as a community of practitioners has grown immensely in recent years. We now have a clear view of the many problems that make cyberspace an attractive domain for warfighters, and of how we could make it less attractive. As we developed the concept for this book, we kept coming back to the realization that the specter of cyber warfare does not overshadow all the good things that are made possible by the internet. The speed and connectivity that enable cyber warfare also enable email, social media, Amazon Prime, and massive multiplayer games. While some might question whether these applications represent positive outcomes for society, this global network has allowed collaboration and communication that was undreamed of a few decades ago and has been the driving force behind massive increases in productivity and wealth creation.

By some estimates, the digital economy, separate and apart from the traditional economy, is growing at three times the rate of the rest of the economy. But as the global consulting firm McKinsey points out, it's increasingly difficult to separate the digital economy from the rest, as every company today is wired up. McKinsey estimates that fully 98 percent of the economy is being impacted by digitization. It is no coincidence then that the companies thriving today are the ones that have taken cybersecurity seriously. In 2018, we saw the first real hits to companies' bottom lines from cyberattacks. The NotPetya malware took billions from companies operating in Ukraine, Europe, and the United States, leading many to report the losses on their quarterly and annual filings with the Securities and Exchange Commission. Yet some, if not most, multinational corporations operating in Ukraine either were not impacted, were minimally impacted, or had some really good lawyers who argued the losses did not need to be reported (more on that later).

Companies such as Microsoft, Apple, and Google, all companies that at one time saw concerns over cyber threats as overhyped, now have religion and are investing in cybersecurity with the zealotry of the converted. They view cybersecurity as a competitive advantage in a market where consumers are increasingly wary of doing business online. Large banks such as Citi,

Bank of America, and JPMorgan Chase also view cybersecurity as a competitive differentiator for both consumer and commercial clients.

The near daily press reports of new incidents and the constant stream of notifications that your personal information has been stolen have created the impression that cyberspace is hopelessly insecure. Yet hiding in plain sight are many examples of companies with big targets on their backs that have been able to constantly defeat even the best nation-state offensive teams year in and year out. While these companies have massive security teams and budgets in the hundreds of millions of dollars, their innovations, many borrowed from the military, are slowly making their way to the wider market.

The offensive advantage in cyberspace is slowly shifting as the defense closes the gap by taking advantage of new technologies, becomes better organized, and begins to understand the value of what is at stake. Accelerating that shift is one of the central requirements for achieving something more like peace and less like war in cyberspace.

Cyber warfare must become both more difficult and costlier to carry out. Cyber criminals, who act as proxies for nation-states as well as cause significant harm with their moneymaking schemes, must have their numbers culled. The barriers to entry for engaging in malicious activity in cyberspace have been going down steadily, year over year. They must be brought back up.

Many who have looked at the specter of cyber war have called for drastic action. "Reinvent the internet" to make it more secure is an often-heard refrain, but no one has yet come up with a plan for how to do that without causing more economic and social harm than the bad actors could do on their worst days. Even sillier are the calls for a "cyber Manhattan Project" or "cyber moon shot." These demands for a massive national effort always lack the same thing: a clear goal.

The Manhattan Project of the 1940s took developing theories of physics, as laid out in a succinct letter from Albert Einstein to President Franklin Roosevelt, and set out an engineering challenge to translate them into an atomic weapon. Kennedy's goal of the "moon shot" was even clearer: get to the moon. Cyber war has no such neat solution, because achieving peace in cyberspace is not a question of solving an engineering problem or reaching a specific location.

Some of the challenges blocking the way to cyber peace are technical, but most, at their heart, are economic. With the right package of economic incentives, the technical problems can be solved. So, while this book will dive into the 1s and 0s to explain the challenge, most of the solutions will be about how to make markets and governments work in the interest of promoting security. Above all, our guiding principle is to avoid solutions that would cause more disruption than the problems they are meant to solve. In cyberspace, this appears to be an easy trap.

The worst example of this tendency came at the end of the Obama administration, when officials at the Department of Justice proposed that companies should weaken encryption to make digital information readily accessible to law enforcement and also, therefore, to criminals. They failed, but many similar ideas are still being put on the table. When things go wrong in cyberspace, such ideas are likely to be introduced and reintroduced and will eventually be implemented if we do not, as a community, develop compelling alternatives.

Above all, as we seek solutions in this space, we are looking for rapid evolution, not revolution. We think there are enough companies that have figured out how to manage the threat that the challenge now is to create the right package of incentives to spread these models and to innovate faster than attackers can. As the cyberpunk author William Gibson said, "The future is already here; it's just not very evenly distributed." In a sense, therefore, the task at hand is to figure out how to more evenly distribute a secure cyber future.

A Different Threat, a Different Model

As we looked for solutions to problems that have long plagued cyberspace, what has not changed is our fundamental premise that cybersecurity is a shared responsibility between government and the private sector, with the onus for protecting computer systems falling on the owners and operators of those systems. Dick first made the concept of a "public-private partnership" for cybersecurity official U.S. policy with Presidential Decision Directive

63 (PDD 63, for those in the know) in 1998. That directive also put in place many of the building blocks for realizing this vision that we still rely on today, such as information sharing and analysis centers (ISACs). Since then, across the Bush, Obama, and Trump administrations, specific policies have been rescinded and rewritten, but the overall thrust of U.S. cyber policy has remained largely unchanged. This degree of continuity across twenty years and four presidential administrations would be remarkable in any other area of public policy. At a time when Republicans and Democrats are sharply divided over climate change, immigration policy, and tax policy (to name a few), it is even more remarkable.

Since the Clinton administration, our cyber strategy has changed very little despite many attempts to come up with a different one. Thus, when we consider how to secure privately owned and operated networks, we return to the basic idea that the companies that own and operate the internet and the things that are connected to it, be they multinational media companies, providers of essential services, or the makers of the tiniest IoT devices, will be responsible for protecting themselves. They will do it through network defense, not offense.

Government's role will be limited, to support the private victims of cyberattacks with law enforcement, information sharing, diplomacy, and, in the rare cases where it is both feasible and in the national security interest, military force. Government will also play a role in helping the private sector help itself, through nudges to encourage investment and cooperation in cybersecurity; through research, training, convening; and, ultimately, through regulation.

Despite twenty years of continuity on this policy, this division of responsibility is often derided in corporate America. Many CEOs are incredulous that they are responsible for defending their companies against foreign adversaries of the United States. "That's what I pay taxes for," echoes out of every boardroom. Leaders in national security often have the same view, believing that it is the responsibility of the U.S. military to defend the nation in cyberspace. They want to equate cyberattacks to nuclear missiles, and argue that it must be the government's role to stop these attacks.

The idea that government should find some magic way to make this problem go away and let us go about our business online is compelling to many. It's also deeply flawed. The cyber domain is fundamentally different from the air domain, as are the threats that lurk within it. Making cyber-security the military's responsibility would require rearchitecting the inter-net to give defense agencies the necessary choke points to try to filter out hostile threats. Doing so would require also granting them unlimited access to the content of traffic, a spy's dream and a privacy advocate's nightmare. Such an approach would likely still fail, and fail while incurring massive costs with tremendous societal disruption.

When cyberattacks do occur, every CEO would like to view it as a na-tional security crisis, shift responsibility to government, and have the military "fire off the missiles." The desire to counterpunch is understandable, but foolhardy. Thus far, the U.S. government has shown remarkable restraint, avoiding engaging in reckless counterstrikes that would broaden conflicts. Whether that restraint will hold we do not know, but we are fairly certain that the utility of such strikes will be low.

Attribution (determining who is behind an attack) is a recurring chal-lenge in responding to such attacks. Advanced threat actors have learned how to keep their computer systems hidden and are able to quickly replace any lost resources with other, likely stolen, computing resources, or make it appear as if another group altogether were responsible for an attack. Thus, counteroffense is at best like firing a cruise missile into an empty tent, and at worst like firing a cruise missile into a civilian apartment complex. And of course, along with relying more on the military, we must also take a dim view of vigilantism in cyberspace, and hope that we will soon see the De-partment of Justice indict someone for so-called hacking back.

Late in the Obama administration, the government finally got out of the business of operating the last government-managed portion of internet in-frastructure, the Domain Name System. With that function now firmly implanted in the private, nonprofit Internet Corporation for Assigned Names and Numbers (ICANN), the federal government has finally com-pleted the internet's thirty-year transition from a science experiment at DARPA (the Defense Department's Advanced Research Projects Agency) to a wholly commercial venture. We spent thirty years getting the government out of operating the internet; we would not want security to be the reason we let the government back in.

What that leaves us with is the approach we have advocated all along: building systems so that most attacks cause no harm, and that allow us to respond to and recover from attacks that do succeed, with minimal to no disruption. We have adopted a different way to talk about this concept: cyber resilience. We also have ideas to share on how it can be implemented.

Cyber Resilience

The best strategies can be summed up with a single word. In the Cold War, we had two such strategies: containment and deterrence. George Kennan's famous "long telegram" took a few thousand words to spell out the strategy of containment, of keeping the Soviet sphere of influence limited. Thousands of papers and books would ultimately be written on deterrence in the nuclear era (and rewritten for the cyber era), but those single-word strategies clued everyone in to the basic ideas. Once set out in the 1940s, they held for almost fifty years with very little variation as times and presidential administrations changed.

Throughout this book, we will come back many times to the theme of working to shift the advantage from the attacker to the defender. This effort should be the overall goal of our national policy, and that of like-minded countries and companies. It's the right idea, but the language of offense-defense theory too readily suggests that cybersecurity is just another problem, such as terrorism or nuclear threats, that the military will deal with.

The reality of the internet as we know and love it today does not lend itself completely to traditional national security approaches. One of the guiding lessons we kept in mind while writing this book was the need to look for solutions by analogy that were not drawn from the world of warfare. This may seem rich, coming from the guys whose last book was titled *Cyber War*, but we believe that if the goal we want to achieve is cyber peace, then we should be looking at solutions to problems outside the fifth domain or any of the other four. If we try to find allegories in the Barbary pirates, or the battle of Fallujah, or the response to 9/11, we will no doubt find them, but they will lead us to one type of solution. Instead, throughout this book we have looked to other areas of study, such as ecology, public health, emergency management, and even psychology. As we have done that, one central theme continued to emerge: resilience. At the corporate level, many leaders are recognizing that their enterprise cybersecurity strategies need to be built around resilience. They must try to prevent every incident they can, but respond and recover rapidly when prevention fails. In his book *Digital Resilience*, RedSeal CEO Ray Rothrock identifies the concept of resilience as "a winning strategy in a losing war," arguing that the threat from cyber actors has made resilience "table stakes for any enterprise interested in survival." Yet while the corporate world is starting to embrace resilience, many in Washington provide only lip service to the concept. Programs and budgets suggest cyber policy is stuck in a war-fighting mentality.

If you do a keyword search on cybersecurity strategies from the last few administrations, you will no doubt find the word "resilience" buried somewhere in the document. But the idea has never been embraced as the central goal of our strategy. It has always been an ill-defined and vague concept. Ultimately, what we want is to be able to ignore cyberattacks, to be able to slough them off and continue on with our business rather than being forced to escalate. Because we insist on finding Cold War parallels, the cyber community often talks about this concept as "deterrence by denial," the idea that we want to make our defenses so good that adversaries will not even try to attack, and if they do attack, it won't be of consequence. We'd propose a slight shift. We want to make our defenses so good, and our architectures so strong, that we do not care about whether we are being attacked most of the time because the attacks have no serious effects.

Cyber resilience must be built upon, rather than be seen as a replacement for sound security fundamentals. When confidentiality, integrity, and availability are compromised, resilience is about the ability to rapidly respond, return to a good state, manage bad outcomes, and learn from the incident so that future incidents are less likely. Here, it is important to note that thinking of "resilience" as the ability to recover to a previous state or to bounce back is too limiting. For resilience to be a useful concept in the field of cybersecurity, it requires that the concept fully embody the idea of returning stronger or better than before.

In the field of psychology, where the concept of resilience has been more fully developed than in any of the other fields that use the term, there is a built-in acknowledgment that resilience is not about returning to a previous state after an individual experiences trauma, but about adapting to that trauma. After the death of a spouse or parent or a child, after the loss of a limb or the trauma of war, overcoming these experiences does not mean forgetting them or getting back to the way you were before the experience. No one could.

Applying this psychological reality to the physical world, Judith Rodin, a psychologist by training and the former head of the Rockefeller Foundation, formulates a definition that works equally well for coping with cyber threats as it does for, say, building resilient cities. Rodin defines resilience as the capacity of any "entity . . . to prepare for disruptions, to recover from shocks and stresses, and to adapt and grow from a disruptive experience." We think that definition transfers aptly to the cyber world.

In the next chapter, we provide a reminder of the threat and the damage that can be done. Then we look at corporations and the progress some of them are making at safeguarding their networks. We examine the potential for improved public-private partnerships and the role of regulation. We ask what the government and the military should do, and we examine the role of the international community. Because cyberspace is ever changing, we then discuss the new technologies and what they could mean for the offense-defense struggle. Finally, we have some suggestions about what you should do at home to secure your corner of cyberspace.

Throughout the book, we will try to show that we have a choice to make about the future we want in cyberspace. In the chapters that follow, we will sketch out why raising the alarm on cyber threats is warranted, and will lay out a plan for how the worst outcomes can be avoided. There are two futures we can choose from. It is up to us to decide which one we want cyberspace to become.

Chapter 2

· · · · · · · · · · ·

ETERNALBLUE, ETERNAL WAR

> The Russian military launched the most destructive and costly
> cyberattack in history. . . . This was also a reckless and indis-
> criminate cyberattack that will be met with international conse-
> quences.
>
> —STATEMENT FROM THE PRESS SECRETARY
> OF THE WHITE HOUSE, FEBRUARY 2018

Lorina Nash rushed her mother to the emergency room at Lister Hospital in Stevenage, England. The doctors said they needed tests to diagnose the problem. They gave Nash's mother a blood test, but then the computers crashed and they could not complete the analysis. The doctors put the sample in the hands of a courier and sent him on a three-hour trip to a clinic whose computers were still working. Lorina and her mom waited in what became a largely empty ER, as most patients were sent away.

Ambulances racing to Essex Hospital were redirected elsewhere, as the Accident and Emergency department there had also stopped accepting patients. At North Hampshire Hospital, the CT and X-ray machines froze. Colchester Hospital canceled twenty-five operations. At Chesterfield Royal

Hospital the problem was the reverse: without functioning computers, patients could not be released and had to spend another night in the hospital. It was May 12, 2017, and the British National Health Service had been hit by a ransomware cyberattack that was shutting down businesses all over Europe and North America, locking down computers and demanding payment in Bitcoin to unlock them.

The attack tool used became known as WannaCry, and seven months later the Australian, British, and American governments identified the culprit as one of the North Korean government's hacking groups, sometimes called the Lazarus Group by Western analysts. While WannaCry captured the media's attention in the United States and many other countries, the events in May were only a prelude to a much more devastating attack a month later by another state actor. Indeed, what was to come was the most devastating single cyberattack in history, so far costing companies more than $20 billion and, more importantly, shutting down key infrastructure.

While WannaCry got the public's attention, corporate and government IT security professionals had already been aware of the growing risk of ransomware. A year earlier, a virus known as Petya (named after a Soviet weapon in a James Bond movie) had demonstrated significant success in attacking Windows-based systems and then spreading encryption throughout the infected network. Analysis of Petya by U.S. cybersecurity firms later revealed that it employed an attack technique based on the National Security Agency's EternalBlue weapon.

Then in late June 2017, malware resembling Petya spread with unprecedented speed around the world, attacking Microsoft servers and then jumping to all connected devices on the affected corporate networks. In major companies seemingly selected at random, and at their facilities in scores of nations, computer screens froze and flashed messages demanding payment. It looked like ransomware again. It wasn't.

Once analysts realized it was not the Petya attack again, they creatively labeled the new attack NotPetya. What cybersecurity experts quickly surmised was that the demand for ransom was fake, a diversion. The attacking software was actually what was known as a wiper, which erased all software on the infected devices. Any device connected on an infected network would be wiped: desktops, laptops, data storage servers, routers, IP phones, mobile phones, tablets, printers.

Operations at major global corporations suddenly ground to a halt. At the pharmaceutical firm Merck, which made more than $40 billion in revenue in 2017 and employed more than sixty thousand workers, production lines froze. Distribution of vaccinations, oncology drugs, and hundreds of other pharmaceuticals stopped. Later, the company would claim the damages cost them almost $900 million.

Maersk, a container ship and port giant, suddenly could not operate the cranes that move millions of shipping containers at its megaports around the world, including New York and New Jersey, Los Angeles, and Rotterdam. Moreover, it had no idea where any given container was, what was in any container, or where any container was supposed to go. Later, the company would publicly own up to $300 million in damages, but a company insider told us that when opportunity costs were accounted for, the true loss was triple that number.

Hundreds of corporations, some in almost every sector, were frozen, including the logistics firm TNT Express (a subsidiary of FedEx), Mondelēz, the snack company, and the DLA Piper law firm. If there had been any doubt that a cyberattack could be global in an instant, that it could disable physical systems, or that it could affect the machinery that keeps the global economy moving, that doubt evaporated on June 27, 2017. Was it cyber war?

A Cyber War by Any Other Name

Whether NotPetya was an act of cyber war depends, of course, on your definition. Upon examination, NotPetya was an operation run by a military unit, specifically the Main Directorate of the General Staff of the Russian Federation's military, often called the GRU or Russian military intelligence. (In the funny-name-game world of cyber wonks, the GRU's hacking team is also known as Fancy Bear.)

The Russian military did not, we suspect, intend to indiscriminately attack global corporations. What it had intended was a crippling attack on Ukraine on the eve of its national holiday, Constitution Day. The GRU had figured out a truly creative attack vector, a channel that could be used to spread an attack.

What the GRU had noticed was that almost every company and government ministry in Ukraine used the same accounting software. Think of the prevalence of QuickBooks in the United States and you will get the picture. Only in Ukraine, the equivalent software was known as M.E.Doc, from the Ukrainian software company the Linkos Group. Like every other similar application, the M.E.Doc program was periodically updated. Updates were pushed out to licensed users from a server at Linkos. The updates were digitally signed by Linkos and recognized by users' firewalls, thus allowing the M.E.Doc updates to pass freely into corporate networks.

So the GRU hacked into Linkos and planted a little something extra in the next update to M.E.Doc: an attack package that exploited a known vulnerability in Microsoft server software, combined with a password-hacking tool and instructions to spread to any connected device on the network, wiping them of all software.

The GRU attack worked almost flawlessly, destroying about 10 percent of all devices in Ukraine, including some in every government ministry, more than twenty financial institutions, and at least four hospitals. *Almost* flawlessly. What the GRU had apparently not recognized (or maybe they did) was that global companies operating in Ukraine would also be hit, and from their Ukrainian offices the attack would spread over virtual private networks (VPNs) and rented corporate fiber connections back to corporate headquarters in England, Denmark, the United States, and elsewhere.

This kind of mistaken collateral damage is not unique to NotPetya or to the GRU. The software used in the so-called Stuxnet attack on the Iranian nuclear enrichment plant reportedly carried out by the United States in 2010 somehow got out into the world, even though the Natanz plant was not connected to the internet or any other network. Stuxnet quickly spread around the globe, was captured by cybersecurity teams in many countries, and was decompiled, with parts of it later reused in new attack tools.

Stuxnet, however, did not damage anything outside of Natanz, because it was written in a way that the only thing it could hurt was the Iranian nuclear enrichment processor. Nonetheless, the fact that the software spread way beyond its target was reportedly one of the motivations for President Obama's subsequent directive, Presidential Policy Directive 20, which allegedly restricted further offensive use of cyber tools without his personal approval. (President Trump is reported to have removed those restrictions in 2018.)

Stuxnet revealed to the world, or at least to anyone who cared enough to bother to grab a copy, one of the most sophisticated attack tools ever, containing more than fifty thousand lines of computer code including numerous tricks never used before (so-called zero-day exploits). NotPetya revealed not a thing about Russian GRU attack tools. It exposed nothing of theirs because it was not their tool. It was America's.

Using Our Weapons Against Us

An obscure, important, and contentious debate among cybersecurity experts concerns whether it's the responsibility of the U.S. government to tell software developers (say, Microsoft) when NSA hackers find a mistake in the company's code that would permit someone to do something new and malicious, such as hack in and copy customer data, steal money, or wipe out all the software on a network. In the parlance of U.S. government cyber-policy makers, this debate is called the "equities issue" because it involves balancing the interests of intelligence agencies trying to attack with the concerns of government departments such as Treasury and Homeland Security that have an interest in more secure corporate networks.

If the government tells the software developer, then the company issues a "patch" that can fix the problem. If the government does not tell them, then it can hack into interesting foreign networks using the vulnerability in order to learn things to protect the country. (The government creates an "exploit," a hacking tool that takes advantage of the poorly written computer code.)

After Edward Snowden stole sensitive NSA information and gave it to WikiLeaks (and the Russians), Obama appointed a five-man group to investigate and make recommendations. Dick Clarke was one of the group that became known as the Five Guys, after the Washington hamburger chain.

The Five Guys' recommendations were all made public, every single word of them, by the Obama White House. One of those recommendations was that when the NSA finds a hole in widely used software, it should tell the manufacturer, with rare exceptions. Those exceptions would be approved at a high level in the government and should be valid for only a finite period. The Obama administration accepted that recommendation.

Microsoft has charged that the NSA knew about a big problem with Microsoft's server software for five years and did not tell them. Instead, the NSA developed an attack tool, or zero-day exploit, and called it EternalBlue. Presumably, the NSA used EternalBlue to get into foreign networks. Only in March 2017 did Microsoft, having just been informed of its software's deficiencies by the U.S. government, issue a patch for the problem.

As is always the case when a software company issues a patch, not every one of its users gets the message or believes the warning that it is a critical patch that has to be installed right away. So, despite the patch, the North Korean authors of WannaCry were successful in using the vulnerability two months later, in May 2017, and the Russian GRU used it again, in combination with other tricks, in creating the June 2017 NotPetya disaster.

Those devastating attacks would almost certainly have been avoided if the U.S. government had told Microsoft years earlier. At least, that is what Microsoft said publicly after it figured out what happened.

Why did the government finally tell Microsoft? Our guess, and it is just that, is that by March 2016 the government had figured out that Russia had stolen the U.S. attack kit, knew about the zero day, and was using it or was about to use it.

It is possible that the Russian GRU stole the zero-day attack tool from the United States in 2016, or perhaps even as early as 2013. We do know that another contractor assigned to the NSA, Harold Martin, was apparently walking out of NSA facilities with highly classified papers and software on a regular basis, according to the charges brought against him by the Justice Department after the FBI arrested him in 2016.

Martin used antivirus software to defend his personal home computer; specifically, he used Kaspersky Anti-Virus. Kaspersky, which is widely used around the world, is made in Russia. According to press reports, the Russian

GRU gained access to Kaspersky's Moscow headquarters and then used the millions of Kaspersky Anti-Virus packages installed on computers around the world to search for documents with certain keywords. (Kaspersky denies that this is what happened.)

Maybe the GRU learned those keywords, which may have been Top Secret Exceptionally Controlled Information code names, from the Edward Snowden treasure trove. In any event, one possibility is that, using a backdoor in Kaspersky Anti-Virus on Harold Martin's home computer, the Russian GRU found a ton of NSA attack tools, perhaps including the EternalBlue exploit.

Now, how would anybody know that the Russian GRU did that? Well, it just could be that Israel's military intelligence Unit 8200 was sitting inside Kaspersky's network watching it all go down. The Israelis would have told the NSA pretty quickly if that happened. It is also possible that the Russian GRU hacked a secret server outside of the NSA that was used to store attack tools, a so-called staging server, in the autumn of 2013. Maybe that was how they got the NSA's crown jewels.

However they got them, they got them. We know that because they posted them online for all the world to see, and use, in the summer of 2016. Posing as the fictional hacker group known as the Shadow Brokers, the Russian GRU started to dole out the NSA's attack tools publicly. It's true that they did not call them the NSA's tools, opting instead to call them property of the "Equation Group," but the NSA PowerPoint slides were kind of a giveaway as to who the Equation Group really was. The Shadow Brokers went on to offer to sell some of the Equation Group's better tricks. The tricks all seemed to date from 2013, which may give credence to the staging server attack as the source of the NSA's attack tools.

The NSA is not the only U.S. government organization engaged in cyberattacks. The Pentagon's Cyber Command is too, as is the CIA. We know a lot more about what the CIA does now because, like the NSA, it also had a major theft and public exposure of its cyber secrets. In the case of the CIA, however, there is little doubt about how the secrets were taken or by whom.

Joshua Schulte, a CIA employee, was arrested by the FBI in August 2017 and charged with passing over eight thousand pages of highly classified information to Julian Assange, who subsequently posted them publicly on the WikiLeaks website. Assange, an Australian who had taken refuge in Ecuador's London embassy, has been accused by numerous American authorities of acting in cooperation with Russian intelligence.

The CIA documents were called Vault 7 by WikiLeaks, and they too revealed numerous zero-day exploits of widely used software, including products of Apple, Microsoft, and Samsung (e.g., allegedly a tool to listen to rooms in which Samsung televisions were installed, even when the television appeared to be turned off). When the documents became public, Microsoft president Brad Smith complained that no one in the U.S. government had told them about the vulnerabilities.

At least one other U.S.-based company had, however, been noticing some of the alleged Vault 7 exploits. For at least six years, cybersecurity company Symantec had been reporting on attacks by a group it named Longhorn. Attack techniques used by Longhorn in more than sixteen countries reportedly match almost exactly in technical detail some of what was revealed in the Vault 7 documents. If that is true, then the CIA might have been exploiting flaws in U.S.-manufactured software for years without telling the companies involved.

WikiLeaks, which is not the most credible source of impartial information, alleged that the Vault 7 documents showed the existence of a CIA program code-named UMBRAGE. This program supposedly involved the CIA using attack tools that it had stolen from other governments in order to leave a misleading trail and cause investigators to believe attacks done by the CIA were, in fact, done by others.

By 2018, the outing of one another's cyber tools and personnel was picking up speed. An anonymous group calling itself Intrusion Truth began to regularly disclose the hacks, tools, and people involved in Chinese hacking groups known as APT 3 and APT 10. It is not yet generally agreed upon among the cyber-expert community who Intrusion Truth is, but it is clear that they are revealing the secret activity of the Chinese government.

What does all of this tell us? First, stealing one another's attack tools may be more widely practiced than was previously thought, and may be done by at least a few nations.

A second obvious observation from these incidents is that the security of U.S. cyberattack units is still miserably poor years after a frustrated President issued an Executive Order (EO 13587) and other instructions to fix it. Most of the theft of U.S. attack tools could have been prevented by simple physical security procedures.

Third, we should not conclude that the Russian GRU *has* to steal U.S. attack tools. They have plenty of good ones they have developed themselves. Their motive in stealing and publicly releasing the U.S. cyber arsenal is to embarrass the United States, make it seem like America is the world's most problematic hacker, and allow nations (including our friends and allies) to go back and identify U.S. intelligence operations against them (thereby creating distrust among allies).

Finally, there is obviously a great deal of hostile activity by the militaries of various nations going on in cyberspace. All of this might not constitute war according to the traditional definition, but it is fairly clear by now that the United States and its allies have been regularly attacked by the Russian military using cyber weapons. The Russian military has not only used cyber weapons to collect intelligence, but has also deployed cyber weapons to damage, disrupt, and destroy physical objects in the real world, beyond the realm of 1s and 0s. And the Russians are not the only ones. To quote the British Foreign Office, the Russians are simply the most "reckless and indiscriminate."

Russia's GRU successfully penetrated the Pentagon's classified intranet, as well as the State Department and White House systems. According to the United Kingdom's National Cybersecurity Center in October 2018, the GRU has engaged in a sustained campaign of low-level cyber war for several years, going back at least to its 2007 attack on Estonia and its 2008 attack on the nation of Georgia.

According to the U.K., the GRU, operating under the false flag name of Sandworm, attacked the Ukrainian power grid in 2015 and again in 2016. Operating under the false flag name of Cyber Caliphate (sounds like an Arab terrorist group, right?), it shut down a French television network, TV5Monde. It attempted to interfere through cyberattacks in the investigations of the Russian assassination attempt in Bristol, England, Russian doping of Olympic athletes, and the Russian downing of Malaysia Airlines Flight 17.

Famously, the Russian GRU penetrated the Democratic National Committee (which admittedly required little skill) as one part of a multifaceted campaign to affect the outcome of the U.S. presidential election. And of course, there was the most damaging cyberattack in history to date, NotPetya, about which the White House issued a rare public statement of attribution regarding a cyberattack.

In one operation in the Netherlands, GRU hackers were arrested in the parking lot of the international organization that investigates chemical weapons use, attempting to hack into the wi-fi. According to Dutch police, the Russian military personnel were in possession of taxi receipts from GRU headquarters to Moscow airport, thus proving that business expenses are the bane of every organization, even cyber-war units.

Whether or not you call all of that activity cyber war, it is objectively a lot of damage being done by a military organization. Much of it fits the definition we suggested in *Cyber War* in 2010 (damage, disruption, and destruction of physical objects caused by a nation-state-created cyberattack). Back then there were commentators and critics who thought such predictions were hyperbolic. By now, however, it seems generally accepted that this kind of warfare can happen. Indeed, U.S. Director of National Intelligence Dan Coats publicly stated that the Russian government had penetrated the control systems of some U.S. electric power companies, that we were in a period similar to the months before 9/11, and that "the warning lights are blinking red."

The Russian GRU's teams such as Unit 26165 and Unit 74455 are not the only military organizations running around cyberspace breaking things. The Chinese People's Liberation Army (PLA) teams such as Unit 61398 and Unit 61486 have penetrated thousands of networks in the United States and tens of thousands around the world. Although President Obama and President Xi signed an agreement to limit cyberattacks on each other for commercial purposes (about which more later), Chinese penetrations of U.S. organizations continue.

Similarly, North Korea's Bureau 121 and Unit 180 have helped to

finance the development of missiles and nuclear weapons with their criminal theft activities around the world, including against the SWIFT international financial transfer system. North Korea has also attacked infrastructure
and businesses in South Korea, including banks and television networks.
The global attack that was WannaCry demonstrated the havoc that the
North Koreans can wreak.

Iran's military, through its Revolutionary Guard Command (IRGC)
and its Ministry of Intelligence, have also been damaging and disrupting in
cyberspace. For weeks in 2012 the online banking systems of the eight largest U.S. banks were shut down by an Iranian attack, which the Justice Department later charged was directed by the IRGC. Iran penetrated the U.S.
Navy Marine Corps Intranet and defied U.S. efforts to evict them for more
than two years. Iranian units took control of networks running systems as
diverse as a water system dam in New York State and the Sands Casino in
Las Vegas.

Iran's destructive efforts also include the 2012 attack on the Saudi oil
company Aramco, which wiped software off thousands of machines, and the
2017 penetration of the Triconex safety-instrumented system of a petrochemical plant in Saudi Arabia, an attack apparently intended to prevent
alarms going off during a planned lethal chemical leak in the future.

And then there is the United States, where in September 2018 the President devolved authority to conduct cyberattacks to the Department of
Defense and instructed the military to "defend forward" to disrupt other
nations' cyber activities. We will discuss that more in chapter 12.

Naming Cyber Warriors

One way in which the U.S. government has decided to respond to these cyberattacks by foreign militaries has been to "name and shame." At the risk of
compromising what are called sources and methods, U.S. intelligence agencies
have permitted Justice Department lawyers to name, show photographs of, and
issue arrest warrants for individuals in foreign military cyber units involved
in attacks inside the United States. This U.S. tactic is intended to demonstrate the extent of the problem, to give the appearance of doing something

about it, and in rare instances to make it possible to arrest and interrogate the military personnel involved. We found no U.S. government or former U.S. government official who thought it would deter further attacks.

Among those military personnel indicted in U.S. courts is Park Jin Hyok of the North Korean Reconnaissance General Bureau. From the People's Liberation Army, Huang Zhenyu was publicly accused and an arrest order was issued for him, among others. GRU officer Dmitriy Sergeyevich Badin is among a host of Russian military officials now sought by international law-enforcement agencies on a warrant from the United States. Ehsan Mohammadi is among the Iranians named by the U.S. Justice Department as having hacked American organizations on behalf of the Iranian government.

Though it has historically been challenging to apprehend foreign hackers because of their ability to conduct cyber operations from their own soil, some of the named military hackers have actually been arrested. Yanjun Xu of the PLA was arrested on a trip to Belgium. Alexei Morenets of the GRU was picked up by Dutch counterintelligence police in that parking lot in the Netherlands.

We have to leave it to your imagination how the United States knows the true names of these and many other foreign cyber military officers, how it obtained their pictures, and how it knows that they were involved in specific attacks. While you ponder that, keep in mind that the important thing here is that these are foreign military officers charged with attacking things in the United States.

Instability in Cyberspace Risks Escalation

All of this activity by Russia, China, North Korea, Iran, and, yes, the United States is suggestive of a dangerous pattern of crisis instability. Most significant hacking used to be done by non-state actors, individuals, or clubs. Now, major attacks are usually the work of some nation's military.

Nations are regularly using their militaries not only to steal secrets, but to damage, disrupt, and destroy sensitive systems inside potential enemy nations. Such operations could easily lead to escalation into broader war, intentionally or unintentionally. The U.S. military, for example, has said that it reserves the right to respond to cyberattacks with any weapon in its arsenal.

To be clear, the recent and current levels, pace, and scope of disruptive activity in cyberspace by the military units of several nations is unprecedented, dangerous, and unsustainable in "peacetime." It cannot continue like this. Either we control and deescalate tensions, or conditions will cease to have any resemblance to peacetime.

If we do not take concerted steps to reduce the risk of cyber war, if we do not engage in a multifaceted program to bring us closer to cyber peace, we risk highly destructive cyberattacks that could cripple modern societies and escalate into the kind of Great Power conflict we have not seen in more than seventy-five years. Thus, we need to make it a major national priority to find ways of defeating nation-state hackers. Some companies may already know how.

There are two lessons we could draw from the NotPetya attack on Ukraine. The first is that nation-state military and intelligence organizations are already taking down major global companies such as Maersk and Merck with cyberattacks. The second lesson, however, is the dog that did not bark. There were other U.S. and global companies in Ukraine during the NotPetya attack, companies such as Hyatt Hotels, Abbott Laboratories, Boeing, DowDupont, Eli Lilly, Johnson & Johnson, Cargill, Pfizer, Delta Air Lines, and John Deere. They do not appear to have been significantly damaged by NotPetya. We turn to what keeps some companies comparatively more secure in the next section.

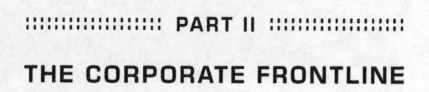

::::::::::::::::::::: **PART II** :::::::::::::::::::::

THE CORPORATE FRONTLINE

Chapter 3

···········

TWO KINDS OF COMPANIES?

If we have data, let's look at data. If all we have are opinions, let's go with mine.

—JIM BARKSDALE, FORMER CEO, NETSCAPE

There are two kinds of companies: those that have been hacked and know it; and those that have been hacked and don't." It's become a staple of keynotes at security conferences, the CISO version of the aristocrats joke. Everyone has a variation of the line, but its originator is Dmitri Alperovitch. Now the chief technology officer and cofounder of CrowdStrike, Alperovitch raised the alarm about nation-state threats when he was at McAfee, one of the largest antivirus companies. Alperovitch wrote some of the earliest reports on Chinese and Russian intrusion sets, uncovering the widespread penetration into American companies by foreign groups. Now, Alperovitch is no longer so sure that advanced persistent threat, or APT, actors are unstoppable.

When the Obama administration concluded its protracted negotiations with China's President Xi over economic espionage in 2015, the Chinese premier pledged to bring an end to the targeting of U.S. companies by his government's spy agencies. Very quickly, CrowdStrike observed that China's cyber spies had not changed their ways. But instead of reporting that the Chinese had stolen data, CrowdStrike made clear that they had detected the attacks and thwarted them. "Seven of the companies are firms in the Technology or Pharmaceuticals sectors, where the primary benefit of the intrusions seems clearly aligned to facilitate theft of intellectual property and trade secrets, rather than to conduct traditional national-security-related intelligence collection which the Cyber agreement does not prohibit," Alperovitch wrote on the company blog.

It was an important contribution to the debate at the time on the effectiveness of the agreement. It was also a bit of a humble-brag. Alperovitch and his cofounder George Kurtz did not shy away from the fact that they had handled the onslaught from China's most advanced offensive groups. When we asked Alperovitch whether he stood by his "two kinds of companies" line, he had a short answer: no.

Of course, Alperovitch is selling something. In June 2018, CrowdStrike announced it had raised another $200 million at a $3 billion valuation. The company will likely go public by the end of 2019. So what Alperovitch is selling, companies are buying. And what he is selling is a platform for rapid detection and containment as well as follow-on incident response services. It's tempting to joke that Alperovitch is now saying that there are three kinds of companies: those that have been hacked and know it; those that have been hacked and don't know it; and those that buy CrowdStrike. That would be unfair to Alperovitch, who sees his company as only one piece of a much larger solution, and one with many noble competitors, including Dragos, Cylance, FireEye, and others in the field.

Alperovitch should be happy. Business is booming at CrowdStrike. Yet he is frustrated. What frustrates him isn't that his technology can't find a market. It clearly has. He's frustrated because he believes more companies that could be secure are not. He has strong evidence that companies following a model of rapid detection and containment are able to stifle adversaries, keeping them from achieving their goals. Those goals may be to steal intellectual property or commit fraud or hold a company's computers for ransom, but they are not, he points out, simply to gain access to the network. That is only one step in a long chain of events that adversaries need to string together to achieve their goal (something we will explore more fully in chapter 4). And doing that against a prepared and determined company is harder than many might think.

Is the Offense Really That Easy?

"I just don't buy that offense has an advantage," says Dave Aitel. Aitel should know. For his entire career, starting at age eighteen at the NSA, he has been on the offense. After six years at the NSA he joined the legendary cybersecurity firm @stake, and then went on to found Immunity, a company that builds hacking tools for penetration testers and government clients. He sold it to the cybersecurity and data center firm Cyxtera in 2018 for an undisclosed sum.

When Aitel worked at the NSA he was one of the last breed of full-spectrum hackers, meaning that he developed exploits, deployed them, and ran them against nation-states' most sophisticated targets. He had a habit of working odd hours, coming in after everyone had left and working until the morning. One time, Aitel got caught up in whatever he was doing and forgot to leave before the rest of the workforce arrived. A disgruntled General Michael Hayden, then the NSA director, arrived to find Aitel's car parked in his reserved spot.

Aitel possesses many fine qualities, but humility is not one of them. So the fact that he does not exhibit the typical hacker bravado should cause a moment of pause. "For the nation-state offense," he says, "you put such a premium on not getting caught that you really don't have a huge advantage." The work he has done throughout his career is painstaking and deliberate. While signals may pass between computers at light speed, for the attacker, moving from reconnaissance through to achieving his objective can take months. And today, the attacker's job has only gotten harder.

When he began his career, the only threats that security tools could detect were those they had seen before and knew were bad. These "blacklist" technologies, like legacy antivirus programs, would scan files against signatures of known bad files and block them. Avoiding these technologies could be as simple as making a single change to the file so that it no longer matched the bad file.

Now, Aitel is worried that the superweapons of his craft are increasingly getting discovered. As we've seen, a zero day is a vulnerability that is not known to defenders and therefore has yet to be patched. Aitel, from an offensive perspective, is concerned that security firms are actually finding zero day attacks with increasing regularity, to the point that detection of zero days is becoming commoditized. "Microsoft's Advanced Threat Detection, CrowdStrike, Kaspersky, the new FireEye stuff, all that stuff actually works and that is a huge change," Aitel says. Thinking from an attacker's perspective, he is not happy about it.

It's getting harder to find vulnerabilities in new systems and even harder to exploit them. Modern trusted systems can actually be trusted. Your iPhone, a ubiquitous commercial device, is far better defended than a state-of-the-art system from Aitel's early days on the offense. Even the latest version of the long-maligned Microsoft Windows operating system is pretty secure.

Better detection and less accessible targets mean that by default, in Aitel's view, defenders now have the advantage. Of course, many companies forgo that advantage by underinvesting in IT in the first place and failing to continue to invest in keeping it secure. "The offense works super hard and they have a mission and they have metrics and they know when they win and they lose," says Aitel, whereas many companies on the defensive simply don't value protecting their assets as much as the offense values stealing them (or destroying them).

Now at a company that makes money defending systems, Aitel wonders how his old employer is going to be able to continue to meet mission demands for intelligence as security gets better. "Offensively," he says, "we aren't planning for the future." He has been a significant opponent of Obama-era rules requiring the intelligence community to disclose vulnerabilities in what's known as the Vulnerabilities Equities Process (the VEP). "The theory of the VEP is that you don't need a huge stockpile of vulnerabilities. But imagine if every zero day you used only worked twice. That's the world we are moving to." For Aitel and his former employer, that is a tough world to live in. For the rest of us, it may mean that we have already started to erode the offensive advantage.

When we wrote *Cyber War* in 2009, we quoted a senior intelligence official who told us point-blank that his teams at the NSA carried out an undisclosed number of missions every month and never got caught. That was then. Only months after *Cyber War* was published, the cybersecurity community, and soon after the general public, began to learn about Stuxnet, the highly sophisticated malware attack on Iran's nuclear centrifuges. Like Stuxnet, other campaigns and malware groups have also been solidly pinned to the NSA. In the case of Longhorn, not only had the group been caught in the act, but Symantec had traced its campaign across forty targets in fifteen countries. What many suspected was seemingly confirmed in stolen U.S. government files released by WikiLeaks. Thus, if in a ten-year period the best in the business within Fort Meade and the CIA have gone from acting with impunity in cyberspace to getting caught with near ironclad attribution, it suggests to us that the offensive advantage has eroded and will continue to.

As we've noted, NotPetya was a devastating attack to FedEx, DLA Piper, Mondelēz, Maersk, and Merck, among others, but many international businesses active in Ukraine either were not hit or maintained operations through the attack and were not forced to disclose any losses. Ukraine is a global center for outsourced IT operations. Samsung, Oracle, Boeing, Ericsson, and Siemens, to name a few, have research and development centers in Ukraine. Microsoft, whose exchange server was the vector of the attack, has offices there. And yet these companies continued to hum along despite attacks that crippled other companies doing business there. The CISO of one U.S.-based global company told us how his team not only stopped NotPetya from spreading beyond their Kiev facility, they quickly identified its origin and shared that information with other companies. How did they do it? "Simple. We patched when we were told to and we segment our network."

This is not to say that cyber defense is easy or cheap. Indeed, the cost of defense is still many times the cost of offense. Those who disagree with that look at the likely cost of designing the Stuxnet weapon used by the

United States to attack the Natanz facility in Iran. We concede, without knowing the details of that classified program, that it was probably ridiculously expensive to execute that attack. The goals of most hackers, however, are more limited and far more easily and inexpensively achieved.

If a hacker's goal is to steal information, hold a company's data hostage for payment (ransomware), permanently delete all the software from the devices on a network (wiper), or flood a network to the point where it cannot operate (a distributed denial-of-service attack, or DDoS), the cost of such an attack against a poorly defended network is shockingly low. Indeed, there are websites on the so-called dark web where hackers sell those attack tools. Remote access tools (RATs) can sell for as little as five hundred dollars. A kit to engage in ransomware could be available for a thousand dollars. These tools will likely not get you into the network of Bank of America or Citibank, but most networks are less well defended than they are. When public announcements are made by software companies or cyber-defense experts about the need for specific steps to block newly discovered attack techniques, most companies do not rush out and patch their vulnerabilities. It is just too costly, too demanding. Thus, attack kits based on vulnerabilities that have been known for years still work on many targets.

So imagine that you are trying to find a way into a network to steal information or money. You could try all the existing hacking tools for a few thousand dollars. Probably that would not work on a smart firm that has fixed all the known vulnerabilities. As the attacker, perhaps you move on to employ a zero-day hacking tool developed or bought for a few hundred thousand dollars. Let's say five hundred thousand. Now, you might get in.

On the defensive side, a bank is spending a thousand times the cost of the half-million-dollar attack tool. Each major U.S. bank spends more than half a billion dollars on cyber defense every year. Arrayed against the cyber-criminal gang's hacker-tool-development team, there are more than several hundred bank and contractor employees defending the network. The attackers are using one piece of software, maybe with several embedded tool kits to help find and extract data they seek. The bank is using upwards of five or six dozen different, layered software tools developed by almost as many different cybersecurity vendors to detect and prevent the attack.

Imagine this contest as an ancient battlefield. Then, there might have been equally sized and equipped armies on either side of the field, each with a hundred thousand troops, cavalry and catapults, spears and shields. When they clashed, thousands on both sides would die. Today in cyberspace there would be a small professional team with one or two attack tools on one side of the field against many times that number of defenders with dozens of variations of shields and nets on the defensive side. The defenders will usually not attack, because they can't. If they are corporations, by law they are not allowed to.

If the attackers fail, they do not die, they move on to the next victim, and they keep going until they get in somewhere and steal data, take money, or stop the company from working. Like a hockey goalie, cyber defenders can lose the game if one puck gets by them. Instead of there being the thirty shots on goal in a two-hour hockey game, there are hundreds of thousands of attempted shots on a major corporate or government network every day.

And if somehow the defenders figuratively rip off the attacker's helmets and see their faces, even identify who the attackers are, often nothing happens. Today, the sophisticated attackers are well masked, but if they are identified, they often have little to fear because they are operating remotely from a country that will not cooperate with law-enforcement requests from the United States or Western European countries. This contributes to the "cybersecurity is hopeless" outlook that we so desperately need to combat.

Ultimately, a bank isn't spending half a billion dollars to keep out one attacker. It's spending half a billion dollars to protect many trillions of assets from more than two hundred advanced persistent threat groups. By one estimate, there are seventy-seven Chinese APT groups alone. And, more importantly, getting into the network isn't the goal. Getting information out or transferring funds or destroying computer resources is, and the companies that are good at cyber defense are amassing an impressive record of denying even the best cyber adversaries these outcomes.

What the Data Says

It's a somewhat odd predicament that in a field based on 1s and 0s, data is often hard to come by. Most companies that have been hacked don't have to disclose it. And, as Alperovitch points out, many don't even know it. What's more, companies that have a solid basis for believing they have succeeded in thwarting their adversaries don't exactly want to stand up and shout it. No CISO wants to invite the wrath of hacking groups who might just pursue them for showing hubris (the things some groups do just for the "lulz," or laughs in hackerspeak, are mind boggling). But some sectors of the economy are forced to disclose breaches of sensitive information. And when that sensitive information appears on the dark web, law enforcement often comes knocking. That means that an ostrichlike approach of sticking your head in the sand when danger approaches, not looking for data thieves, and hoping no one knows you were attacked won't always work.

If you have been paying any attention to cybersecurity news over the last five years, you might conclude that every major health-care provider was hit by a Chinese attack and lost their subscriber database. When health-care providers lose data on the people in their health plans, they are required to notify their customers and report to the Department of Health and Human Services. In turn, HHS helpfully reports it on their website.

Todd Inskeep, a longtime fixture in the cybersecurity community, decided to dig through the reports to find out what they showed. Now a consultant at Booz Allen Hamilton, Inskeep is often called in to be an interim CISO at companies after they have been hacked and have fired their full-time CISO. Inskeep is firmly convinced that most breaches are preventable. Oftentimes, the mistakes companies make that let attackers in are painfully obvious, at least after the fact. But many in the community will contend that if attackers are thwarted on one attack path, they will simply find another and eventually win. Inskeep thinks the data tells a different story.

When Inskeep and other researchers at Booz Allen looked at that data, what they found suggests that many of the largest health-insurance companies have done a pretty good job at keeping their customer data safe. While Anthem, the second-largest health insurer in the country, lost all of its subscriber data in 2015, some 78 million records, over the last five years the companies in the number one and number three positions in the market did not. Those companies, United Health and Aetna, respectively, lost a total of 12,000 records to cyber incidents. United Health, in fact, lost zero (though the company did report a small number of losses of files that had gone missing). Four of the remaining top ten health-care companies also reported zero losses to cyber theft. The three companies that round out the top ten reported a total of 37,000 lost records out of the 28 million records those companies hold.

Is it possible that these companies had major losses that neither they, nor law enforcement, nor the cybersecurity ecosystem discovered? Maybe. Is it possible that they simply weren't targeted? Unlikely. A health-care record fetches a pretty high premium on the dark web because it lets criminals commit insurance fraud, a highly lucrative enterprise. And so, the more likely answer is that these companies, motivated by a financial incentive not to have fraud committed against them using the information they store, have actually been able to manage the threat. And given the scrutiny health care has received and the intelligence assets placed against discovering Chinese intrusions, it is also unlikely that these companies were hit by state actors that managed to keep their thievery from being discovered.

We reached out to several of these companies to gain their perspective on the issue. Jim Routh, the longtime chief security officer at Aetna (now part of CVS Health, where he retains the same role), agreed to talk. Like most people in the field, Routh understandably does not want to incur the wrath of the cyber gods by proclaiming that his company hasn't been hacked, but he does agree that it is a reasonable conclusion one could draw based on the available data.

There is an old saw in cybersecurity that being in the field is like being chased by a bear. You don't need to outrun the bear, you just need to outrun the other companies in the field (so that the bear will eat them). Aetna's approach to outrunning the bear (proverbial or Russian) is to focus on innovation. Routh has one of the best records among CISOs and is constantly innovating to keep it. Aetna goes well beyond the requirements passed down to it by government agencies or its customers, rapidly creating controls that are not part of regulatory requirements or even part of voluntary frameworks. They track threat actors, study their tactics, techniques, and procedures, and work to understand the criminal ecosystem that supports them.

While Aetna has a pretty good record, Routh isn't about to give up and go home if an APT actor gets past him. Routh's goal is to achieve resilience, that is, to keep a security incident from undoing his company, halting production, or undoing its reputation. "Resiliency isn't about avoiding a breach, it's about preventing bad outcomes," Routh says. Yet so far, he seems to have avoided a breach.

To do that, Routh and his team are constantly changing the attack surface and modifying the environment so that even if attackers get in they can never be sure of their footing on the network and can never rest, knowing that they will be able to maintain access. Aetna deploys upwards of six hundred different controls, and changes which ones are deployed every day. They have three hundred machine-learning models running across nine platforms to control their security. They do red teaming (attacking their own network to test for security problems) every quarter. Authorization decisions on Aetna's network are made by a centralized machine-learning program that takes into account sixty different attributes before granting access. If it all sounds complicated, it is. "I teach a class for our auditors on how to test the mathematical efficacy of our controls," Routh says. "When I talk about continuous, behavioral-based authentication, regulators think it is voodoo."

Of course, it's not voodoo. And it's not luck. And of course, Aetna isn't the only company that is doing it. Beyond the health-care industry, it's possible to find many other examples of companies for which there is no public information to suggest that they have been breached. That may mean that they have pretty solid security programs, but it also may mean that they have even better lawyers. Under U.S. federal laws, only health-care records currently have a mandate that losses be disclosed to the individual record holders and made public. Disclosure of other types of personal data are required by laws in all fifty states, but these laws are limited to credit cards, Social Security numbers, and other personally identifiable information.

Large swaths of malicious activity are never disclosed or counted, from simple account compromise to the theft of intellectual property that undergirds our economy. That's because such disclosures are required for public companies only if they are judged (by the company) to be a "material risk" under vague guidelines issued by the Securities and Exchange Commission. In our analysis of public information on cybersecurity incidents, we found that less than a majority of the companies that make up the *Fortune* 500 had reported any significant cybersecurity incidents in the last decade. That means that the majority of the companies with the biggest bull's-eyes on their backs have either succeeded in keeping the adversaries at bay or convinced their lawyers that whatever was taken did not merit a disclosure.

For a small number of companies on that list, we have full faith that they have invested sufficiently and smartly to manage the risk and protect their most valuable assets. For others, we know for a fact that they have lost their crown jewels. Unfortunately, that knowledge is protected by classification rules that prevent us from publicly naming companies that the U.S. intelligence community has identified as victims of China's multiyear effort to steal our nation's most valuable secrets.

It is difficult to square the fact that in 2013 (the last year numbers were released) the FBI and other federal agencies made more than three thousand notifications to U.S. companies that they had been breached with the relatively small number that have copped to it publicly. Keith Alexander, the former director of the NSA and the first commander of Cyber Command, has called China's intellectual property theft "the greatest transfer of wealth in history." While we agree with that assessment, looking at the data on companies that have actually disclosed when they have been hacked does not add up to an honest picture of the losses we have sustained.

Given this reality, any list of companies that have been hacked is going to be imperfect, and identifying companies that haven't is even more difficult. Yet we think there is solid evidence that some companies are effectively managing ongoing campaigns carried out by the most advanced and persistent actors. Battling those actors takes advanced skills and equal persistence on the part of defenders. It requires using threat intelligence and tracking actors inside networks. It requires building out a cooperative community to create a global detection grid of adversary behavior. But most companies aren't being attacked by APT actors. For large swaths of the economy, "good enough" cybersecurity is a relatively straightforward proposition.

Getting the Basics Right

James Mickens is one of the funnier people ever to work in cybersecurity. A computer scientist by training, Mickens did a stint publishing off-the-wall commentary on cybersecurity issues until leaving Microsoft for a teaching position at Harvard. Describing himself as "like a petty, sarcastic version of Neil deGrasse Tyson," Mickens explained the universe of computer science to his readers. In one of his pieces that has become part of the folklore of cybersecurity, "This World of Ours," Mickens explains how to think about cyber threats. "Basically, you are either dealing with Mossad or not-Mossad," writes Mickens, referring to Israel's much vaunted intelligence agency. "If your adversary is not-Mossad, then you'll probably be fine if you pick a good password and don't respond to emails from ChEaPestPAiNPi11s@virus-basket.biz.ru." If it is Mossad, on the other hand, Mickens would like you to understand that "YOU'RE GONNA DIE AND THERE'S NOTHING THAT YOU CAN DO ABOUT IT," because if Mossad or another APT actor is coming after you, they aren't going to stop until they get what they want.

On both ends, Mickens is exaggerating for effect, but, as with much satire, there is a kernel of truth. In chapter 18, we will talk about what individuals need to do to protect themselves online: it is a bit more involved than just using a good password, but it is possible. On the other end of the spectrum, we will discuss in chapter 4 what companies that are consistently defeating even the most advanced adversaries are doing. We maintain it is possible. In the middle, of course, between practicing good personal cyber hygiene and threat hunting for adversaries inside your network, is where most companies need to be.

In 2011, the Obama administration put out a broad legislative proposal to regulate cybersecurity in critical sectors. After Congress refused to pass it, thanks to lobbying by an implacable U.S. Chamber of Commerce, the White House cyber team began to think about how they could nudge companies to invest more, and more intelligently, in cybersecurity without requiring them to do so. The idea was simple. If you can't regulate, the next best thing is for government to simply put out voluntary standards and urge companies to meet them. And so the National Institute of Standards and

Technology (NIST, pronounced like "mist") Cybersecurity Framework was born.

The framework takes the immensely complicated task of securing an enterprise and breaks it down into manageable chunks. Everything a company needs to do to protect itself fits into one of five core "functions": Identify, Protect, Detect, Respond, and Recover. These functions provide a basic lexicon that everyone in the company from the board to the coding team can understand. Each function is further broken down into categories that cover high-level activities such as asset management in the Identify function; data security in the Protect function; continuous security monitoring in the Detect function; breach planning in the Respond function; and communications in the Recover function.

Each category is broken further into subcategories that specify a desired outcome. For instance, under the Identify function, the first subcategory under Asset Management is "Physical devices and systems within the organization are inventoried." The subcategories are then referenced against existing standards documents such as the Center for Internet Security's Critical Security Controls, or NIST's own technical guides, known as the 800 series of special publications.

Critics of the framework will, somewhat justifiably, note that its list of five functions, twenty-two categories, and ninety-one subcategories, which tie, in turn, to hundreds of detailed technical controls, doesn't provide a ready starting point for companies that do not know where to begin. The team that developed it at NIST would argue that companies need to understand their own risk and risk appetite, and then develop their own security profile by selecting what security controls are appropriate for their desired level of risk. One thing NIST has made clear is that the framework was never meant to be a checklist. But for those companies that are looking for a simple list, there is good data to point the way.

Every year Verizon's cybersecurity division puts out its Data Breach Investigations Report, the VDBIR in acronymland. The VDBIR brings a much-needed dose of data to the opinion-driven, everybody-is-an-expert world we live in. When Inskeep looked at last year's report, some basic facts jumped out at him. He saw clearly that most attacks involved weak or stolen passwords—81 percent, according to the VDBIR. So he put strong pass-words or, better yet, multifactor authentication at the top of a list of five things most companies should do. If guessing a password or finding a stolen password wouldn't get an adversary in, the data suggested to Inskeep that attackers next went to spear phishing.

Symantec's Internet Security Threat Report concluded that 71 percent of organized groups, the really advanced nation-state and hacker-for-hire groups, relied on email to initiate their attacks. Data in the VDBIR agreed, showing that 66 percent of malware was delivered in email attachments. So Inskeep looked at how to address that. He proposed two controls: one set of technical controls like email filtering, and one set of controls focused on employee training.

Knowing that adversaries would not give up and take their hacking skills elsewhere if he blocked credential theft and spear phishing, Inskeep next looked to protect systems that could be remotely exploited. Instead of trying to protect everything, he thinks companies need to focus on where adversaries will go to gain access if they are thwarted on the two most com-mon pathways. Locking down, monitoring, and patching vulnerabilities in internet-facing systems would pay real dividends.

Finally, if you can't keep an adversary out of your systems, you want to keep them from moving across your network. Inskeep found convincing data from CrowdStrike that showed that most adversaries used known vulnera-bilities to allow them to move laterally within a network. Finding these vul-nerabilities and patching them should, therefore, be a priority. So he made it fifth on his list.

Will doing these things stop Mossad or, more importantly, the Russians and the Chinese? No. There is a reason the acronym APT has caught on to describe them. Advanced persistent threats are, if anything, persistent. But it will certainly make their job harder. No group is going to waste a zero-day exploit if they can use Metasploit, an open-source penetration-testing tool, to gain access to your network. Forcing them to burn a zero day is in the interests of both individual companies and the defense community at large because it increases the cost of the attack.

Denying the easy attacks means there will be fewer attacks overall. If newbie criminal hackers can't gain a foothold by successfully carrying out easy attacks, they may never develop advanced skills. This kind of basic cyber hygiene isn't necessarily easy or cheap, and it doesn't mean that companies won't need to invest in detecting and response, but it will cut down on the number of adversaries that can make it into company networks and will increase the work factor for those that do. But fundamentally shifting the balance toward defenders requires finding technical and other innovations that give defenders a decisive advantage.

In the next chapter, we look at how the best companies in the industry combat the threats that good cyber hygiene will never be able to stop.

Chapter 4

. . . .

THE KILL CHAIN

If some animals are good at hunting and others are suitable for
hunting, then the gods must clearly smile on hunting.

—ARISTOTLE

Possibly the greatest innovation in cybersecurity over the last decade
wasn't a technology but a white paper. "Intelligence-Driven Computer Network Defense Informed by Analysis of Adversary Campaigns and Intrusion Kill Chains" was written by Eric Hutchins, Michael
Cloppert, and Rohan Amin, a group of researchers at Lockheed Martin, the
large defense industrial base (DIB) company. The paper was released in 2011
with little fanfare at an obscure conference, the International Conference
on Information Warfare. "This wasn't Black Hat or RSA," says Amin, now
the CISO at JPMorgan Chase. "We had no idea that it would take off the way
it did." But take off it did, launching numerous imitators and dozens of companies, which have built technologies to help their customers find, fix, and
finish adversaries inside their networks.

We sat down with Amin in his office at JPMorgan headquarters in a
skyscraper high above Park Avenue. The building was remodeled in 2011 to

give it a West Coast, tech-friendly feel, complete with coffee bars (two), coworking desks (many), meeting and phone pods, as well as LEED certification for responsible environmental construction. If the image of someone who works at JPMorgan conjures up a Brooks Brothers suit and a Hermès tie, you would be disappointed to find that jeans outnumbered slacks by two to one. The reality for JPMorgan, like every other global bank headquartered in Midtown or in the Financial District, is that the venerable old bank is now a tech company that lends and invests money. That means they need an office environment that will attract the tech talent like Amin that the bank needs and have had to slacken the dress code accordingly.

Five years into his stint at JPMorgan, Amin already outlasted most CISOs in the field. Of course, Amin is far younger than most of his peers, part of a new breed of CISOs who, unlike an older generation that came into cybersecurity through IT, law, the military, or law enforcement, have spent their entire careers in the field.

Amin began working at Lockheed in 2002, right after graduating from the University of Pennsylvania with a BS in computer and telecommunications engineering and an MS in telecommunications and networking. Working at Lockheed, a company that's consistently under threat from the most skilled nation-state actors, gave him early exposure to what we now call advanced persistent threats. "In the early 2000s, people were still in the 'worms and viruses' state of mind, automated threats that were indiscriminate," says Amin. "But we were seeing focused adversaries with hands on keyboards, a person whose job it is to steal our info."

A few years in, Amin and others on Lockheed Martin's computer incident response team (CIRT) began to develop the kill-chain process. "We were seeing a whole bunch of Chinese intrusion sets targeting the DIB and we were tired of this victim mentality, woe-is-us, nothing-we-can-do, defeatist attitude." Built into that victim mentality was the idea that the attackers had the advantage. Amin and his team were looking for a way to flip that around.

Amin and his colleagues took inspiration from the Air Force, which coined the term "kill chain" to break down the process from locating a target to putting a bomb on it: find, fix, track, target, engage, assess. In applying the concept to cybersecurity, the Lockheed CIRT wanted to disrupt the effectiveness and efficiency of their adversaries in cyberspace. "We also were exposed to thinking from JIEDDO," says Amin, referring to the Joint Improvised Explosive Device Defeat Organization, a mid-2000s effort to deal with the threat from roadside bombs in Iraq and Afghanistan.

In building out the kill chain, the Lockheed team began with the same phases that JIEDDO used to break down the stages of a terrorist's building, placing, and detonating a roadside bomb: reconnaissance, weaponization, and delivery, everything "left of boom." They replaced "detonation" (the boom) with "exploitation," the stage where an attacker gains initial access, having defeated perimeter security protections.

Stages of the kill chain

Many cyber practitioners would see the failure to stop exploitation as a victory for the attackers, but the Lockheed team viewed it as the point at which the attackers were on their home terrain. To the right of exploitation, they capture three more phases: installation, command and control (C2 in the diagram above), and actions on objectives, the things an adversary needed to do to actually get what they wanted, whether that was to steal intellectual property or to destroy the network.

The paper the Lockheed team wrote turns the idea that offense has the advantage over defenders on its head. What the writers suggested was that attackers needed to string together an intricate series of events to achieve their objective. Defenders, on the other hand, only had to detect and stop them at any one of several possible stages. This kind of thinking proved to be revolutionary.

Today, it's hard to avoid the kill-chain concept in cybersecurity. "I often sit in on tech pitches, and at least half the time the pitches reference the kill-chain model," says Amin. "Usually, they have not done their homework and have no idea I cowrote the paper they are citing."

Breaking the Links in the Chain

Thinking like an attacker is the oldest advice in cybersecurity. Yet few of the good people who work in cyber defense seem capable of doing it. If you think like an adversary, it quickly becomes clear that there is a lot more work involved in going after a well-defended target than it would seem. And while there are now many different models of the kill chain under different names, such as the "attacker life cycle," to avoid copyright infringement against Lockheed, the basic model is largely the same. And it always starts with reconnaissance.

If you are going to hack Lockheed Martin or any other firm, you had first better do some research. This initial reconnaissance might involve using a network scanner to look for vulnerabilities, but it probably begins with a few tools that everyone reading this book already used today: Google and LinkedIn. Attackers are going to find out everything they can about the company. Where are its offices? Who are its employees? How is it organized? What software do they use? What systems do they run?

If defenders make it hard to conduct reconnaissance on the company by limiting information about who its employees are and what systems they operate, adversaries may give up and move on to other targets. If corporations plant false information, say fake employees on LinkedIn with profiles that point to technologies they do not use and fake email addresses for contacting them, companies can detect the reconnaissance in the early stages by noticing attempts to access those systems or contact those nonexistent employees.

After reconnaissance, an adversary needs to weaponize what they have learned, taking information about the company in question and putting together a plan to gain access to it. That might involve looking for a known vulnerability in a hardware or software system at the company and then buying or building malware to exploit the vulnerability. Weaponization is hard to counter directly, but the next stage, delivery, is not.

Most sophisticated attacks today rely on spear phishing, sending an email to a specific and unwitting employee at the company, with malware attached inside a pdf or other document. Sometimes the email provides a link to a website, where the malware will automatically download. If the attack is unsophisticated and reuses malware known to antivirus companies, a simple matching of the payload to fingerprints of known malware can block it.

If the attack tool is new or changed in any way, companies such as Fire-Eye can "detonate" the attempted spear phishing by quarantining the suspicious email and then automatically clicking on each pdf or link and seeing what happens. If the attachment proves harmful, the system will block it. Other companies will do the same thing for web links by seeing what they download when they connect to the link and determining if it is malicious. Still others will rate the website in the link for trustworthiness and will prevent employees from connecting to untrustworthy sites.

These systems are, of course, imperfect, and sophisticated adversaries will test their payloads against these defense tools before using them against high-value targets. That's why companies that have adopted the kill-chain model haven't given up on training their employees as a line of defense.

There is a cartoon that has circulated in the IT security community for years. It shows a boxing ring. The emcee for the match, gesturing toward a formidable stack of computing equipment in one corner, announces that "In this corner, we have firewalls, encryption, and antivirus software, etc. And in this corner, we have Dave!" In the opposite corner is an overweight, slovenly, middle-aged man with a silly grin and a T-shirt that says HUMAN ERROR. Poor Dave represents that one guy in every organization who just can't resist a clever (or not so clever) hook in a phishing email. Dave finds the offer for a free vacation or the policy report from a D.C. think tank he has never heard of just too tempting to resist.

Since the cartoon first appeared in 2014, the tech stack in the right-hand corner has evolved considerably. Today, the buzzwords it would hit would include "machine learning," "advanced AI," and "virtual detonation chambers," but Dave is largely the same. There is no training Dave. No matter how many PowerPoint slides you make them click through or security-awareness videos they watch, the Daves of the world will always click. But there is training that works for most other employees.

Companies that have made their employees a strong line of defense have done so by targeting their own staff with simulated attacks. They send emails trying to trick the staff into clicking on links or opening documents from sources that look like what an attacker might use. If they fall for it, instead of getting the document they wanted to read or the website they wanted to reach, they get a "You got phished!" message. Their company's security team and, usually, their manager also get notified. If they do that too often, there may be consequences such as a day of unpaid leave. Once bitten, twice shy.

Of course, there is still the problem of Dave. If one thousand employees resist clicking on the phishing email but Dave still does, the attacker has found their way in. To combat this problem, companies have realized they need not just to train their employees to spot spear phishing, but also to use their employees as a detection system. Let's say Dave clicks on an email that is also sent to his coworkers, and someone else recognizes it as spear phishing. Companies such as Cofense offer a button that can be embedded into their clients' email, so the staff recipient can click to report phishing.

Some recipients of the spear-phishing email may have been in a meeting when the email arrived in their in-box. Others may have seen the email and thought it was uninteresting. But a few vigilant employees may have seen it, decided it was a phishing attempt, and sent it off to the IT department, or clicked that Cofense button. If the company is lucky and Dave has not clicked on it yet, they may be able to delete the message to him before he sees it or they may place it in quarantine to be examined later.

Sometimes the spear-phishing email is so good that even the best-trained employee in the world would click on it. The attacker may have really done his homework and found out a supplier the company uses. They may have compromised that supplier's less-well-defended network and gotten into their email system. The spear-phishing email might then not come from an unknown or spoofed email address. It might have come from someone that poor Dave is emailing with all the time. It might even come wrapped inside a document that they were expecting their supplier to send, like a monthly bill. No amount of user training is going to stop that. But compromising Dave's computer doesn't mean that the offense has won. In the traditional kill-chain model, they haven't even gotten halfway in.

Once poor unsuspecting Dave has clicked on the pdf, the malware hidden in the background will try to take over his computer. It will attempt to implant itself deep in the operating system. But defenders can both prevent the installation or, if it fails, detect it. Sandboxing techniques, such as software that quarantines suspicious messages, can be used to keep the malware isolated, so it cannot gain control of the system. Endpoint protection applications from companies like Cylance block any activity that their models deem to be suspicious. Endpoint detection and response, from companies such as CrowdStrike, installed on Dave's system will watch for anomalous behavior that may indicate it has been compromised.

These companies' products seek to block the adversary as it exploits vulnerabilities in an attempt to execute code on Dave's system, install malware, communicate back with its controller, and move across the network, the next steps in the kill chain. At the most advanced companies, teams of highly skilled individuals are looking for these whispers of ghosts lurking in their machines.

The Hunters

The concept of threat hunting is fundamental to the kill-chain model. While each step in the kill chain provides an independent opportunity to detect the adversary activity, companies that are looking inside their systems for evidence of an intrusion not only have the ability to detect it, but also to stop it. That is why companies are working to break up the steps of the kill chain into many more.

The MITRE Corporation isn't a large company compared to other defense contractors, but it is an important one. MITRE is a nonprofit that manages government-funded research-and-development centers. Because of that, it might be working to employ artificial intelligence to detect the early signs of disease outbreak for the CDC, or it might be figuring out how to make the wings of a drone into solar collectors, to allow them to fly indefinitely. Competitors on the global stage, be they foreign corporations or foreign governments, want the intellectual property and state secrets that MITRE is determined to guard closely.

In 2009, the MITRE Corporation had its first significant breach. Gary Gagnon was its CISO. While many CISOs would have called in an incident response firm and started updating their résumés, Gagnon is not your typical CISO. Against his initial instincts, he green-lit an audacious idea from his incident response team, who argued that instead of trying to get the adversary out of the network quickly, they needed to keep the adversary inside their network, to try to understand their intent and interests. They proposed firewalling off the intruder to limit what information he could access, and then doing their own man-in-the-middle attack to compromise his command and control and learn his tactics and techniques.

"I've been on the job for three months, and I'm like, 'Holy shit, you've got to be kidding me.'" But Gagnon saw the value in the intelligence he could collect. "So, I said I will do this once, but I will never do it again." But he did do it again. In fact, he did it more than two thousand times.

That first incident made Gagnon realize that the attacks his company was suffering were not opportunistic, but rather well planned. "The mindset of most defenders is that it is random rather than a planned objective that can be understood. Most companies believe that the aggressors are not targeting them." But they are, and Gagnon now had the data to know it with confidence.

Gagnon thinks about cyber adversaries in terms of uncertainty. Attackers breaking into his network knew that the information they wanted was at MITRE, but they didn't know where to find it on the network. The attacker's job was to drive down that uncertainty by gaining a foothold on the network and then mapping it and moving laterally across it until he could find and extract the data he wanted. Gagnon's approach was to reintroduce uncertainty. To do that, he began a multiyear deception campaign to trick the adversary into wasting time and revealing his tools and techniques while Gagnon's threat-hunting team watched.

"In the world of deception, all deception is good," says Gagnon. And that's why he is not shy about discussing MITRE's deception campaign. "The fact that we are communicating to the public that we use deception as a tool starts reintroducing uncertainty. If an adversary gets in our network, how do they know if they defeated our controls or if we let them in? If they exfil data, how do they know whether it is real or whether we planted it?"

Gagnon and MITRE went all in on deception, building out what they called their "fun house": a "house of mirrors where we can let the adversary play." By 2010, they had a fully replicated model of all of MITRE's infrastructure. They captured the data they collected on adversary activities and transformed them into indicators to feed their sensors, but they also developed Collaborative Research into Threats (CRIT), a database that captures a wide range of adversary activity. Around 2014, the folks at Fort Meade suggested that MITRE study what they had learned and see how it could be used to inform the defense.

Gagnon's team created a chart that exploded the traditional concept of the kill chain. Instead of the standard seven steps (three to the left of exploitation and three to the right) the chart his team showed Gagnon depicted an expanded version that broke out the three steps to the right of exploit into nine distinct steps matched with the behavioral characteristics that could be used to detect the adversary at each stage. It was an epiphany for Gagnon.

"I already knew that I didn't want to play the cybersecurity game at the exploitation phase. That's vulnerability of the day," explains Gagnon. "I'm not worried about the compromise. What I worry about is what happens after the compromise."

Breaking down the right of exploit into nine steps that were based on five years of observing how adversaries actually acted showed Gagnon something surprising: attackers did not change the tools or tactics they used once they got inside the network, right of exploit. In many cases, attack groups were utilizing common tools that they have sometimes used for years. What that meant is that defenders were making it all too easy to operate inside their targeted network, yet this was the piece of cyberspace that defenders could actually control. Defenders could shift the balance in their favor considerably if they could figure out how to detect and disrupt adversaries on what was tantamount to home turf.

Gagnon immediately publicly released the chart. "I wanted to build a community around adversarial behavior right of exploit. It was now a tractable problem for me. It went from 'I don't know what is happening' to 'There are now nine objectives the adversary is trying to achieve.'" Gagnon's team also identified what tools the adversaries were using against them and where there were gaps in their detection capabilities. "That became an investment framework for us." Gagnon went shopping for new endpoint products that could fill these gaps. He dubbed the chart the ATT&CK Matrix, for adversarial tactics, techniques, and common knowledge.

Since 2014, the ATT&CK Matrix has continually evolved. Today, ATT&CK breaks down the steps an adversary needs to take within the network to eleven separate stages, so that threat hunters can look for signals that might indicate privilege escalation, in which adversaries try to gain administrative rights, or lateral movement, in which adversaries attempt to move across the network from their initial point of access. MITRE has further broken down each step in the chain into more than two hundred tactics to look for. Building on the kill-chain model in this way shows just how difficult the adversaries' job can be if the threat hunters are looking for them.

Collective Defense

The ATT&CK framework is ultimately an attempt to create collective defense among companies threatened by advanced adversaries. As such, it is an evolved example of the most dreaded phrase in cybersecurity: "information sharing." Information sharing often feels like the dead horse in cybersecurity that continues to be beaten well past the point where anyone could get any further use out of the concept. But in reality, information sharing has been the focus of cybersecurity policy for twenty years because it is both so important and so hard to get right.

We discussed the value that a single corporation got by pooling the insights of its employees on what might be a spear-phishing email. Now, imagine the value that corporation could get if it shared those insights with its peer companies and in return received insights from those companies' employees? That might really put the hurt on these companies' common adversaries. Why? Because if the companies are not sharing this information, the adversary is free to use the same email message, from the same account, with the same payload, delivered using the same URL, exploiting the same vulnerability, and communicating back to the same command-and-control infrastructure, across multiple different companies.

If one company discovered it, no big deal; one thousand others would not. But if these companies are sharing information among themselves, and a discovery of the attack by one means that every company will know about it, the attacker will need to be much more careful and selective. The attacking group might need to develop separate attack patterns for every target. That would be a lot of work.

By sharing the spear-phishing email, or malware, or any other indicators of compromise, defenders are hugely increasing the workload of the attacker. When the kill-chain methodology is combined with information sharing across every stage, the attacker's advantage can almost totally be erased. Of course, sharing this kind of information is difficult and it can be hard to justify against the many priorities within an enterprise's cybersecurity organization. After all, sharing a piece of malware with other companies in your sector doesn't directly benefit you. It benefits you only if, in return, the companies you share with also share with you. Some have described this as a tragedy of the cyber commons. Fixing the problem by incentivizing information sharing has been the focus of over a decade of government policy and dozens of academic and think-tank papers.

When PDD 63 called for the creation of the first information sharing and analysis centers to be created by the private sector, Dick Clarke hoped that the private sector would be able to muster the resources to build just one center. Since then, more than a dozen industry-level organizations have sprung up. The most successful of these is the Financial Services Information Sharing and Analysis Center (FS-ISAC). Encompassing almost all of the financial services industry in North America (and therefore most of the world), the FS-ISAC has addressed the sharing problem by creating tiers of membership. At each higher tier, newer, better, higher-quality information is shared among the members on that level. The trick is that you get it only if you can give in kind. The largest, most sophisticated members of the financial services industry formed the Financial Systemic Analysis & Resilience Center (FSARC), a separately chartered organization that works directly with the federal government to share intelligence.

For its part, MITRE has helped to stand up a series of regional information sharing and analysis organizations, nonprofit groups that pull together companies in the same geographic area to encourage them to build information-sharing processes. These efforts have enjoyed some success, but have also led many smaller, less sophisticated companies to the conclusion that they cannot undertake the time and effort of sharing information on their own.

Here is where vendors like CrowdStrike have stepped back into the picture. Instead of needing to set up a process to share a piece of malware discovered by CrowdStrike on one of your computers, why not have Crowd-Strike do it for you? Better yet, why not have CrowdStrike pull that discovery back to its cloud and share it with all its customers so they can block it before they are ever even infected? This is the concept behind CrowdStrike's intelligence-sharing offerings and those of its competitors.

Many of these competitors want to go one step further. Cybersecurity often draws in the civically minded. A large portion of professionals in the field got their start in military, government, or law enforcement. For them, "the mission" never changes, no matter whom they are working for. It remains always to stop the bad guys. And so, even when an economist might argue that it is not in the rational interest of a security-tool vendor to share information with other tool vendors, they do.

Rick Howard is a 1982 graduate of West Point whose last job in the Army was to lead its computer emergency response team. The chief security officer of Palo Alto Networks, Howard works for the kind of company that might argue it could do it all for its customers. Palo Alto offers a full range of network and device-security tools that are some of the best in the business. But instead of making the case that all you need is Palo Alto's suite of products, Howard pushed his company and its competitors not just to share information among their customers, but also to share it with one another.

Howard persuaded his then CEO, Mark McLaughlin, also a civic-minded West Point graduate, to start the Cyber Threat Alliance (CTA). Together with Symantec, McAfee, and Fortinet, Palo Alto agreed that under the CTA banner, these companies would each agree to share the new threats they discovered with one another. What is more, this would be no soft agreement. Membership would require sharing a thousand unique pieces of malware a day. The requirement was so high that only serious players could join. It had an effect that Howard intended. Rather than selectively choosing what to share each day, many of these companies chose to automatically share everything they found. Howard's goal was simple. He wanted to make it so that an adversary could only use a piece of malware or another element of attack infrastructure once before it was discovered and shared globally. In short, he wanted to achieve herd immunity.

Today, CTA members are sharing about four million indicators a month. "Seventy percent of those indicators come with some kind of context around them," says Neil Jenkins, CTA's chief analytic officer. "It's not just a file hash and an IP address, it's context about what industry is being targeted, what country is this being seen in, what attack framework or TTP [tactics, techniques, and procedures] is it using." And all that information is getting shared with every vendor that is a member. "If that information is getting shared and put into our products, we can protect thousands of companies and millions of individuals."

The idea (and execution) was so compelling that the Obama administration's long-serving cybersecurity coordinator (and Rob Knake's long-suffering White House boss), Michael Daniel, decided to become the organization's director when he left office. In Daniel's view, there was nothing else he could do outside of government that would have the impact that realizing the Cyber Threat Alliance vision would. Since taking over, Daniel has added another dozen members, including major players in the space, such as Cisco, Sophos, and Rapid 7. While he has yet to pull in CrowdStrike or many of the other endpoint vendors who view their intelligence as a competitive advantage, he keeps trying. Many of those companies' customers (including the federal government) are placing pressure on them to join for the simple reason that the best endpoint detection system in the world isn't likely to be as good as the ten next best combined.

Chapter 5

• • • • • • • • • • • •

THE TECH STACK

Software was not built to be used, it was built to be bought by someone at the top.

—STEPHEN O'GRADY, FOUNDER, REDMONK

I n the movie *Amadeus*, a young Wolfgang Mozart asks the emperor how he liked a new piece of music that the prodigy had just played for him. "Too many notes," the emperor replied. In Mozart's case, however, the many notes were all tied together in movements that together formed a coherent symphony conceived by one individual and then played on almost a hundred instruments, each chiming in at the right time for an overall intended effect. We are far from achieving that level of orchestration in cybersecurity. The whole of the cybersecurity technology landscape adds up to less than the sum of its parts.

Silicon Valley is seldom accused of lacking ambition, but in the case of security, few pitches that promise to revolutionize anything in cybersecurity make it to a live meeting with investors. Instead, venture-capital firms have chased relatively quick wins from marginally improving existing cybersecurity products. The "10x" improvement that Google looks for in its venture investments has not been achieved even by Google, whose new cybersecurity platform, Chronicle, looks altogether undifferentiated. Instead, Silicon Valley and venture-capital firms around the country have funded thousands of cybersecurity companies with massive overlap in capabilities that are targeted to a small set of buyers in the financial sector.

The large financial institutions spend huge amounts on scores of these products, both to placate regulators and to protect their assets from cyber criminals. All these tools are, however, a nightmare for most large enterprises to integrate and manage, and impossible for smaller companies to try. For every new regulatory requirement or emergent threat there is a new tool that someone wants to sell them.

You will never know how popular you are or how many friends you have until you become a CISO at a large-cap financial institution. Then your best friend from high school whom you haven't spoken to in twenty years will show up at your office with a new business card. He's doing business development for a new cybersecurity tool he just has to show you. A lot of the time, the tool might actually address a threat or close a regulatory requirement. So you decide to buy it and add it to all the other security technology in your tech stack. The problem is you then need to manage and run it.

One consulting firm we have worked with is doing brisk business helping clients come up with strategies to eliminate tools. They are often able to show customers that there are features in other products they already have that could replace one or more of their stand-alone products. Mostly, though, they work with clients to sort out which tools they really need and can actually use, on the theory that a small handful of managed tools will be more effective than a large number of unmonitored machines that go *bing!* Their record was reducing eighty-plus tools down to eight. That may be the right approach for some companies, but for those who are in a constant battle against advanced threat actors, new tools are constantly needed to combat new threats, protect new classes of assets, and generally stay one step ahead.

A utility company we know is in the process of a massive technology rebuild. They began with the largest set of security requirements they could come up with, drawn from the NIST 800 series of technical guides (and many they defined themselves that aren't yet captured in the technical docs), some 614 controls in all. They then began looking for tools that implement multiple controls. In the end, they ended up with 114 different tools. Sixty-seven are one-offs. The other 47 are designated as primary, meaning that they cover multiple controls. Six programs tie it all together, analyzing data across multiple tools using behavioral analytics. Few companies have the resources or patience for this kind of multiyear, multimillion-dollar integration effort.

The problem may be best illustrated by looking at what it takes to secure a simple desktop or laptop computer, what the security community calls endpoints or hosts. Gartner, the IT advisory firm, tracks twenty-two different categories of endpoint technologies, everything from legacy antivirus to virtual private network software. At a dinner Dick Clarke had with leading corporate CISOs in 2018, he asked how many different tools they were deploying only to endpoints. The low was six. The high was thirty-two, the median in the high teens. This many tools bog down systems and causes problems with compatibility. Many security programs are now being given a budget not for how much they can spend, but for the percentage of memory and processing power they are allowed to take up.

You might think that the obvious answer would be for customers who need to integrate all these tools to start demanding that vendors check off multiple boxes on their requirements list. You'd be right. That is what Sounil Yu has been trying to get industry to do.

The Cyber Defense Matrix

Sounil Yu works for a large financial institution, the identity of which is one of the worst-kept secrets in cybersecurity. He spends his days looking for new technologies that can help his bank do cybersecurity better, faster, and cheaper. The bank has a security budget on the order of $400 million per year. Yu's job is to figure out how that gets spent.

Every start-up that wants to pitch a cybersecurity product to his employer goes through him: thousands of solutions, each one claimed by their inventors to be unique. Lots of jargon, little differentiation. To help himself sort through the mess, Yu began to organize technologies pitched to him into what he dubbed the Cyber Defense Matrix. The matrix tries to capture everything that a cybersecurity program needs to do at a high level. Yu pivoted off the NIST Cybersecurity Framework's five functions: Identify, Protect, Detect, Respond, and Recover (what he calls "Things that I do"). He put those across the top of his matrix. Down the side, he wrote out the five common asset classes: Devices, Apps, Networks, Data, and Users (what he calls "Things that I care about"). He then started to fill in the matrix with technologies.

When he was finished, it showed heavy concentrations of technologies in areas like device protection, but huge blanks on the matrix for anything to do with recovery. Few products covered more than one space on the grid, and finer-grain analysis would show that no product could do everything necessary within a single square (despite claims made by their marketing department). When he took the analysis beyond the traditional company IT network and looked at tools for monitoring the security of employee devices or supplier networks, most of the grid was blank. None of this made sense. By some estimates there are more than three thousand security product companies. If three thousand companies were building security products, why were they clustered so closely together and not filling out his matrix? Moreover, how would companies other than the five or so largest banks ever amass the resources and patience to integrate and manage this mess?

Yu quickly concluded that what the market needed was platforms. All these tools did one of four things: sensing, sense making, decision making, and acting. Many of them did all those things (or tried to do all of those things) in a single, neat package. That approach created two main problems. First, it meant that every tool that required sensing needed its own sensor and every tool that would take an action needed its own actuator. Second, it meant that when it was sense making, it was making sense of only the data it collected from its own sensors. Sensors and actuators need to be deployed to networks, devices, and applications, and thus need to be managed. They are hard to get deployed and difficult to maintain, but the real value of these products was in the data analytics and artificial intelligence that made sense of the data and could decide what to do about it. So Yu made a pitch to decouple the security stack.

His epiphany was that a sensing and actuating platform could do the bidding of multiple analytics and orchestration tools. At a conference sponsored by the endpoint vendor Tanium in 2016, he made the case that vendors like Tanium could provide the platform for sensing and actuating for any number of analytics or orchestration tools. Companies such as McAfee, Cylance, and CrowdStrike could pull the data they needed from the Tanium sensor and then send actions to the Tanium actuator based on their analysis. Tanium could provide antivirus software "powered by" McAfee or Trend Micro, or insider threat detection "powered by" Exabeam. Tanium did not bite.

Like almost every other company in the field, Tanium wants to be "the platform," a do-it-all, single-vendor product, not "a platform" that other vendors would use. Tanium raised another $200 million last fall at a valuation of $6.5 billion, to bring its total raise to $800 million. The trouble is that even $800 million in venture funding is not enough to build out all the capabilities on Sounil's matrix.

Venture Tourism and Thin Peanut Butter

If anyone can be blamed for this state of affairs it is Silicon Valley. And if we reserve a special place in cybersecurity hell for the enablers of vice, then Sand Hill Road should burn. The tech start-up battle cry of "Move fast and break things," originally coined by Facebook CEO Mark Zuckerberg, has been pushed by the venture capitalists of the Valley in an effort to build large, monolithic monopolies at the expense of consumers, regulations, ethics, and cybersecurity. And move fast and break things they did, from the now antiquated concept of stable employment to a free press to U.S. elections.

All the while, the push to get products out the door and fix security later has led us to our current predicament. The idea of building in security, i.e., making products secure from the start rather than bolting security on after products are built, has long been championed by the security community. It never made sense to the "visionaries" in Silicon Valley, but when the prevailing winds of tech euphoria started to slacken as the breaches piled up, the venture-capital world became interested. It was like a fire department that both sets the fires and charges to put them out. Billions have gone to cybersecurity companies. Billions will continue to flow. Yet we remain far from a high level of cybersecurity. A significant part of the problem is the venture-capital model we have in this country for funding cybersecurity research and development.

In an attempt to understand how we reached this point, we sought out Bob Ackerman. In some ways Ackerman hasn't gone very far. He started out studying computer science at the University of San Francisco and now he sits a few miles away in an office on the Embarcadero almost under the Bay Bridge. In other ways, however, he has traveled the history of cybersecurity and is helping to shape its future.

From his early days working with UNIX and the pioneering BSD operating system to designing what a mobile phone/computer would look like at the technology company InfoGear years before the iPhone materialized, Ackerman went on to form his own ecosystem for venture investment in cybersecurity. Today that system includes DataTribe, AllegisCyber, and Founders Equity. The three firms together and his many successful investments in the field have earned Bob the nickname Mr. Cyber on Silicon Valley's venture-capital row.

DataTribe, based in Baltimore (near the NSA) and San Francisco, is Ackerman's vehicle to identify unmet needs in the cybersecurity product market and then to create teams, do research, and start companies to meet those needs. "I'm not an investor," Bob explained. "I build companies." In doing this seed and A-round investing, he draws heavily upon recently retired NSA staff.

Allegis is his vehicle for later-stage investment in cyber companies, B- and C-round money. Founders Equity is "for the ones that got away," a fund to buy stock in privately held cyber companies from early-stage employees looking for some cash before the companies go public.

Cybersecurity, along with other IT and biotech in general, attracts venture-capital (VC) money like bears to honey. Indeed, most applied cybersecurity research is funded by VC investors hoping to back the next unicorn on its run from start-up to billion-dollar valuation on the stock market. Although Ackerman is the quintessential cyber-VC guy, he sees some real downsides to the fact that investor money has flooded into the field.

"Visionary sheep" is what Ackerman calls the many venture-capital firms that think they must invest in cybersecurity start-ups. "The problem is most of them know nothing about cybersecurity, they just want 'a cyber' in their portfolio," he told us. "They're doing venture tourism" in the world of cybersecurity. "There are really only about a half dozen venture-capital firms who understand the field, the technology."

The result of this financial tourism is overinvestment and too many VC companies mindlessly following their competitors' activities, Ackerman contends. "It totally disrupts the economics of innovation."

Staffing those firms with the limited supply of cybersecurity experts and software engineers has, in the words of Ackerman, "spread the peanut butter too thin" on too many pieces of bread. It also makes it difficult for the corporate buyer to sort through a sea of look-alike, sound-alike firms competing for the attention and dollars of chief information security officers.

Many of the three thousand cybersecurity companies "are a feature, not a firm," he said. They solve one narrow problem and really should be part of a platform company offering a mutually supporting mesh of integrated security products. In a rational world, many of the start-ups would be folded into larger companies, but the desire of VC investors to force their firm to someday become a billion-dollar unicorn prevents such needed consolidation. Thus, while VC funding was a way to have private-sector money fund research and development in cybersecurity, it has now become an impediment to efficient market forces. Luckily, if the cyber-products industry can't solve the problem, there is hope that the IT-products industry, with some gentle encouragement, just might.

Building Security In

Sounil Yu's presentation at the 2017 RSA, the annual corporate cybersecurity conference held in San Francisco's Moscone Center, was titled "Solving Cybersecurity in the Next Five Years." He took a poll at the start to ask how many people thought it was possible. Only a handful of the hundred-plus attendees raised their hand. Undeterred, Yu made his pitch. What he meant by "solving" wasn't that cybersecurity problems would go away, but that they would be manageable, that the situation was improving, and that companies would achieve resilience in the cyber realm.

There is a concept borrowed from the military called the OODA loop, for observe, orient, decide, act. It was meant to help military leaders at the field level figure out what to do when bullets are flying and grand strategy has been tossed out the window. At each stage of the kill chain, the attacker is going through the OODA loop, figuring out where he is, where he needs to go, and how to get there. In order to defeat the adversary, Yu argues that defenders need to "get inside" the attacker's OODA loop, to respond faster and more nimbly.

Right now, though, security is well outside the attacker's OODA loop. It may take an attacker a day to infiltrate a system and two hundred days for the security team to find it. Security is slow. It introduces delay and approvals. The true cost of security isn't just or even mainly that it sucks down a decent percentage of the IT budget, but that it slows down businesses from making money. What's faster than the attacker's OODA loop? The business cycle, the pace that companies want to move at when unencumbered by security.

Again, pivoting off the NIST Cybersecurity Framework, Yu provides a history lesson in cybersecurity. In the 1980s, as information technology became affordable to the corporate world, enterprises started incorporating it into every facet of their business. As IT got spread around the corporation, it became hard for companies to know what assets they had and how to manage them. Security was largely in the form of asset-management programs. Yu therefore labels the 80s the "identify" decade.

Then came the 1990s, when viruses and worms started to emerge, and we introduced measures to "protect" our IT assets. That's when we got antivirus software and firewalls, secure configuration and vulnerability management. (Yu notes that when consultants say that their clients' security programs are literally stuck in the 1990s, that is what they mean: relying on antivirus and firewalls and hoping for the best.)

In the 2000s, we saw that attackers were able to bypass antivirus, firewalls, and other protective controls, and we needed a way to detect when that occurred. Thus were born technologies such as intrusion detection systems (IDS) and security information and event management (SIEM), which helped organizations home in on unusual activities detected in their logs. Security organizations shifted to include threat management programs and started building security operations centers staffed with personnel to continuously monitor and act upon alerts created by these detection systems.

Finally, to bring us to today, we are in the age of response. We realized that our detection systems were far from perfect; our analysts were overwhelmed by false positive alerts. We are instructed to "assume the breach," hunt for threats, and try to contain them. In this current age, we see the emergence of incident response capabilities, which manifest largely as a capability delivered through people with some technology to assist. We also see the emergence of hunt teams to seek out intrusions. Security organizations become more integrated into the overall risk-management programs so that the wide range of security issues can be properly prioritized among competing demands for personnel and resources.

By now, you should see where this is going. If the 1980s were the Identify decade, the 1990s were the Protect decade, the 2000s were the Detect decade, and the 2010s were the Respond decade, then the 2020s will be (drumroll, please . . .) the RECOVER DECADE! But instead of thinking of recovery as a long, drawn-out process of rebuilding after an incident, Yu thinks that recovery really means resilience, the rapid adaptation to emerging threats by systems that can fail safe. He sees a series of technologies that are coming online to make enterprises more resilient: content distribution networks like Akamai, Docker containers that allow applications to be spun up and spun down securely, serverless architectures, immutable infrastructure, and, of course, the cloud. None of these things are security tools, but all of them help businesses make changes to their IT environments quickly when problems arise.

Yu quotes Ryan McGeehan, who ran incident response at Facebook, as saying, "Larger swaths of risk are quickly being eliminated at newer companies, at earlier and earlier stages. And usually not because security was the goal." These technologies nullify attacker persistence on infrastructure by rebuilding it frequently, shifting some measure of advantage from the offensive to the defensive side. They provide visibility and make anomalies easier to detect by providing rich data on the state of security. In short, these technologies are being designed with security built in.

While Yu notes that since the 1980s, security and IT have been diverging and CISOs and CIOs are increasingly reporting to different leaders (and at one another's throats), he sees trends such as DevOps, bring your own device, and the ever-present specter of shadow IT bringing them back together. DevOps, short for "development and operations," shortens the software development life cycle by bringing the development team and the operations team in closer alignment so they can rapidly push out new versions of software. The fact that employees tend to prefer to carry around one device and not two has forced most companies to allow work to be done on personal devices. Shadow IT, the information technology systems that workers use to get jobs done that are not provided by or sanctioned by the company's IT department, has long been considered a problem in traditional security organizations. But some companies are starting to embrace these trends despite the apprehension of their security teams. If carried out with security in mind, they are finding, doing so has security benefits.

Yu argues that by embracing trends in technology rather than fighting against them, security can harness the speed of modern businesses as a weapon to be wielded against malicious cyber actors. With DevOps, companies may be releasing updated versions of their software dozens of times a day. That means that when bugs are discovered, they can be fixed immediately. It also means that bugs may be eliminated in rewrites before an attacker can identify and exploit them. The concept of chaos engineering pioneered at Netflix has corporations running a constant stream of experiments to test the resilience of their systems. Bring-your-own-device policies can let companies bring their employees' personal phones and computers under protection, rather than allowing devices to be used for some work purposes but well outside employers' control. Shadow IT is usually a sign that existing and approved technologies are too slow for business.

By embracing the speed of business, Yu believes that security will in fact be able to get inside the attacker's OODA loop. Simply put, business moves faster than the attacker. The new resilient designs that enable businesses to move that quickly are largely being built in the cloud.

Cloudy with a Chance of Security

There is a bumper sticker that is ubiquitous on the back of laptops at hacking conventions like Black Hat and DEF CON. With a wink and a nod, it reads: MY OTHER COMPUTER IS . . . YOURS. Stealing computing resources from universities, corporations, and individuals used to be common practice, even among the "gray hat" hacking world that was more interested in research and less in criminal profit. While cyber criminals still use stolen computer resources for mining cryptocurrencies and for carrying out DDoS attacks, when they need real computing power or to hide their tracks, they turn to the same company that you do for your socks and kitchen supplies: Amazon.

With a stolen credit card or a compromised account, criminals can spin up a virtual server on Amazon as easily as you can buy an ebook. According to data from Spamhaus, a nonprofit corporation that tracks online spam propagation, Amazon is one of the worst sources of all kinds of malicious cyber activity. Out of its data centers spew many of the ads for CheapPills and Ponzi schemes that clog up your junk mail folder. Amazon's servers host many of the domains that cyber criminals try to get you to click on.

Of course, Jeff Bezos isn't relying on spam or botnets to make his billions. As with the internet itself, the cloud has turned out to be a neutral medium, a mirror that reflects the intentions, good or bad, of those who are using it. So, like email or the World Wide Web, the cloud quickly has become vital to both legitimate businesses and the cyber-criminal underworld. Like every Silicon Valley start-up, criminals are making the most of cheap or free computing power. While the cloud has made it easier and cheaper for cyber criminals to do what they do, it has also made it immeasurably easier for companies that do not have thousands of people and security budgets with nine digits to implement best-of-breed protections online.

There are, of course, trade-offs. Larry Zelvin, a senior security executive at BMO Bank and a former senior White House and DHS official, worries that the cloud could be what ball bearings were to the German war effort in World War II, the single point of failure that when successfully targeted destroys the whole economy. When Rob Joyce, then head of Tailored Access Operations (TAO) at the NSA, gave a talk at the 2016 USENIX Security

Symposium about how to defeat an APT actor, he cautioned against throwing everything into the cloud and hoping for the best. "You need to remember that 'the cloud' is just a fancy way of saying somebody else's computer."

For some companies or government agencies, that will mean they will never trust what is going on beneath the hypervisor that creates the virtual computing environment in which their applications live, and they will choose to build their own. For most companies, owning your own servers doesn't reduce risk. It increases it.

Ed Amoroso, AT&T's longtime chief security officer, now an independent consultant, cautions against trying to replicate the security practices of the select few companies with these capabilities. "The *Fortune* 50—the companies that have five hundred to seven hundred people on their security team—when they say they aren't moving to cloud or they are going to build their own, what it ignores is that ninety-nine percent of the businesses and organizations out there bear no resemblance in any way to these large banks." The obvious question a company asks, he says, in making the decision to move to the cloud is, "Are we better than Amazon?" Ninety-nine times out of a hundred, the answer is going to be no.

For the rest of us, the cloud has the potential to bring the same kinds of security programs we discussed in chapter 4 to small businesses and even individual users. If you can't afford to spend hundreds of millions on your cybersecurity or hire a thousand people to guard your IT system, the second-best thing is to outsource the security of your computing infrastructure to companies that do.

Like the banks, Amazon, Google, and Microsoft all have security budgets that dwarf the GDP of Palau. They have global security operations centers working twenty-four hours a day, three hundred sixty-five days a year, working in eight-hour shifts that follow the sun around the world. In stages, each company has gotten religion on security, recognizing that their business models were predicated on being able to provide a security environment that was as good as, if not better than, the security environment in a traditional IT shop.

Early adopters of cloud services complained that using cloud services left them blind. They no longer knew anything about the state of security on the computers that ran their most critical operations. So Amazon, Google, Microsoft, and others began to make the data available. Now, businesses can get an instant, real-time snapshot of the state of their security and can use cloud computing power to analyze the data provided. Cloud providers are also being clear where their responsibility for security ends and where their customers' begins.

All major cloud services will provide their customers raw computing power. "Elastic" computing, which can shrink or expand based on demand, is what makes many regard Amazon as the leader in the space. Instead of a company building its own data center or stuffing servers into its closet, Amazon builds and maintains the computing environment and leases it to the company on a metered rate. It has proven the perfect solution for start-ups that need infrastructure on which they can build their own applications.

This type of cloud computing is known as infrastructure as a service (IAAS). Amazon and other leaders have also started to sell platform-as-a-service offerings that provide the coding environments on which to build applications. Far and away the best way to rapidly increase security is to move from local computing to software as a service (SaaS).

Salesforce, one of the early successful SaaS providers, never sold its customer relationship management platform as a software package you could install on your own computer. In fact, early on, Marc Benioff and his team made up company T-shirts that had a big no-smoking-style circle and slash symbol (think *Ghostbusters*) over the word "software." The only way to use Salesforce was (and is) to use a web browser to access it. The software sits safely on Salesforce's servers. It can't be downloaded by cyber criminals to look for vulnerabilities. When Salesforce discovers a problem, there is no delay between when the patch is ready and when it is installed. Malicious actors have no window through which to attack the weakened software.

The New York Cyber Task Force has repeatedly called out cloud computing as one of the best ways for the defender to gain leverage over the attacker. Amoroso, a member of the task force, identified a series of advantages that cloud technologies have over traditional IT environments. First, they offer greater automation: tasks like securely configuring devices are done automatically for you in the cloud. Second, cloud technologies are "self-tailoring," meaning that once services are selected, they automatically work together without needing to patch cables together or install software. Third, they have "self-healing characteristics," meaning that when things go wrong, cloud technologies will automatically switch over to back up infrastructure.

Cloud providers all offer different levels and different approaches to security. Google largely bakes security into its offering. Its security features can be adjusted, but come with Google Cloud offerings. Microsoft provides basic features, but offers additional security monitoring on a per-user basis for its SaaS offerings like Office 365, a popular suite for email and word-processing applications. Amazon provides a solid baseline by monitoring its own infrastructure and providing data on the state of that infrastructure to users, but allows third parties to sell security as a bolt-on to its core offerings in its marketplace. Google is so confident in its security capabilities that, instead of arguing that it shouldn't be expected to be able to stop government intelligence organizations, it is actively working to protect its customers from them and will notify individual Google account holders if they are being targeted by an APT actor.

The danger with cloud computing is that it is concentrating risk in the hands of a few players that now have a near monopoly. Almost all SaaS providers start out building their services on top of Amazon Web Services or Microsoft Azure and many stay that way. Netflix, now in a heated rivalry with Amazon Prime for eyeballs in the streaming wars, uses Amazon, as do other giants of the internet age such as Airbnb. Dropbox, the online file storage company, until a few years ago was also an Amazon customer.

What this concentration of risk means is that a problem at Amazon (or Microsoft or Google) could be a problem for everyone. Researchers discovered flaws in the chips relied on for most computers built in the last twenty years. These vulnerabilities, dubbed Spectre and Meltdown, would allow an adversary to access data being processed by a vulnerable computer chip even if the software being run was fundamentally secure. Because the cloud is "multitenant," meaning that multiple companies or users are running on the same hardware, there is the potential that an adversary who could compromise a vulnerability like this could access multiple sets of data at once.

While patches have been issued and workarounds put in place to keep cloud assets secure, the underlying concern remains. Attackers have found vulnerabilities that allow them, once they have gained access to a virtual machine at a cloud provider, to break out of that virtual machine in what is known as a VM escape attack. Researchers at CrowdStrike uncovered the high-profile VENOM vulnerability (virtualized environment neglected operations manipulation). The vulnerability was found in a popular open-source virtualization package used by almost all cloud providers. Luckily, the vulnerability was discovered in a security review, not through adversary activity, and users of the vulnerable software package were quick to put patches in place.

Since the VENOM vulnerability was discovered, a new layer of protection has been put in place for most applications that run in the cloud: containers. Just what they sound like, containers run on top of virtual machines and keep applications running in the cloud from interacting with other applications running in the same virtual machine. Thus, a vulnerability in one piece of software running inside a container would not let an attacker gain access to data in another. Instead of installing lots of software in system libraries throughout a computer, containers like Docker or Kubernetes keep all the files for the software to execute within the container.

For advanced threat actors, compromising the security of a cloud provider to get to your data may be something they are more than willing and able to do. Thus, the cloud may not be the right solution for all applications. The U.S. government, while taking a "cloud-first" approach in the Obama administration, has been noticeably slow to make the transition, instead consolidating its own data centers. Where it has made a big push on the cloud (i.e., inside the intelligence community), it hired Amazon to build out and run cloud infrastructure that only it could use. The reality is that for most purposes, the security bang for the buck you get by moving to the cloud is well worth accepting the residual risk. After all, being able to walk into your own data center and see that there are thousands of lights blinking back at you and that no one has stolen your servers provides no guarantee that there is not a team of APT actors silently riffling through them.

To Code Is to Err

When we spoke to Ed Amoroso a decade ago for *Cyber War,* we asked him what he would focus on if he were made "Cyber Czar for a day." He had a one-word answer: software. Poorly written software was then and is now ultimately responsible for many of the ills that plague cyberspace. Amoroso said that if he were in that position, he would direct government R&D to focus on reducing error rates in software and to develop tools to make it more secure. In *Cyber War* we lamented that DARPA, whose predecessor organization had funded the development of the early internet, didn't seem too interested in securing its invention. That began to change shortly after we published *Cyber War,* thanks in part to Mudge Zatko.

When Dick got tasked with figuring out a national strategy for cyber-security in the late 1990s, he asked colleagues at the FBI who some of the good-guy hackers were that he should talk to that could explain to him all the bad things happening in cyberspace. That led to a meeting at John Harvard's Brewery in Cambridge with members of the hacker think tank the L0pht. Mudge Zatko was the de facto leader of the L0pht.

With Dick's prompting, Zatko and other members of the L0pht team were asked to testify before the Senate, where they stated in matter-of-fact terms that they could take down the entire internet in thirty minutes, refer-encing abuse of the Border Gateway Protocol (BGP), which is used to route internet traffic between communications carriers and is still in use, vulner-able, and being exploited today.

Zatko, with long brown hair, sitting in the middle of the long table, flanked on either side by his fellow hackers, looked much like Jesus at the Last Supper. A decade later, his flowing locks had given way to a serious, D.C. professional haircut. The famed hacker looked like many other govern-ment functionaries in his official portrait, with a tight, square-knotted tie, standing with a straight back in front of an American flag.

When Zatko got to DARPA he doled out some of the funding he had to efforts to secure code. Zatko came from a background of breaking and ex-ploiting software and systems. In thinking about the problem of cybersecu-rity, he identified that many of the defensive software solutions being offered were actually adding to the problem rather than reducing it. Taking a sample of almost 10,000 pieces of malware collected from the late 1980s to 2008, he showed that the average number of lines of code in malware stayed consistent at a relatively tight 125 lines.

Meanwhile, security software such as a unified threat management platform now encompassed more than 10 million lines. In a case of the cobbler's son having no shoes, the code in security tools appeared to introduce new vulnerabilities at a far higher rate than other classes of software. Put another way, the security software was easier to exploit than the nonsecurity software.

Looking at the vulnerabilities added to DoD's watch list, which tracks existing vulnerabilities in the armed-forces-deployed computer systems, over a monthlong period in the summer of 2010, Zatko identified that six of the seventeen vulnerabilities tracked that month were in the security software the DoD had deployed. He showed that over longer periods, the percentage of vulnerabilities in security products would change from a low of 18 percent to a high of 44 percent. As if attackers didn't have an asymmetric advantage on their side to begin with, the DoD (and commercial industry) were introducing more risk and vulnerability than they were removing by deploying modern defensive security software.

Although coding has improved in recent years, it used to be a rule of thumb that there would be at least one to ten errors in every thousand lines of code. Zatko found that in some specific cases, such as NASA's code hygiene for mission critical space systems, that rate had been cut to between one and five. But given that Windows 10 has approximately 50 million lines of code, it is easy to understand how there could be a lot of lines that could spawn vulnerabilities.

After repeatedly getting complaints about how easily hackers and researchers, such as the L0pht, were finding errors in Windows, Steve Lipner at Microsoft developed a system called secure development life cycle (SDLC) to check code before publishing it. It became an informal industry standard and it did improve things a little. Companies also sprung up to vet code. We worked with one called Veracode, out of Bedford, Massachusetts. Parts of some large enterprises such as Boeing and Wells Fargo told their software vendors that they would not buy their software unless it had been checked by Veracode. IBM, WhiteHat, Black Duck, and other companies offer similar and related services.

Developers, the people who actually write the code for bosses who wanted it done yesterday, found SDLC and third-party vetting a cumbersome process that slowed them down. There was all that waiting around to get the results of your coding, then the time for fixing your mistakes. In the new, fast-paced world of DevOps, new code could be requested by a manager one day and go live on the network within twenty-four to seventy-two hours. There was no time for security review. Veracode's answer for that in 2017 was something called Greenlight, a software package that figuratively looked over the code-writer's shoulder as they were writing. It warned them immediately when they had failed to do something properly. There was no waiting for days. Other companies followed suit with similar real-time code vetting.

Still, however, there were errors. Not everyone had their code vetted for security, and the code reviews don't always find all of the issues. Even if security bugs were found, the developing company still had to decide whether they would actually change the code and what the cost would be to thoroughly test and vet the changes to ensure they didn't break things for their customers. Others who had vetted code would sometimes have to change it later to add a feature, and they would forgo security checks of the modified code. To err is human.

So maybe the solution is to take the human out of the loop on code development. Google, with its AutoML program, was using artificial intelligence in 2018 to write code for neural networks, i.e., AI to write AI. Developers Fan Long and Martin Rinard at MIT experimented in 2015 with machine learning not just to spot errors in code, but to fix them on the spot by having the AI write a patch. Meanwhile, at Rice University in Houston in 2018, Swarat Chaudhuri and colleagues were sketching. Actually, they were using a type of AI they call "sketch learning," which uses neural networks to recognize patterns and judge intent behind a question. Their goal was to have AI that could guess what kind of code you wanted or needed based upon your brief description. The AI would then put together Java code to respond to your request, drawing on what it had learned by looking at previously written Java code in the large GitHub depository of code. The Rice project, called Bayou, was funded by the Defense Department and Google. Microsoft was also funding work at Cambridge University in 2018 in which AI was attempting to determine human intent and then finding or generating the appropriate code. That project, called DeepCoder, is designed to grow from developing a snippet of a few lines for a minor component of a program to gradually tackling larger tasks.

All of this work is still early days of what we believe is the future of secure coding, indeed the future of all code writing. Machine learning, especially if it were ever to be powered by a quantum computer, could eventually examine vast amounts of existing code and learn enough from that process to write large-form programming on its own. That is a huge step from what is going on today with AI writing APIs or snippets of programs, but we can see the path to that outcome.

While this sounds exciting and promising, there are still significant issues to overcome. For instance, just because a computer can write code doesn't mean it will be secure code. AI/ML is notorious for "unknowingly" incorporating biases based on their models. Think of facial recognition scanners that are trained only on Caucasian faces and then become really good at identifying different white men, but think all other races are the same (this actually happens). To this end, the biggest promise is "proven" code. That is code that is mathematically proven to be constrained in its execution.

Formal proofs are well known in mathematics, but only beginning to be applied at meaningful scale to software. Coq, OCaml, and other proof languages are gaining traction. According to Dan Guido at Trail of Bits, the state of the art for formally proven "safe" systems is up to about fifty thousand lines of code. That is large enough for microkernels, which are often found in embedded systems, but a long way off from the multimillion lines of code in modern operating systems and even individual applications. Yet it's a start. By formally defining and verifying modular components of code, these pieces of code may be used as trusted building blocks, providing strong footing for less secure software running on top of them.

Meanwhile, as we wait for our AI overlords to start writing better code, Zatko and his wife, the data scientist Sarah Zatko, have started rating today's software for how well it is constructed. At the request of the White House in 2015, they set up the Cyber Independent Testing Lab to automate the process of rating software quality to, in his words, "quantify the resilience of software against future exploitation." They hope to give consumers the ability to compare products and distinguish those that are built with security in mind from those where security is, at best, an afterthought, and to pressure developers to harden their products. By doing so, they would take away the low-hanging fruit from attackers, upping the skill and time necessary to discover vulnerable products.

The Pieces Are There

Buried in the three thousand cybersecurity vendors are many of the solutions needed to stop most malicious actors from doing significant damage. Using the cloud and security as a service can help simplify some things. The pieces that are still missing seem to be coming or could be developed in the next three years or so. Some of those missing pieces include software to write software (error-free) and advances in orchestration that can truly bring all security devices together to orchestrate all defensive software. We need a solution to the seeming paradox that there are both too few and too many security products on the market. There is still a lot of white space on Yu's Cyber Defense Matrix, but there are also too many narrow feature set solutions to specific cyber risks, offered by such an incredibly large number of vendors that even giant corporations have a hard time sorting through the technologies, selecting best in breed, and integrating them.

Large corporations, the federal government (still the single largest buyer of cybersecurity products), and the VCs could do four things to make it easier for their people trying to defend networks to maximize the benefit of the existing solutions. First, VCs should require new companies to make clear where they add value in the existing cybersecurity landscape. Every presentation should include a slide in each pitch deck requesting funding that places the new technology in the Cyber Defense Matrix. Buyers of technology should not take meetings with companies that can't explain where they fit in. Going a step further, product companies should rigorously track which controls and regulatory standards they meet or help meet and, where there are no defined control sets for what they do, define them.

Second, buyers should refuse to purchase technologies that are not designed to be open and plug-and-play compatible. While there are some open-source efforts that may get to Yu's vision of commodity sensors and actuators, the industry needs to adopt this as the model for how technology gets deployed. We also think that for the midmarket buyer, investors should look at consolidating companies that can offer full suites of capabilities tailored to specific markets (think a baby Symantec for health care).

Third, buyers should place pressure on security product makers to up their game in secure coding. If an independent testing lab rates a security product as failing to meet basic standards of code hygiene, it should not have a market. Buyers should insist on security being built into the design of new IT-enabled products, rather than letting them be rushed to market only then to be hacked and later modified for security.

Fourth, we need to move away from product evaluations done in labs and soft-feature comparison to cooperatively sharing data on product successes and failures. Malcolm Harkins of Cylance has suggested that we need a process for publicly sharing data when security products fail to detect incidents, the same way we learn that a faulty sensor was responsible for an aviation incident. If Cylance or CrowdStrike or another endpoint detection platform failed to detect a compromise in an incident, that attribution of failure should be made known.

Thus, we are left believing that technology itself is not what is lacking to rectify the offense-defense imbalance. It is leadership thinking holistically about the nature of the cybersecurity challenge and looking for systemic solutions, cooperation among large enterprises facing similar risks, and an awareness in corporate and governmental leadership that cybersecurity is expensive, essential to the operation of any major entity, and demanding of a continuous and creative whole-company approach. More than anything else, it requires a drastic shift away from the attitude that security is hopeless and that adversaries win as soon as they gain a foothold in your network.

Chapter 6

\.\.\.\.\.\.\.\.\.\.\.

CYBER RESILIENCE:
THE BEST BAD IDEA WE'VE GOT

There are only bad options. It's about finding the best one.

—BEN AFFLECK AS TONY MENDEZ IN *ARGO*

The attacks started out small. The first wave of distributed denial-of-service (DDoS) attacks, at the end of 2011, was just probing and planning, stress testing the capabilities of the world's largest financial institutions. Over the next nine months, the attacks would occur only sporadically, a day here and there, but in September 2012 the frequency and severity of the attacks went up. The websites of U.S. banks such as JPMorgan and Bank of America were flooded with traffic on an unprecedented scale, and, oddly, at predictable intervals, Tuesday through Thursday from 10:00 A.M. to 2:00 P.M., New York time, as if someone was trying to send a message.

Media outlets, with the help of unnamed officials in the Obama administration, quickly pointed to Iran as the culprit, believing the attacks were a response to the Stuxnet malware that had disrupted Iran's nuclear enrichment program several years earlier. Phones began to ring throughout the White House West Wing. At every level from CEO down to CISO, the banks wanted the government to do something to stop the attacks.

The Obama administration selected a limited response. Rather than escalate tensions with Iran by striking back in cyberspace or sending a carrier group through the Strait of Hormuz, the administration chose to treat the attacks like any other mildly disruptive internet activity. The Department of Homeland Security coordinated remediation, sending information on the attacking IP addresses to ISPs and hosting providers so they could notify the owners of infected accounts to get them to delete the malware and slow the attacks. The State Department issued démarches to foreign governments to request their assistance in shutting down the attacks. No proverbial missiles were fired in cyberspace. The banks were not happy.

Not liking the response they got, the banks took their case to *The Wall Street Journal*. "We'd like them to act," declared one unnamed bank official. But act how? What this and other unnamed bank officials wanted the government to do was to either "block the attacks" or "take down the network of computers mounting them." As simple as these options sound, for both technical and legal reasons, the U.S. government did neither.

While the DDoS attacks against the banks were allegedly carried out by Iran, the malicious traffic did not stream out of servers located in Tabriz, Isfahan, and Tehran, which would have allowed for both easy attribution and blocking at national borders. Instead, the attackers commandeered computers all over the world, most of them in the United States. Using malware that homed in on vulnerabilities in popular blogging platforms, the attackers had gained access to large numbers of accounts on servers at hosting providers, companies such as GoDaddy or HostGator, and then used their powerful processors and high bandwidth to generate and deliver attack traffic to the banks.

In order to "block" this traffic, the U.S. government would have had to be sitting in between the attacking computers and the target computers. While blocking the attacks sounds appealing, the reality is that the United States has open borders in cyberspace. No agency of the federal government sits at the internet exchange points, where the undersea cables come up onto land, to inspect each packet of internet traffic. Without such a capability, the U.S. government is simply not positioned to block malicious traffic to protect banks or any other companies. Nor should we want such a system to be built. While China has a Great Firewall, a vast system of traffic inspection and interception deployed at the borders of China's internet and throughout the country, calling the system a firewall suggests, erroneously, that it has value for cybersecurity when it is in fact a tool for censorship and surveillance. Similarly, a Great Firewall of the United States would be an ineffective tool for cybersecurity, but a very useful tool for domestic spying and censorship, something we as Americans should be concerned about giving to our government.

Taking down the botnet through more aggressive means was also not practical. Directing the U.S. military to knock the attacking computers off the network would have meant launching a military operation against targets both in third-party countries such as Germany, Canada, and France, as well as in the United States. It is difficult to fathom the implications of the U.S. government taking such an action (there are still likely lawyers in the bowels of the Eisenhower Executive Office Building sorting through this). Foreign governments could reasonably label the activity as an act of war. American companies and individuals would rightly view it as an unreasonable invasion of their privacy without due process.

The attacks continued until May 2013. In the end, the banks were able to keep their websites up by investing in their information technology infrastructure so they had the capacity to service the legitimate requests of customers and filter out or respond to the malicious requests. DDoS mitigation companies such as Akamai and Cloudflare signed a lot of contracts. While CEOs continued to demand that the government make the problem go away, many of their chief information security officers quietly thanked their friends in government for not doing anything. The attacks got them the money they needed to make security investments that were long overdue. In that year's filings with the Securities and Exchange Commission, not one of the banks listed the attacks as having a material impact on their business, despite having previously called for the United States to treat them as acts of war.

If the U.S. government had chosen a more aggressive response, the ramifications could have been far-reaching. A tit-for-tat escalation with Iran would likely have prevented the nuclear deal achieved two years later. On cybersecurity, a stronger response would have settled the question of who is responsible for protecting the private sector in cyberspace in favor of making it a government responsibility. That determination would have had far-reaching consequences for the future of the internet.

Over the last thirty years, the U.S. government has worked to get out of the business of running the internet, turning over operation of the backbone to commercial providers in 1995. The final piece of transitioning the operation of the internet to the private sector took place in the fall of 2015, when the Commerce Department ended its contract for the operation of the internet root servers, the systems that allow the translation of domain names like goodharbor.net to the 1s and 0s that computers understand. As a nation, we should be hesitant about inviting the government back onto the network.

A Different Domain, A Different Strategy

Pretty much as soon as computers were invented, those who invented them saw the dangers of their misuse. And not long after that, all those involved recognized that protecting computers from malicious actors was going to look different from other national security missions. In other domains, national security is primarily, if not exclusively, the responsibility of government. Private companies may build weapons and Americans have variously been asked to plant victory gardens, build bomb shelters, and say something when they see something, but otherwise citizens have had limited roles in confronting national security threats. After 9/11, more than anything else President Bush just wanted average Americans to "keep shopping and traveling." Cybersecurity is altogether different. Cyberspace is a largely privately owned domain and it is fundamentally about the exchange of information, much of which is meant to be private. Thus, government's role and the private sector's role were inevitably going to look very different from how they did in other domains.

As the United States was just beginning to recognize a host of new threats in the post–Cold War era, President Clinton asked Robert Marsh, a retired Air Force general, to lead a study on what to do to secure critical infrastructure, including cyber threats. That study, released in 1997, called for the development of a public-private partnership. "Because the infrastructures are mainly privately owned and operated," Marsh wrote, "we concluded that critical infrastructure assurance is a shared responsibility of the public and private sectors." Dick Clarke and his team at the NSC reviewed the report and drafted Presidential Decision Directive 63 (PDD 63) in the spring of 1998. That document set out the basics of how the United States would approach cybersecurity for the next twenty years.

Like every presidential policy document issued on cybersecurity since, PDD 63 outlined how a partnership between industry and government to manage cyber and other threats to critical infrastructure would work. It called for the creation of the first information sharing and analysis center and set up an analogous organization in government. Each successive administration has modified or added to the policy. President Bush rescinded PDD 63, replacing it with Homeland Security Policy Directive 7 (HSPD 7), and then expanded cybersecurity policy with a host of other directives and strategies. When a bipartisan group chaired by Jim Lewis at the Center for Strategic and International Studies made recommendations on cybersecurity for the next President in the lead up to the 2008 election, their basic advice was simple: "Do not start over." Once President Obama came into office, he ordered a sixty-day review of cybersecurity policy, which largely concluded that the new administration should build on, not replace, what Bush had done. The public-private partnership needed to be "enhanced" and "evolved," but would remain the cornerstone of the nation's cybersecurity efforts. And to the surprise of many in the field, President Trump has also continued to build on his predecessors' work, even going so far as to positively cite Obama-era policies and programs in his own executive orders and strategies.

Over twenty years later, the idea of "public-private partnership" and "shared responsibility" are often met with a collective groan from those in the industry. The phrases are soft and well worn, recited in every politician's keynote address at cyber conventions and packed into the press releases that accompany every new policy announcement. As the scope and scale of cyber incidents have grown, if we have learned anything it is that government's role in protecting private companies from even the worst nation-state actors is and will remain limited. Part of the struggle with this approach, however, has been an unwillingness to fully accept its implications. The concepts of partnership and shared responsibility have remained fuzzy. Government strategies tend to avoid spelling out precisely how responsibilities will be shared because government officials have a hard time telling American citizens that, when it comes to cybersecurity, the buck does not actually stop in Washington.

Yet, as national-level incidents occur, those divisions of responsibility have grown clearer. Whatever policy documents say (or don't say), the fundamental responsibility for the protection of the nation's networked systems falls on the private-sector owners and operators of those systems, with the government in a supporting role. In short, private companies must protect themselves. The government may provide assistance, but its responsibilities are to do the things that only the government can do, such as investigate crimes, collect intelligence, and wage war. Companies are responsible for fending off denial-of-service attacks and filtering out malicious traffic. The government will arrest criminals and level sanctions.

Many on the political right have criticized this approach, arguing that cybersecurity is part of national security, the government's most basic responsibility. It should not be left to market forces or private interests, they argue. Moreover, they say private companies, in the business of making money, are not properly incentivized to take on this responsibility. They pay taxes to fund national defense and should not be left to protect themselves from foreign criminals and nation-state actors who wish to do the United States harm. These arguments all seemingly have merit, but they do not lead to a workable solution for the nation's cybersecurity. That's because all of these ideas would be cures worse than the disease. They would destroy more value than they would protect.

With all the talk of cyber threats, it is easy to forget that the benefits of internet connectivity are far greater than the risks that come with it. In developing an approach to cybersecurity, it is important to stay focused on preserving and extending the internet as a platform for increased efficiency, economic transactions, and the exchange of ideas. Any workable approach must address problems in ways that increase the value derived from the network. As appealing as it may seem on the surface to have the government step in and take cybersecurity out of the boardroom and off the balance sheet, the costs and consequences of an expanded government role would be far worse.

Can the Private Sector Bear the Cost?

In the summer of 2014, JPMorgan Chase was hacked. Jamie Dimon, CEO of the Wall Street bank, went on the offensive in the media, defending the company's investment in cybersecurity and pledging more. With unusual candor, Dimon publicly shared the fact that his company spent more than $250 million a year on cybersecurity. By any measure, this is a larger number, but the denominator is important. JPMorgan is the largest bank in the United States. Its assets total more than $2.5 trillion. In 2017, income exceeded $24 billion, on revenue of almost $100 billion. How much is too much to protect these assets?

In judging whether a company is spending enough on cybersecurity, an often-used metric is the percentage of spending on information technology compared to how much is spent to protect this enterprise. Modern banks, after all, tend to look like IT companies on the inside. No other industry has embraced the many digital revolutions with the rapidity of the financial industry. JPMorgan spends $10 billion per year on technology and employs fifty thousand technologists, one in every five of its employees. By comparison, Facebook's total number of employees is thirty-five thousand. Google, sixty-one thousand.

To protect their investment, JPMorgan spends $600 million per year. On a dollar-for-dollar basis, JPMorgan spends about 6 percent of its IT budget on IT security. Within the field of IT security, that is in the average range. A company building capability could easily spend more than that in any given year, as could a company with critical assets targeted by advanced actors, as JPMorgan clearly is.

Is it too much? Many pundits and politicians have begun to ask at what point, given the security risks, the internet has caused more problems than it has solved. Simple math suggests that when the cost of securing a network exceeds the value derived from being on that network, it no longer makes business sense to be online. We are far from that point.

In recognition of the cyber threat his company faces, Dimon said that he would likely double the amount that JPMorgan spends on cybersecurity. While spending at this level would put the company squarely in the middle of the pack on expenditure, smart investments could allow a company working at the scale of JPMorgan to spend less. Poor decisions could require more. Even at half a billion dollars of spending, the investment is worth it because of the incredible value unlocked by networked technology. Thus, we return to the idea, so seemingly unfair, that the private sector can afford to pick up the cost of protecting itself and that government should, unlike in every other domain, take a supporting role.

The Home Depot Model

While many in government may wish to assign primary cybersecurity responsibility to the private sector, actual national strategy is vague when it comes to the details of which side is doing what. Many in the cybersecurity community (including both of us) gave the Trump administration a certain amount of credit for building on the work of previous administrations in the National Cyber Strategy released in 2018. As if on cue, the strategy completely dodged the question of where government's role ends and the private sector's begins. Instead of clarifying roles and responsibilities, the strategy stipulates that "the Administration will clarify the roles and responsibilities of Federal agencies and the expectations on the private sector related to cybersecurity risk management and incident response" at a later date.

While the Obama administration never released a formal strategy that spelled out the President's approach to cybersecurity, it did ultimately get more precise about what private companies could expect from government and vice versa. The best articulation was in a 2013 speech by Michael Daniel, then the President's cybersecurity coordinator, who made clear at the RSA cybersecurity conference that private companies are responsible for their own network defense. The government will provide support and do the things that only government can do. As Daniel explained, there is a broad spectrum of activities the federal government might take in response to a significant cyber incident:

- DHS, with the support of FBI, NSA, and other agencies, might intensify information sharing efforts and provide technical assistance to companies that are victims of an attack;
- The State Department might use diplomatic channels to call upon countries to stop this activity;
- Using other tools, federal law enforcement may investigate, attribute, arrest, and prosecute perpetrators;
- The FBI or the Secret Service could work through the courts and companies to stop U.S. infrastructure from being used in the attack;
- The Department of Homeland Security might coordinate with foreign governments to get infrastructure participating in the attack shut down;
- The executive branch might issue financial sanctions or visa restrictions against foreign hackers involved in efforts to disrupt our networks and critical infrastructure;
- And if warranted by a cyber incident's effects, the President might call on the U.S. military to take action.

Daniel's scenarios can be boiled down into a short list of potential actions that the government could take, including sharing information on threats, providing technical assistance, using diplomatic tools, investigating the crime, using legal action to stop the attack, issuing economic sanctions, and, on a very bad day, using military force inside or outside cyberspace. None of these response options look like what Daniel framed as the government "riding in on a white horse" in response to an incident. The government's strategy is basically taking a cue from Home Depot: You can do it. We can help. Private companies remain fundamentally responsible for protecting their own assets and systems.

The Dangerous Allure of a National Protection System

Keith Alexander is not convinced by this line of reasoning. He is unequivocal in his belief that private companies protecting themselves from nation-state threats is not working. Now the CEO of the venture-backed cybersecurity start-up IronNet, he works in a suburban office park not far from Fort Meade. The company's motto is "The mission continues." General Alexander is not the only person at the company to come out of the U.S. intelligence community, and it is clear that he still thinks about cybersecurity questions in terms of U.S. national security and not shareholder value (likely to the chagrin of his VC backers). "I flipped through this before you arrived," he told us, dropping a pocket copy of the Constitution on the table. "It still says that the purpose of the Union is to provide for the common defense. There is no parenthetical that says 'except in cyberspace.'"

Alexander has been making the case that we should no more expect U.S. companies to defend themselves from Russian cyberattacks than we should from Russian nuclear bombers. Writing in the *Financial Times* with Jamil Jaffer, he notes: "In no other context do we rely on private-sector actors to defend themselves against national-level threats. After all," he continues, "we don't expect Walmart or Tesco to put surface-to-air missiles on top of their warehouses to defend against Russian bombers. Yet when it comes to cyberattacks, we demand exactly that from JPMorgan and Barclays."

It's a compelling but somewhat flawed argument. Cyberattacks, as disruptive as they are, are not Russian bombers carrying nuclear warheads. Cyberspace is also an altogether different domain than the air through which nuclear bombs fall and missiles fly. If we could change the fabric of air to prevent bombs from falling, or after one bomb has fallen block all others like it, those would be preferable options to either placing missiles on the roofs of Walmart or creating a potentially world-ending nuclear deterrence strategy (it was called MAD for a reason). Moreover, distinguishing between criminal attackers and foreign nation-state groups is becoming increasingly difficult, as some criminal groups are every bit as sophisticated as the best nation-state groups today and are often hired by foreign governments.

By now, it should be clear to anyone that the Department of Defense is not magically protected from cyber threats. If there are classified capabilities that the Pentagon won't share with the private sector, nobody should be too upset because they don't appear to work very well. Moreover, the DoD, like the big banks, is benefiting from the large infusion of new technologies from the private sector. Sharkseer, the Pentagon's cutting-edge new intrusion detection program, is in fact an amalgamation of many dozens of different commercially available products. To be clear, Alexander is not calling for government to take over defense. Ultimately, what Alexander seems to be calling for is a tighter coupling of industry and government so that intelligence can be shared and collective action can be taken. We wholly agree with and endorse that approach.

While Alexander isn't actually arguing for a fundamental shift in responsibility, others have. Alan Charles Raul, the former vice chairman of the Privacy and Civil Liberties Oversight Board, makes the case in *The Wall Street Journal* that "Cyber defense is a government responsibility." Raul draws an analogy to the creation of the U.S. Navy in response to the threat of the Barbary pirates in 1794, arguing that government similarly has responsibility today, when commerce is threatened by "digital Barbary pirates." Raul argues that "Congress and the President must immediately order the Department of Homeland Security, FBI, and Secret Service—and the State Department—to protect American commerce from attacks, as the Navy and Marines protected U.S. maritime trade off the coast of Tripoli 200 years ago."

Raul is dismissive of the approach of government partnering with the private sector and sharing information, and against a regulatory approach. He falls back on the notion of having government inspect internet traffic. He suggests that the federal government should make Einstein, a program run by the Department of Homeland Security to protect federal agencies, available more broadly.

As the spate of breaches at federal agencies from the Office of Personnel Management to the State Department indicate, Einstein is no panacea. While the name "Einstein" may suggest that it is somehow smarter than other network defense tools, details on the program's function and operations, as revealed in a series of privacy impact assessments that are publicly available, make clear the program is simply a combination of commercially available tools that monitor where internet traffic is coming from and going to, detect intrusions, and block them using known signatures of malicious activity. The advantage this program has is that it can use classified signatures, thus possibly bringing knowledge of adversary capability and intention derived from intelligence collection.

The idea that government should create a national system to protect the private sector and that this system should make use of the capabilities of the National Security Agency is not a new one. In fact, the program that houses the Einstein system at DHS suggests a grander scale than simply protecting federal agencies. It is called the National Cybersecurity Protection System. In the Bush administration, most of the focus of the Comprehensive National Cybersecurity Initiative in 2008 was on the idea of using intelligence to provide an advantage to network defenders. That approach met with limited success. If companies want these signatures, they can have them today. In 2013, President Obama signed an executive order creating a program called Enhanced Cybersecurity Services that gives this classified information to commercial service providers to protect their customers. Five years later, uptake rates have been low.

Other countries may yet try to make this approach succeed. In countries that do not value privacy and freedom of expression, concerns over the government's ability to read communications at will are not an obstacle. In countries where private companies hold less sway, slower, less reliable internet communications are less of a concern (though they will no doubt have an impact on economic competitiveness and foreign investment). Yet for one last reason, relying on this approach is likely to be a mistake: it won't work.

As the speed and volume of network traffic increases, the ability to meaningfully inspect it at the internet's choke points goes down. The increasing ubiquity of encryption makes the task all but impossible, as the content of traffic is not readily available for scanning. This technical reality has put the British government in the ironic position of calling for traffic to move unencrypted, an act that would be counterproductive from a cybersecurity perspective.

While governments talk about creating national perimeters in cyberspace to secure their nations, as we have noted, industry is moving in the other direction. Perimeter approaches at the company network level (let alone the national level) were declared dead long ago. As we discussed earlier, cutting-edge companies in cybersecurity today are doing three things:

looking at traffic moving *within* company networks for signs of malicious activity; detecting malicious activity on individual computers (endpoint detection); and making product purchases and architecture decisions to favor the defender. Initial judgments about whether a packet contains malicious content must be made in the context of the company or organization being targeted, something no government agency anywhere in the world is equipped to do. If what is required to achieve cybersecurity is to monitor internal company traffic, to place software on each individual computer, and to make smart architecture decisions, what role is there for government in this business?

The Glassiest House

Even before he became national security adviser, John Bolton wanted to blow things up in cyberspace. Always a hawk, Bolton, in what should have been his twilight years, ramped up his rhetoric. In the month before his surprise ascendance to the White House, Bolton argued forcibly that the United States needed to go on the offensive against Russian, Chinese, and Iranian cyber units. Nobody paid much attention until after Bolton was tapped, when Corey Bennett, an enterprising reporter at *Politico*, dug up Bolton's speeches and op-eds and asked the cyber cognoscenti for comment. Once in office, Bolton quickly demolished the Iran nuclear deal and tried to derail negotiations with North Korea with a predictable call for unconditional surrender prior to beginning negotiations. Bolton likes conflict. Having called for the United States to get muscular in cyberspace, he then set about systematically dismantling the cyber office at the National Security Council. He sent the well-respected cyber coordinator Rob Joyce back to the NSA.

Ultimately, though, weak coordination (or no coordination) at the White House could give Cyber Command a freer hand. Instead of huddling in the Situation Room or meeting via teleconference to organize a whole-government approach to an unfolding crisis in cyberspace, now the Pentagon can simply let the proverbial missiles fly. Of course, as it turns out, few people in the Pentagon are thrilled to be unshackled. That's because no one with any knowledge of how cyber offense is conducted thinks that "counter cyber" or "defending forward" works very well. The community also worries about the very real potential for blowback.

In theory, counter-cyber activity might work like this. An Iranian hacking unit sipping a Red Bull in a nondescript office complex outside Tehran attempts to gain access to an electric utility in New Jersey. Maybe they are conducting reconnaissance so they can black out the Northeast in a future conflict. Maybe they want to steal the schematics for a new interchange and share them with the utility planners in greater Tehran. Maybe it was Tuesday, they were bored, and their scans turned up an insecure system. Whatever the reason, they start hammering away on the log-in for a web server at the utility. Perhaps the NSA picks up on this activity in its routine collection. Perhaps the utility notices the failed log-in attempts. Either way, the Iranians have carried out an attack on the United States and it is time to fight fire with fire.

Of course, the Iranian hackers didn't attempt to connect directly from their computers to the New Jersey utility. Instead, they hid their tracks through a series of hop points. These might be compromised computers in homes and small businesses. They might have used a commercial or consumer-grade virtual private network or one of the many censorship circumvention tools designed to allow people behind national firewalls to roam the web freely. Or, if they were hip to the latest trends in the cyber-criminal underworld, they might have used a stolen credit-card number bought for fifty cents on the dark web to set up an Amazon Web Services account and purchased all the computing power they needed. Chances are, they used several of these techniques to create a string of hop points.

What that means for the counteroffense team at Fort Meade (or, in some darker fantasies, at the utility) is that hitting the Iranians back just became pretty complicated. At the very least, the last hop point used to access the utility's server was in the United States. Chances are high that several were. That creates a jurisdictional nightmare that the courts will need to sort out. Warrants will need to be issued. The FBI will need to be brought in. Certainly, it forestalls the idea of destroying that computer. Before the trail leads to Tehran, it probably winds its way through servers in at least one other country (after all, Iran does not do much business with the United States).

Maybe it leads to computers in our once and future allies Germany and France. Maybe it leads to a server in our sometimes adversary China. Either way, following that trail comes with a boatload of geopolitical risks. Dropping a "cyber bomb" on those servers is not a viable response, at least in the near term.

If the legal and diplomatic questions can be worked out, maybe, just maybe, the counter-cyber team can follow it all the way to the laptop resting on the knees of the Iranian hacker. Now what? Time is short. He's about to shut down the virtual machine he is working in and reboot. Should the counter-cyber team brick his device? That will teach him! Oh wait, he's got a dozen different computers he works on. Hmmm, you say, maybe we need to ratchet things up. Let's see whether we can take out the power in all of Tehran. That would create deterrence!

While the counter-cyber team is preparing to black out Tehran, its colleagues on the other side of the wall at Fort Meade have been busy. They think the right thing to do is to maintain persistence on the Iranian hackers' device and gather intelligence. After all, destroying a six-hundred-dollar laptop will not hurt the Iranians too much and taking down the power grid in Tehran for a single attempt to gain access to a server in New Jersey would not actually be proportional. Better to know what the Iranians are doing than to do virtually nothing to stop them and, in so doing, go blind. The utility in New Jersey might have made a different decision, of course. If unshackled from the laws that prohibit hacking back, it might very well have decided it needed to do something punitive. Private companies escalating in the cyber arena create the likelihood that they will start a war that the United States military will need to finish.

Recognizing both that current law prohibits any form of private-sector activity on a company's own network and that companies have a legitimate gripe, Congress has tried to craft a law. A proposed law, the Active Cyber Defense Certainty Act, is, in fact, quite sensible, to the point that it makes such operations totally unworkable. Under the proposed act, companies wouldn't be allowed to do anything destructive or retaliatory, but they could "hack back" to establish attribution and find out what was taken. Before a company went off its own network, it would need to notify the FBI's National Cyber

Investigative Joint Task Force. The company would have to share what type of breach occurred, who the company would combat with its active defense measure, how it is preserving evidence for further investigation, and what steps it is taking to minimize harm to third parties. All that would give it a "defense" against charges of violating the Computer Fraud and Abuse Act, but not immunity from it. In the circumstances where intelligence collection or tactical or retaliatory action is called for, it is likely a better idea for companies to rapidly pass off information on the incident to government and to have government take those actions when it is in the national security interest. There are limits to the value of offense and dangers in overrelying on it.

Michael Sulmeyer, a senior cybersecurity policy official at the Pentagon in the Obama era, has a neat way of summing up the problem with looking to offense as the solution to the cybersecurity dilemma. On the speaker's circuit while at Harvard's Belfer Center, he would break down the problem in a straightforward manner. "We all know the old saying 'Those who live in glass houses shouldn't throw stones.' Well," he would continue, "let's just assume that in cyberspace the U.S. government has the best stones, the sharpest, the shiniest stones, really great stones. But let's also recognize that we live in the glassiest house. So sharpest stones, glassiest house. Will we really care that we can send our supersharp, awesome stones through somebody else's window when they can throw a cinder block through our glass house?" Usually, that ended the desire of anyone in the audience to argue that hitting back in cyberspace should be a major part of the solution.

Gaining Leverage

Many historians have tried to come up with theories to predict why wars begin, but perhaps the one with the greatest explanatory power is offense-defense theory. In his classic *The Causes of War*, Stephen Van Evera of MIT offers convincing evidence that the question of whether offense actually has an advantage over defense is not as important as whether aggressors believe that they have an advantage. On the eve of World War I, combatants widely believed that the ability to move troops around rapidly on rail gave an advantage to the offense, not realizing the reality of the trench warfare to come, where defending machine-gun nests would cut down advancing troops by the millions. Allan Friedman and Peter Singer argue that the belief in a first-strike advantage is as misguided today in cyberspace as it was on the eve of the First World War.

As they point out, significant attacks require high levels of expertise and may require months if not years of planning. The outcomes may be difficult to achieve, hard to predict, and possibly unknowable. And, of course, there is some small risk that you will be caught and arrested or at least kept from ever traveling outside the authoritarian states that give you shelter. Thinking along these lines, shifting the advantage decisively to the defender will require increasing the work factor for the attacker; increasing the skill level necessary so that it is harder to gain a foothold, as it were, in the cyber-criminal world; increasing the uncertainty around success; and decreasing the rewards and increasing the risks of engaging in cyberattacks. When a group of Wall Street security executives thought about how to achieve these outcomes, they realized they needed to borrow an idea from the moneymakers on the trading floors: leverage.

For over a generation, the center for cybersecurity policy has been Washington, D.C. That makes sense for most policy issues because Washington is, after all, the seat of government. And so, when the people who write task force reports on various topics assemble, they usually do so at a D.C.-based think tank like the Brookings Institution or the Center for Strategic and International Studies. Cybersecurity, as we are learning, is different. If the main responsibility for cybersecurity falls to the private sector, then figuring out a path forward might better be done in the seat of business, not government. Thus, the New York Cyber Task Force was born.

Phil Venables and Greg Rattray are both longtime fixtures in cybersecurity policy circles. Venables, a computer scientist by training, has spent his career in security at banks and has been at Goldman Sachs for close to twenty years. Rattray, a political scientist by training, is a retired Air Force colonel who had a hand in many if not most of the early efforts to combat cyber threats at the Pentagon and at the White House. Rattray is now a senior executive at JPMorgan. To the problem of cybersecurity, Venables brings a deep understanding of what it takes to protect an enterprise in cyberspace; Rattray, who has, among other things, advised ICANN on security, thinks about security from the perspective of the internet as a war-fighting domain and a global ecosystem. Together with the dean of the School of International and Policy Affairs at Columbia, Merit Janow, they conceived of the task force. To run it, they could think of only one person.

We meet with Jason Healey in his office at Columbia University in the Morningside Heights neighborhood of Manhattan. It's on the thirteenth floor and his office number is 1337. Asked whether he got that office and number assigned to him at random, Healey is somewhat coy. If you invert "1337" it looks somewhat like the word "LEET," hackerspeak for someone who is "elite." Healey, who is quick to say that he is not a hacker, is certainly elite in the field of cyber policy. His office is filled with well-worn copies of every book ever written on cyber warfare. On the back of the office door is hung a speaker hoodie from Black Hat, and there are about fifty lanyards with speaker badges from DEF CON, RSA, and other top cybersecurity conferences.

Healey has spent his whole career in the cyber domain. He went to the Air Force Academy intending to be a fighter pilot, but realized pretty quickly that he didn't have the eyes or reflexes to fly in combat. He turned down his pilot training slot and went into intel, where he got his last choice for training, in Signals Intelligence. That turned out to be a good thing because U.S. Air Force Signals Intelligence was at the leading edge on cybersecurity in the 1990s. His early exposure had come from the Morris Worm, the Cuckoo's Egg, and the Solar Sunrise incident. (Healey is steeped in this history and has written *A Fierce Domain*, the definitive book on these incidents.) Hired by Venables at Goldman to be its first computer emergency response team (CERT) coordinator in 2001, Healey became immersed in defense of the corporate world. Rattray, then director for cyber threats in the defense directorate on the National Security Council staff, recruited Healey to be his counterpart on the Homeland Security Council. After his two-year stint was up, Healey returned to the private sector, working again for Venables at Goldman and then later with Rattray at a consulting firm. For a brief stint at the Atlantic Council he worked with neither of them, but once at Columbia he was again with the two people who had done the most to shape his career.

Healey's academic focus at the Atlantic Council had been on how to get defense better than offense. Venables had, in the corporate world, been looking at the same problem. His obsession was how to improve security by, in his words, "decreasing the cost of control" within the enterprise. How can you automate, take the user out of security, create efficiency, and keep resources for what matters? Coming from a national security perspective, Rattray took a broader view of the entire ecosystem. Healey remembers Rattray asking questions in the 1990s that no one else in the military did, such as "What is the failure mode of the internet?"

Looking at a chart from *The Economist* on the most effective ways to combat climate change, Healey thought what was needed was a similar list for cybersecurity. He sent out an email asking colleagues for examples of what had made the biggest difference in helping defenders regain the advantage in cyberspace. Once the task force started its work, he continued to drill down on the list, eventually producing about 115 innovations in technology, policy, law, and operations that would have shaved off some of the attacker's advantage. Policy changes such as safe-harbor provisions for sharing cyber-threat data among competitors despite antitrust concerns made the list, as did technical innovations such as the growing ubiquity of encryption and hardened operating systems.

Stepping back from a fold-out chart of the list taped to the wall in his office, Healey is still stunned by all the white space where other solutions should be. "In this field, we all know that the defense operates at a disadvantage. What's remarkable," he continues, "is how long we have known it." Healey quotes Lieutenant Colonel Roger Schell from memory. Schell, when he was at the NSA, developed the Rainbow manuals that guided early cyber-defense operations. "Few if any contemporary security controls can stop a dedicated team from accessing information sought." Schell wrote that in 1979. "Nineteen seventy-nine!" Healey yells. "We have known this for forty years and haven't been able to do anything about it. . . . I used to say that the cyber defense was the Chicago Cubs of the internet, but now nobody has as long a losing streak as we do."

Yet, as we have noted, there are signs that the attacker's advantage is eroding. What we need to do now is collectively make investments that will further erode that advantage. The members of the New York Cyber Task Force concluded that leverage should be the cornerstone of our national strategy, that the collective efforts of public- and private-sector partners needed to be focused on those factors that could most dramatically shift the advantage from the attacker to the defender. While we view the concept of leverage as a key component of cyber strategy, it is a means to an end, not the end itself (the end being resilience). Still, the recommendations that the task force made provide a road map for building resilience. On the corporate level, they recommend (as we do) improving governance, embracing the cloud, investing in secure software, and automating as much cyber hygiene as possible. For government, they want agencies to focus on aligning market forces to promote security by harmonizing regulation, promoting transparency, and creating incentives for cybersecurity, such as federally backstopped insurance and funding for research and collaborations that the market will not fund. Of course, all of this is easier said than done.

Only Bad Options

In the movie *Argo*, Ben Affleck as CIA operative Tony Mendez leads a mission to smuggle six State Department employees out of Iran after the fall of the embassy in 1979. Mendez came up with a plan to disguise the employees as a Canadian film crew filming a fake *Star Wars* knockoff. In the movie, based on a true story, we watch Affleck pitch the idea to Philip Baker Hall as CIA Director Stansfield Turner and Bob Gunton as Secretary of State Cyrus Vance. Both government officials are shown to be skeptical. After running through the other escape plans that the agency considered and rejected, Affleck levels with his superiors: "There are only bad options. It's about finding the best one." Hall as Turner deadpans, "You don't have a better bad idea than this?" Bryan Cranston, playing Tony Mendez's fictionalized boss, delivers the closing argument: "This is the best bad idea we have, sir—by far." With that, the mission is approved.

While a fictional account, the approval process as depicted in the movie rings true to many people working policy in Washington. There are never any good options. If there were, we would not need the apparatus we have developed for managing the national security of the United States. Instead, it is always about finding "the best bad idea." All national security decisions are about making trade-offs, nowhere more so than in cybersecurity, where every policy choice has the potential to impact our economic prosperity and our most cherished values of freedom of speech, freedom of expression, and the right to be free from unwarranted search and seizure.

Cyber resilience, prioritizing network defense and making the private sector bear the costs of absorbing these attacks is, at first blush, an unappealing prospect to most CEOs. After all, as General Alexander points out, the first responsibility of the federal government is to provide for the common defense. Yet every time policy makers unpack how government could take on this responsibility, private-sector enthusiasm quickly begins to fade because of the unintended consequences of government involvement. On cybersecurity, there are only bad options. Private responsibility for network defense with government support is the least bad one. To get private companies to build their own resilience (and therefore the resilience of the nation and of cyberspace), a series of mechanisms is necessary. Sometimes corporations need a little nudge. And sometimes they need a big shove.

:::::::::::: **PART III** ::::::::::::

THE GOVERNMENT'S
SUPPORTING ROLE

Chapter 7

· · · · · · · · · · ·

NUDGES AND SHOVES

The Government in Corporate Cyberspace

> As they commit to this activity, the Federal Government can
> and will help them, in the spirit of a true public-private partner-
> ship. The Government will not dictate solutions and will eschew
> regulation.
>
> —NATIONAL PLAN FOR INFORMATION SYSTEMS
> PROTECTION, THE WHITE HOUSE, 2000

By the start of the Obama administration, it was clear to many in
government and on the Hill that market forces alone were not driving the private sector to protect the nation's vital systems against
sophisticated criminal groups and foreign nations. So, with support from
Democrats in the Senate, in May of 2011, the White House delivered to
Congress a comprehensive legislative proposal that would have granted the
Department of Homeland Security authority to regulate critical infrastructure for cybersecurity, from oil and gas companies to stadiums.

Industry was not supportive. The U.S. Chamber of Commerce quickly
made it its mission to kill the bill and succeeded, arguing that with the
economy still fragile after the financial crisis a few years earlier, regulating

cybersecurity would hurt one of the few sectors of the economy that was thriving: information technology. They espoused the mistaken view that cybersecurity regulation would stifle innovation and was a jobs killer. In case the message wasn't clear, the Chamber of Commerce hung giant banners between the pillars of its headquarters, which faced the White House across Lafayette Square, that spelled out J-O-B-S. The idea alienated many of the tech executives who had donated both money and technical talent to elect the President. As the legislative proposal failed to gain support on the Hill, by the summer of 2012 the administration quietly began to plot a different approach.

At that time, cybersecurity nominally fell under John Brennan, the deputy national security adviser for Counterterrorism and Homeland Security (and later CIA director). Brennan, by his own admission, mostly focused on the first half of his title, the administration's Catholic conscience on the targeted killing of terrorists. He delegated most of the Homeland Security mission on a day-to-day basis to his deputy, Heidi Avery. Avery is not a household name by any measure. A career intelligence official, she managed to coordinate the Obama administration's response to Deepwater Horizon and a series of major natural disasters without raising her profile above a single blog post. And so, in her stealthy way, so as not to undermine what was now a long-shot effort to get the legislative package through Congress, Avery quietly assembled a small team to see which elements of the legislative proposal the President could accomplish through executive action.

Executive orders allow the President to direct agencies to take actions that align with existing laws. The CSIS commission report, "Securing Cyberspace for the 44th Presidency," had suggested that the President draw on existing regulatory authority, such as the EPA has over water systems or DHS has over chemical plants, to regulate for cybersecurity. Avery asked staffers in the NSC cyber office to pursue this strategy. They didn't expect that the idea of regulating for cybersecurity would meet resistance within the administration.

Any regulation issued by a federal agency gets reviewed by the small but powerful Office of Information and Regulatory Affairs. OIRA is housed inside the Office of Management and Budget in the ugly, 1960s-era New Executive Office Building, directly north of the Eisenhower Executive Office Building that houses the NSC staff. Pennsylvania Avenue was seemingly a dividing line, with the national security team on one side advocating regulation and the Chamber of Commerce and OMB on the other, dead set against it.

When the NSC team went to meet with OIRA to get them on board with the idea of issuing an executive order to expand regulation on cybersecurity, the response that they got was lukewarm.

Jasmeet Seehra, a career official and experienced Washington hand, was surprised that, after failing to get a bill passed because it had been labeled a job killer, the President would sign on to using his authority to unilaterally expand regulation. Unemployment was still hovering around 8 percent. "I know it's none of my business," the career official said, "but you guys remember it's an election year, right?" Instead, she suggested, might they think about a "nudge"? No one in the room had any idea what she was talking about. She pulled out a copy of a book called *Nudge: Improving Decisions About Health, Wealth, and Happiness*, and suggested they do some reading. The book was coauthored by her boss, Cass Sunstein.

Sunstein, a Democrat, was not necessarily a fan of regulation. A former colleague of President Obama's at the University of Chicago Law School, Sunstein had advocated for simple but not always popular ideas, such as subjecting regulation to cost-benefit analysis. With the economist Richard Thaler, Sunstein had written *Nudge*, arguing that government may be more effective when it shapes voluntary action rather than when it sets mandatory requirements. On his first date with his future wife and former UN ambassador Samantha Power, he told her his dream job was to run OIRA and implement these ideas.

The nudge the NSC team came up with was the NIST Cybersecurity Framework, discussed in chapter 3. It was meant to spur voluntary efforts by private-sector companies to defend their own infrastructure and, most agree, was largely effective at doing that. The National Strategy for Trusted Identities in Cyberspace, which we will discuss in chapter 8, was a nudge to get industry to solve the long-standing problems that keep things like health records from being brought online and make it burdensome to carry out certain financial transactions. Urging industries to create their own mutual information sharing and analysis organizations was also a nudge.

All of these nudges contributed to some corporations improving their cybersecurity, and there are many more nudges that government should consider, but to get companies to perform critical roles in our economy to the level of defense that is now possible, they may need to be pushed a bit harder. Let's call it a shove. We think it's time to reopen the regulation debate and to think anew about how the government should be interacting with the private sector to further erode the offense's remaining advantages.

Evan Wolff is one of the leading cybersecurity attorneys in Washington. What that means is that by day he helps his clients respond to cyber incidents, including directing investigations and advising on notifications under state, federal, and international requirements. By night, as a former MITRE data scientist and Global Fellow at the Wilson Center, he thinks and writes about how his clients can mitigate the threat of cyber incidents in the first place, including what can be done to build an effective collective defense. From experience, Wolff recognizes that only rarely would the teams behind security incidents stop at nothing to reach their targets. In fact, the forensics usually shows that the basic blocking and tackling of cybersecurity was not done, making it easy for the attacker. Fundamentally, what Wolff sees as missing isn't any one or group of security controls, it's an economic model that would force companies to take on the full societal cost of poor cyber-security, along with better coordination with federal and industry partners. In the language of economics, we need to make companies "internalize the externalities" of protecting data, protecting networks, and establishing secure communications, says Wolff. "Until we internalize those externalities," he believes, "we aren't going to begin to get the industry part of the collective defense down."

Contrary to the current political dogma, regulation doesn't kill innovation, it can create it. When markets are not valuing what we as a society want them to value, regulation can create whole new markets. The common refrain from industry is that regulation can't possibly move fast enough to keep up with innovation. We can find many examples where twenty-year-old security standards are still applicable and still have yet to be broadly implemented. We also see a growing reluctance to use digital products and services by consumers and businesses because of security risks.

The tide seems to be turning on this issue. Twenty years ago, when President Clinton released the first national strategy on cybersecurity, it "eschewed" regulation. Three years after that, the Bush strategy took largely the same stance. The Obama administration, as we've seen, pulled a regulatory proposal after the Chamber of Commerce went on a jihad to stop it. And yet, as the losses start to mount in cyberspace, the Trump administration's cyber strategy was silent on the topic of regulation. Surprisingly, the Department of Homeland Security's 2018 cybersecurity strategy actually said it would use its regulatory authority: "DHS must, therefore, smartly leverage its regulatory authorities in tailored ways, and engage with other agencies to ensure that their policies and efforts are informed by cybersecurity risks and aligned to national objectives to address critical cybersecurity gaps."

Smartly leveraging existing regulatory authorities in tailored ways is exactly what government should be doing. What doomed the Obama legislative proposal to failure was a bid to centralize all regulation of cybersecurity at the Department of Homeland Security, instead of taking the sector-by-sector approach advocated by the bipartisan group behind the CSIS commission. In that approach, DHS would regulate only the sectors it already has responsibility for, such as the chemical, pipeline, and maritime industries, leaving other sector-specific agencies that understand their industries to regulate them.

Although Clinton, Bush, and Obama eschewed, rejected, or declined to establish a federal cybersecurity regulatory regime, there is a mountain of cybersecurity regulation created by federal agencies. Banks, nuclear power plants, self-driving cars, hospitals, insurance companies, defense contractors, passenger aircraft, chemical plants, and dozens of other private-sector entities are all subject to cybersecurity regulation by a nearly indecipherable stream of agencies including the FTC, FAA, DHS, DoD, FERC, DOE, HHS, DOT, OCC, and on and on. Variation in federal regulations should be a result of conscious policy choices, not the incremental accretion of rules written at different times with little central guidance. It is time to step back and assess which of these agencies and regulations have been effective.

What we would like to see is either a comprehensive law passed by Congress or an executive order issued by a President. Where regulations are purposefully different to address specific industries, that is the intelligent, nuanced approach. When regulations differ because regulators have not consulted with one another, that is mismanagement. Eating up greater and greater percentages of security spending with duplicative regulatory compliances is in nobody's interest. For companies with multiple regulators, a streamlined process for verifying compliance, not just for eliminating duplicate requirements, is necessary. The financial sector has been developing a good model for how to coordinate oversight with the Federal Financial Institutions Examination Council.

The law or order would establish basic cybersecurity regulatory principles and best practices for federal regulators, as well as just enumerating what regulations exist. Among the best practices could be guidelines for such policy issues as accountability, audits, incident reporting, government information sharing, bug bounties, identity and access management, third-party code security reviews, continuous monitoring, public notifications, supply chain security, and personnel certifications. Above all else, though, the key principle that needs to be followed is that regulations need to be outcome-based, by telling regulated entities what they need to achieve, not how to do it.

In other areas, we have done this before. After 9/11, when experts worried about other ways that terrorists could use our infrastructure against us as weapons, as al-Qaeda had done with airplanes, many people focused on the chemical industry. Massive volumes of highly toxic chemicals were stored all over the country, often in close proximity to population centers. Through the Chemical Facility Anti-Terrorism Standards (CFATS), the Department of Homeland Security worked in partnership with industry to develop a program that fundamentally reduced the risk to the American people. It did not mandate that facilities relocate or switch to safer production methods, but it had the effect of causing companies to make those decisions. If by necessity you must store toxic chemicals in downtown Boston, then the program mandated that you implement security at such a level as to thwart an attack on the facility by trained terrorists. Instead of hiring paramilitary forces and hardening their complexes, most companies chose (wisely) to relocate or switch processes.

In the nuclear reactor domain, outcome-based security is achieved through the use of a design basis threat (DBT). While the details of what makes up the DBT used by the Nuclear Regulatory Commission are classified, the basic idea is that nuclear facilities need to be able to detect and delay an adversary composed of a certain number of actors with a certain type of skills bearing a certain set of weapons and tools. Replicating this model would be straightforward for cybersecurity, where red teaming is a well-established practice. One effective regulatory approach might be for government agencies to certify the capabilities of red teams and then for those red teams to conduct tests of companies.

One of the best examples of how to do outcome-based regulation is already being intelligently applied to combating cyber threats. Regulation E of the Electronic Funds Transfer Act requires that banks reimburse consumers for fraud losses. Contrary to popular belief, it's not that your checking account is insured by the Federal Deposit Insurance Corporation that keeps you from being liable for fraudulent charges. Instead, the banks must accept those costs. Originally established when check fraud was the dominant way criminals took money out of the financial system, the rule works equally well now that threats have mostly morphed into online account compromise.

We think, as a basis, mandatory breach disclosure is a start. In some version of a truth and reconciliation commission process, companies should be required to disclose all losses of intellectual property going back ten years. Moving forward, the Securities and Exchange Commission should establish a process to adjudicate public disclosures in a timely manner so that investors are made aware when the intellectual property they are banking on may be used by foreign competitors.

Breach disclosure alone has not had the hoped-for effect of preventing personally identifiable information (PII) from being stolen. Equifax, after disclosing the largest data breach in U.S. history in 2017, recovered its stock price in less than a year. We think it is necessary that the fines for losing PII be significant enough to make companies think twice about storing that data.

The Ponemon Institute, a cybersecurity think tank, puts the cost of a data breach at $141 per lost record. Those costs, incurred through disclosure, class-action lawsuits, state-level fines, and improved security, have not been sufficient to get companies to make the necessary changes in operations and investments to prevent such losses. If, instead, companies knew with certainty that they would be paying, say, $1,000 for every record they lost, that would begin to align incentives.

The prospect of high fines may still mean that many companies will simply choose to take their chances and accept that if they are breached they will lose it all. Trying to force companies with bad cybersecurity out of business should not be the goal. Nonetheless, we think companies should have to prove that they have the resources to pay those fines.

Congress should steal an idea from environmental policy by requiring companies that store PII to purchase bonds that would cover the full societal costs of the loss. Oil tankers operating in U.S. waters must have a Certificate of Financial Responsibility issued by the U.S. Coast Guard National Pollution Funds Center showing that the vessel's owner has the financial resources to cover the cost of cleaning up a spill.

Such massive policies mean that the underwriters are going to want near certainty that they will never be paid out. Thus, we now have double-hulled ships and other improvements that have made spills such as the *Exxon Valdez* a thing of the past. If we treat data like oil spills and require companies to cover the full societal costs of losing data, the market will do the rest by ensuring that spills of data become exceedingly rare.

These diverse regulatory models could be applied differently depending on the sector and the harm that government is trying to prevent. We are certain, however, that the blanket conclusion that regulation is anathema to innovation is wrong, that voluntary collaboration can be enhanced by a regulatory baseline, and that a lack of security is holding us back from fully benefiting from the digital revolution.

If Washington Won't Regulate, States Will

While successive federal administrations have shied away from coherent and coordinated cyber regulations, while various federal agencies and departments have developed their own regulations covering the cybersecurity of specific industries, while Congress has remained largely in gridlock on cyber regulations, state governments have acted.

California has required since 2012 that businesses have cybersecurity programs, and in 2016 its attorney general, Kamala Harris, concluded that failing to implement the Center for Internet Security's Critical Security Controls "constitutes a lack of reasonable security." (The CIS recommends twenty specific areas for controls.) In September 2018, Governor Jerry Brown signed SB-327, requiring that by January 1, 2020, manufacturers of devices sold in California must implement "reasonable" security features. Given that California's economy is the fifth largest in the world, that will mean that most device makers will be compelled to comply with the new law.

Not to be outdone, other states have pursued cyber regulations. Ohio enacted legislation in 2018 that provides protection for businesses against tort suits following a successful cyberattack that obtained personally identifiable information if the corporation had a cybersecurity program based on the CIS Critical Security Controls and the NIST Cybersecurity Framework (so-called safe harbor). New York's Department of Financial Services (DFS) Regulation 500 has since 2017 applied to foreign banks, state-chartered banks, insurance companies, and other financial entities, requiring a cybersecurity program, a qualified chief information security officer, multifactor authentication, encryption, application security, supply-chain vendor review, asset inventory, and continuous monitoring or annual penetration tests. It also recommends the NIST Cybersecurity Framework and requires an executive to sign off for the efficacy of the company's cybersecurity plan.

Some of these state regulations are commendable ways of guiding recalcitrant corporations to the minimum essential steps to protect themselves, their customers, and the general health of the cyberspace on which we all rely. Unfortunately, many of the laws vary significantly on important issues such as when there is a legal requirement to notify the customer or the government about a possible hack. The multiplicity of varying state regulations combined with the numerous federal rules does provide corporations and their lobbyists with grounds for complaint that it is all just too hard and expensive to track, understand, and implement.

If ever there was an example of interstate commerce it is the modern corporation's information technology network. With the exception of small businesses, corporate cyber activity is almost always multistate, involving distributed offices, data centers, IT vendors, and customers. Thus, there is a good case for creating superseding and uniform federal regulation. There are only two problems: Congress, which is hyperpartisan and concerned about committee jurisdictional fiefdoms within each house; and the lobbying groups such as the U.S. Chamber of Commerce, which blindly and in a knee-jerk manner oppose any new cyber regulation with the erroneous mantra about stifling innovation.

Until the Congress and the lobbyists can begin to act in the national interest, there is the risk that any new uniform federal regulations they might pass would actually water down some state laws and be less effective. Thus, we may, for now, be better off with progressive states such as California and New York writing rules that end up being de facto national standards because most major companies fall under their jurisdiction.

Getting Some Backbone

We have been arguing in this book that corporations can now achieve a fairly high level of cybersecurity if they spend enough, deploy state-of-the-art IT and cyber solutions, and adopt the right policies and procedures. Even the power grid, government agencies, and the military could achieve enhanced security. However, in the unlikely event that all of that happened, we would still have a problem.

A foreign nation-state could still cause a high degree of chaos by attacking the backbone of the internet itself, rendering it useless or at the very least only sporadically available. Without the internet, few other pieces of the economy would work. The three remaining problems are, naturally, described by three acronyms: DDoS, DNS, and BGP.

In the attacks against the banks, the Iranians used a distributed denial-of-service attack. In the more recent attacks, variants of the Mirai bot used thousands of surveillance cameras as platforms to flood the Domain Name System (DNS) and disrupted large parts of the internet. A worse DDoS can easily be imagined and executed, effectively knocking off-line key infrastructure by flooding internet connections. At a certain level of flood, the companies that specialize in stopping DDoS attacks, such as Akamai and Cloudflare, will be overwhelmed.

If, as in the case of the Mirai bot, the flood is directed at specific DNS-related IP addresses and at certain companies that specialize in outsourcing Domain Name System look-up services, then that key part of the internet backbone will not work and it will be impossible for some users to find their way to web pages, for some email to reach its intended recipient, or for some of the countless networked devices in our homes and offices to function. Mirai was a relatively small attack compared to what could happen.

While the DNS tells your email message or the server supporting your browser where to go on the internet (or on your corporate intranet) to find the address you are looking for, there is a completely different system used by the internet service providers who own and operate the big fiber-optic pipes that are the backbone of the internet. That system, the one that tells Verizon or AT&T how to route a message to get to a server that is not on their own network, is called BGP (it means Border Gateway Protocol, but just say BGP like everyone else). BGP is still the biggest security flaw in the internet, even twenty years after Mudge Zatko testified that he and the other members of the L0pht could take it down in thirty minutes.

Think of the BGP as like the Waze app. It tells internet traffic what the route is to get from where it is to where it wants to go. If you get onto the internet by connecting to Verizon in the United States and you want to read a web page of the Australian Football League that is on a server in Australia that connects to the internet by using the local ISP Telstra, Verizon will consult the BGP tables. There they will find the routing to the football club. It may be from Verizon to AT&T to Telstra.

The problem is that essentially any internet service provider in the world can contribute to the BGP. So, what if China Telecom posted on the

BGP table that the Aussie football server was actually on their network? Then your computer would connect to China Telecom while looking for Australia. And that is what has been happening.

According to Chris Demchak of the U.S. Naval War College and Yuval Shavitt of Tel Aviv University, China Telecom has been messing around with the BGP tables. For instance, in February 2016 and for six months after, all traffic from Canada to South Korea was misrouted through China. In October 2016, some traffic from the United States to Italy went through China. In April 2017, the pathway from Norway to Japan was altered to go through China. In July 2017, it was the connection from Italy to Thailand. You get the picture.

While traffic is going through China, that traffic (emails, for example) can be copied or sent into a black hole. The Chinese are not alone. Russia and other countries have also been regularly redirecting internet traffic that was not supposed to go through them. Iran has been grabbing traffic for secure messaging apps such as Signal. While such messages are encrypted, the "To" and "From" metadata could be interesting to the Iranian secret police.

China Telecom's attempts to redirect traffic through China is greatly aided by the fact that it operates eight internet points of presence (PoPs) inside the United States and has its own West Coast fiber running from Hillsboro, Oregon, to Morro Bay, California. Needless to say, AT&T does not have PoPs in China, nor cables running from Shanghai to Dalian. China would never agree to that, because in a crisis the United States could really throw the Chinese internet into chaos by playing with the BGP tables and grabbing their traffic.

Whatever you think about the potentially beneficial or pernicious effects of cybersecurity regulation of U.S. companies, the very backbone of the internet, made up of the long-haul fiber-optic cables and the routing systems, should be secured so bad guys trying to mess around with the DNS and BGP routing systems would have a harder time. The way that could be done would be for the Federal Communications Commission (FCC) to regulate this internet backbone, the DNS, and the BGP systems to require some basic security functionality. They refuse to, once again, out of an ideological antipathy toward regulation thinly guised as a fear that regulation would impede innovation.

Cyber Insurance—A Moneymaker

Do you chew Trident or Dentyne gum? Do you like Philadelphia Cream Cheese and sometimes put it on Ritz crackers? When no one is looking, do you eat all of the Oreo cookies in the roll? Or when you have a cough, do you pop in a Hall's lozenge? Then you already know some of the products of a big, multinational food company you've probably never heard of: Mondelēz. Production of all of those necessities of life came to a crashing halt because of the NotPetya attack we discussed in chapter 2. Mondelēz, however, had insurance and, therefore, assumed that it had transferred its risk and that its claim to cover some of its $100 million in losses would be honored. Not so fast.

Zurich, the big Swiss insurance company, refused to pay out. The Swiss said that NotPetya was an act of war, an attack carried out by the Russian military and, therefore, excluded from the insurance policy. Thus, the debate about what is and what is not cyber war has gone into a courthouse and the future role of cyber insurance may be decided over who pays for the losses on the day the Oreos stopped.

The outcome in the case is important because many corporations rely on insurance as part of their overall risk strategy. Moreover, cyber insurance could play an even bigger role if it were combined in some creative ways with regulation, as we will discuss later. The last ten years have seen a burgeoning of the cyber risk insurance market. Corporations and even city governments have attempted to transfer risk to insurance companies by buying up new cyber insurance policies. There was a lot of hope among cybersecurity experts that this trend could be a way of nudging corporations into improving their security by linking insurance coverage to some meaningful security measures. Alas, that has not happened. Instead, a lot of insurance companies have a newfound source of profit and that income has actually worked against meaningful security improvements.

At first, staid old insurance companies were fearful of covering cyber risk. They put riders in the existing casualty and loss policies that exempted damage from cyberattack. They did so because there was no actuarial data: no reliable record of how often attacks occur, what losses from the attacks typically amount to, or how attackers actually execute their breaches. To insurance companies used to being able to predict with more than 90 percent accuracy when you will get into a car crash and how much it will cost them, cyber was a scary place, a terra incognita.

Gradually, however, some companies dipped a toe, not five or ten toes, in the water. They covered a few kinds of costs and only up to fairly low dollar amounts. They would pay for a cyber incident response team, maybe for the cost of giving customers some relatively useless credit monitoring service postbreach. Maybe they would pay out on some legal costs and cover some business continuity losses. What the insurance policies would not cover were the two most expensive effects of cyber breaches: reputational damage and intellectual property theft. If China steals your research-and-development secrets, you are on your own.

Most of the carriers began to require some assurance from their clients that the insured party had taken some minimal cybersecurity measures. What they almost never did, however, was to bother to check on whether the corporations were actually doing what they claimed to be doing. As one insurance company official told us, "We can always check after they file a claim and if they weren't living up to the minimum practices they said they were, we can just deny the claim."

Insurance companies could, of course, require continuous monitoring software to report on a company's state of security and compliance in real time. Doing this would be the cyber insurance equivalent of the Progressive automobile insurance policies that involve installing driver behavior monitors in cars. Why wouldn't insurance companies want that kind of information? Money.

After years now of selling limited cyber coverage, most insurance companies have found that doing so is profitable. While they do not sell anywhere near as much cyber insurance as life, casualty, home, or auto insurance, they keep a much higher percentage of the premiums they collect when they sell cyber insurance. The payouts to the insured are a smaller percentage of the revenue than in most other forms of insurance. So why rock the boat when you are making money?

Most insurance, somewhat oddly, is not regulated at the federal level.

Health-care insurance is, of course, or was until the Trump administration made a hash of the Affordable Care Act. Almost all other kinds of insurance are supervised by insurance commissioners in the fifty states. Some states elect their insurance commissioners, as in California. In others, governors appoint them. In New York, the Department of Financial Services doubles as the insurance regulator.

What worries some of the state insurance commissioners we have talked with is the prospect of the often-discussed "cyber Pearl Harbor" or the "cyber 9/11." What they mean by that is there could be a large-scale, catastrophic cyber event that would not be covered by one of the many outs and exclusions the insurance companies have put in their policies. The commissioners worry that a major cyber event could cause companies to pay out so much that they might become insolvent and unable to continue to pay out for other damages. Thus, the commissioners are beginning to think about a new law similar to the Terrorism Risk Insurance Act, TRIA.

Enacted after 9/11, TRIA provides a partial federal-government financial backstop to the insurance industry in the event of a major terrorist attack that exceeds the financial ability of the insurance industry to respond to claims. A "Cyber War Risk Insurance Act" is one example of a possible useful new regulation. It could provide a partial federal financial backstop to the industry in case of a national cyber event. It would also be an opportunity to create some meaningful compliance standards for insured entities.

We would suggest that corporations would be eligible for such CWRIA-backed insurance only if they had installed such features as an approved continuous monitoring system to perform asset discovery, assess the state of critical patches, and conduct vulnerability assessments. Companies that went out of compliance for more than thirty consecutive days would lose coverage until they remedied their deficiencies. Now that would not be a federal mandate, but it would be one hell of a nudge, maybe even a shove.

Comey Versus Cook

The employees were looking forward to the holiday party, but then one of them, assisted by his wife, started shooting everybody. It was December 2, 2015, in San Bernardino, California. Syed Farook and his wife, Tashfeen Malik, killed fourteen and wounded twenty-two, before being chased and killed by local police. The FBI was immediately called in to lead the investigation.

By February, the FBI was saying publicly that it could not open one of the iPhones used by the terrorists. The devices were set so that after a few failed attempts to open them with a PIN, the phones would wipe all data. FBI Director James Comey called upon Apple to develop software that could be used to bypass the PIN and unlock the devices. Apple CEO Tim Cook, correctly in our view, refused, saying that Apple could not be compelled to weaken the security of its own products. Comey took Cook to court.

The backstory was that Comey had been campaigning inside the Obama administration for new legislation that would require companies that make encryption software to build in ways that the government could decrypt the code. It was an idea that had gone down in flames twenty years earlier, when Congress rejected a proposal for a so-called Clipper chip that would permit a court to unlock encryption upon petition by the government. After months of lobbying inside the administration, Comey had lost. The Obama administration would not undercut encryption. Then San Bernardino happened, and Comey saw his chance to get a court to give him what the White House would not.

How could anyone possibly deny the FBI's request to help it in an ongoing investigation of such a heinous terrorist attack? Comey and his supporters at the Justice Department claimed they were not seeking a legal precedent, they were just worried about this one case. There were, however, hundreds of other iPhones involved in other cases that the FBI or local police could not open. What happened next tells you a lot about the value of encryption to cybersecurity. Far from supporting Comey and the FBI, former high-level national security officials came out of the woodwork to support Apple, including former CIA and NSA directors. We were part of that chorus. What we were all saying was that encryption is essential to secure private-sector networks and databases. If Apple created a way to break the encryption on its devices, malicious actors would find a way to use it too.

In a heated debate at the RSA security conference in 2016, Dick Clarke asserted that the government was looking to create a bad precedent and that, in fact, it already had classified means to open the phone. All that the FBI needed to do was to "drive up the Baltimore-Washington Parkway to Fort Meade," the home of the NSA. John Carlin, then the assistant attorney general for national security, strenuously denied it was about precedent and asserted that there was no existing method of opening the device available to the government. Comey told the same story in congressional hearings.

Then, while Comey's case against Cook worked its way through the courts, the FBI announced that it had opened the iPhones with the help of an Israeli security firm. The court case ceased. Much later, the Justice Department Inspector General reviewed what had happened and concluded that while Comey and Carlin were denying that the government could open the iPhones, the FBI actually had the capability all along. The IG declined to investigate whether Comey had knowingly misled Congress or, alternatively, that no one in the FBI had bothered to tell their leader that he was wrong as he went around the Capitol for weeks saying no capability existed. The latter possibility seems unlikely.

The takeaway from this tempest in a Capitol teacup is that even national security officials, or maybe especially national security officials, think that encryption is a sine qua non for corporate cybersecurity, but do not think government should have a role in it. Many national security officials were even willing to break ranks with the FBI to stress this point. Of course, no discussion of the virtues of encrypting everything would be complete these days without mentioning that a lot of companies are having their networks encrypted involuntarily and not by the government.

Calling for a Ransomed Friend

"I have a friend whose company just got hit. All of their data got encrypted. Do you think they should pay the ransom?"

We have had more than a few calls like that. We usually say that the answer is probably yes, you should pay, unless you have multiple, reliable, backup databases. Then our callers often respond, "Okay, then do you know where I can buy some Bitcoin?"

In 2017 and 2018, there was a near pandemic of ransomware in North

America and Europe. According to the Royal Canadian Mounted Police, sixteen hundred ransomware attacks were occurring each day in Canada in 2015. By the fall of 2016, the attacks almost doubled. As we said, a pandemic.

Hackers could easily buy attack kits that would find vulnerabilities that allowed them to go from publicly facing web pages or email servers into an entire corporate network. There they could deploy something else easily procured on the dark web: software that finds and encrypts all data stored on a network, including emails, Word and Excel documents, Salesforce, Oracle, SAP files, everything. Then comes the ransom offer.

Want the key to unlock everything we encrypted? Then send us one hundred thousand dollars' worth of Bitcoin. Although Bitcoin was supposed to be a safe way of doing business because it involved a publicly viewable blockchain record, it has actually turned out to be easy to use it to hide money flows. Bitcoin is the coin of the realm when it comes to ransomware, allegedly very difficult to trace.

Faramarz Savandi and Mohammad Mansouri knew how to do it. The two Iranians wrote their own version of ransomware software and it became known as the SamSam kit. The two men hit about two hundred networks in the United States over two years and collected more than $6 million in Bitcoin. The damage that their ransomware did to networks was estimated at $30 million. Among their victims were numerous hospitals and medical facilities (MedStar Georgetown, Kansas Heart Hospital, Hollywood Presbyterian, LabCorps), and city governments and agencies (Atlanta, Newark, the Port of San Diego).

In Atlanta, Mayor Keisha Bottoms declined to pay the fifty-thousand-dollar demand. Most of her city's services, including some police functions, were down for a week. One estimate put the cost of coming back online at $17 million. The two Iranians were also active in attacking networks in Canada and the United Kingdom. They remain at large and are believed to be living well in Tehran. There are numerous others in many countries engaged in the same profitable trade, which has been estimated to have produced more than a billion dollars in revenue in the last few years from thousands of ransoms around the world performed by dozens of attack groups.

So, back to our caller. Why do we often tell them to pay up? There is honor among thieves, and if you pay, you usually get back to business pretty quickly. If the ransomware thieves did not free up your network when you paid up, then word would get around and no one would pay. After all, they have their reputation to maintain. You can, however, get around them sometimes.

It's all about how good your backup is and how long you can afford to have your network down. If you back up your data every day, you may well have backed up the malicious software that later infected your network. Hackers are waiting a week or so after they get on your network before activating their encryption software. By so doing, they get in your backup. If you simply mount your backup after your data is involuntarily encrypted, it will just happen again, only this time you will have lost your backup as well.

The solution is to keep multiple backups of varying ages, to keep the backups segregated into discrete modules so that everything is not in one master file, and to keep so-called golden disks, the clean originals of key applications, web pages, etc. Then you can experiment with gradually restoring your network, assuming your corporation can be off-line for forty-eight or seventy-two hours. If you can't be, you may have to pay up. As we have been saying for years, cybercrime pays, at least if you are willing to live in Tehran or someplace similar and never use your ill-gotten gains to vacation somewhere nice that has an extradition treaty with the United States.

Andy Ozment, a former White House and Homeland Security official, has provocatively proposed that ransomware may be one of the more useful regulatory mechanisms we've got, essentially imposing fines on companies that have not invested in basic cybersecurity. It is a compelling argument, but we think it is time to remove the incentive for cyber criminals to use ransomware by having a government law or regulation that bans paying the ransom or institutes a fine in addition to whatever ransom is paid.

Ransomware is funneling billions of dollars to the underground economy. As DEF CON cofounder Jeff Moss has pointed out, even if most of those billions of dollars go to buying Maseratis and leather jackets in Moscow suburbs, the remaining millions are going to buying more and better capabilities, expanding teams, and attracting more criminal groups to the business. We need to stop funding the development of our adversaries.

In the next three chapters we will look at how smart government intervention in the markets could solve the problem of identity theft and the workforce crisis, and secure the power grid. We will also look at how the government can do a better job of regulating its own security.

Chapter 8

||||||||||

IS IT REALLY YOU?

Tell me who are you? (Who are you? Who, who, who, who?)
'Cause I really want to know (Who are you? Who, who, who, who?)

—PETE TOWNSHEND

here is no doubt that over time, people are going to rely less and less on passwords," the CEO of Microsoft told the crowd assembled at RSA.

With that, Microsoft announced that it was working with the cybersecurity firm RSA to roll out its SecurID technology on the Windows platform. Internally, Microsoft was moving to a "smart-card system" and testing a "biometric ID-card" that would allow facial, iris, and retina recognition as a means to grant access to computing resources.

Of course, this was all in 2004. Bill Gates was still Microsoft's CEO. To his credit, and contrary to legend, he never suggested that passwords would go the way of the dodo, only that we would rely on them less. What Gates was proposing then was two-factor authentication, or even multifactor authentication: your password and a card with some sort of biometric data on it. You would type in your password, stick in your card, and the computer would read the biometric data and match it with the biometrics you were presenting (your fingerprint, iris, etc.).

The obstacles were numerous. Many people did not like giving up their biometrics. The reader devices were unreliable. Users lost their cards a lot. Implementation was expensive. And in the end, users still had to remember a password.

And so the password did not die. It procreated. Today there are some ninety billion passwords in use around the globe, and that number is growing. By corporate policy and with enough prodding from the tech media, people are creating more, not fewer passwords. Password-manager applications, such as Dashlane, 1Password, and LastPass, make it relatively easy to create and remember unique and difficult-to-break passwords. Application-specific passwords are automatically generated in the background by many applications, and the primary form of authentication for the growing number of smart devices is still the password.

When Gates made his speech in 2004, the available alternatives to passwords were awkward. They introduced friction into the user experience and did not always work. Requiring the same card to access a building and to use a computer caused problems when people forgot to take them out of their computers when they left the office to go to the bathroom or the cafeteria, something no amount of scolding could fix.

At about the same time, the federal government made a similar move. President Bush signed Homeland Security Presidential Directive 12 in August 2004, which called for federal government agencies to issue smart cards for both physical access (opening doors and getting through security) and logical access (gaining access to computers). The directive gave agencies a generous fourteen months to implement the program. A decade later, data reported to Congress showed that only 62 percent of federal employees had been issued and were using the smart-card technology. Redoubling efforts after the breach at the Office of Personnel Management, federal agencies finally hit the target of 85 percent coverage in the fiscal year that began in October 2016.

The governments' misfire on implementation did not inspire the private sector to move to smart cards for password replacement or augmentation. Simply put, these technologies were too hard to implement and too difficult to use. A few years after Gates's 2004 speech, however, a new technology emerged that people almost never are without because they almost never put it down: the smartphone.

I (Am My) Phone

The first iPhone hit the market on June 29, 2007. The first Android phones would come out a little over a year later. These devices would quickly address many of the problems that people had with other tools used for multifactor authentication. They could be used to receive text messages containing secondary security codes. When fingerprint readers started to become widely adopted by smartphone makers around 2013, smartphones could then be used to meet the trifecta for multifactor authentication: 1) something you have (the smartphone itself, registered to you); 2) something you know (still the good old password or a one-time number sent to your phone); and 3) something you are (a fingerprint or, now, your face with the integration of facial recognition software). Companies such as Okta and Duo, now darlings of Wall Street for their successful IPOs, make implementing and using multifactor authentication on smartphones for multisite single sign-on relatively simple.

Yet, for all these technical advances, adoption has been slow and may even be stalled out. Although Microsoft makes two-factor authentication freely available to its customers, an independent survey recently reported that only 20 percent of subscribers to Microsoft's Office 365 suite of productivity applications are using any form of multifactor authentication. Surveys of other platforms have found similar results. As we have noted, upwards of 80 percent of data breaches still involve weak or stolen passwords.

While the most sophisticated adversaries are not going to give up and go home if they run into a second authentication factor, many lower-level criminals clearly would be forced to move on to other, softer targets. While multifactor authentication may be costly to implement and add friction to the user experience, it is even more annoying to adversaries. There is likely no other technical solution that would do as much to frustrate attackers, increase the skill level necessary to carry out attacks, or slow down attackers.

Yet no amount of imploring seems to move the needle on multifactor authentication.

The problem of passwords won't go away until some combination of two things happen: multifactor authentication without a password is forced on companies and their customers, or multifactor authentication becomes something that takes place seamlessly in the background. On the first front, we are starting to see more companies make the push. Banks, which are financially responsible should cyber criminals drain your bank account, have all the incentive they now need to require the use of two-factor authentication. Many are adopting "push" models that don't require users to do anything to set up two-factor authentication. Banks validate your phone number in the background and then send a text message with a one-time code you must enter to log in to your account.

Of course, there are multiple ways criminals can capture a text message and use it to log in to an account, from compromising the underlying SS7 telephone network to compromising the phones or computers that receive the text messages. So, what Google, Duo, ThreatMetrix, and the Department of Defense are each separately working on is taking multifactor authentication well beyond three factors.

Using advanced analytics, these efforts can take dozens or even hundreds of factors to make decisions about granting an individual access to computing resources. As these technologies come to fruition, getting access to your accounts may only involve tapping on an app or clicking on a log-in button while data analytics go to work in the background to check whether the device you are using is the same one you used last time, whether your location makes sense, whether your typing speed as you shift from uppercase to lowercase is consistent with the pattern established on you over time, and a host of other factors.

Moreover, authentication is becoming something of a sliding scale instead of a simple yes-no, binary decision. Once you are allowed inside a network and using your account, behavior out of pattern will get flagged and you will then be asked for additional verification. If, for instance, you are not in the habit of transferring money to Poland, you may get a prompt to enter a password or a call might even be placed to your phone with a live human operator, who may ask you questions, such as about your prior use of your account.

All these measures are likely to make the password, as Bill Gates predicted, less central to the authentication process. And there may even be some hope for a passwordless future. Jim Routh at Aetna is in the process of eliminating passwords for his twenty-million-plus subscribers using Trusona, a passwordless authentication app. That just leaves one huge problem: validating the true identity of the account owner.

Identify Yourself

People who work on identity management like to draw distinctions among "authentication," "authorization," and "identification." The solutions Bill Gates talked about in 2004, smart cards and tokens, are authorization solutions that give or deny access to restricted accounts and computer resources. Okta, Duo, and other multifactor solutions are also authorization solutions. They are asking, is the individual (or device) requesting permission to access this system presenting the required information and executing the required actions? If so, they grant access. If not, they don't. What they do not do is affirm that you are, in fact, you.

Validating that your email address is assigned to you is not something that Okta does. That's the responsibility of the HR department, and for that they require you to bring in your passport and driver's license. Your bank may require you to do the same when you open an account, or answer challenge questions online based on information that credit bureaus have collected about you. These are what is known as "identity-proofing" events, where you prove that you are in fact you, establishing a unique identity.

The problem is that these events are one-offs for individual accounts. There is, as of yet, no way to assert your identity (and keep anyone else from asserting your identity) across the internet. And that is what allows for a host of ills, from Social Security and insurance fraud to fake social media accounts that manipulate elections. If multifactor authentication would frustrate adversaries in carrying out attacks, making it harder to steal identities and therefore benefit from cybercrime, it could take away the motivation in the first place.

We already have the means to use a single identity across multiple internet platforms, what is called federated identity. Facebook, Google, and others have used the fact that almost everyone has an account at one, the other, or both to insert themselves into the authorization process for a host of sites ("Sign in with Google" buttons seem to be almost everywhere). But neither Google nor Facebook actually know who you are, so their ability to authenticate you as *you* is only as strong as the information you provided to them when you registered your accounts. While both companies are making some attempts to validate new accounts by checking names against provided phone numbers and then texting those phone numbers, criminals have proven adept at beating these systems. Burner phones make it all too easy for criminals to hide their identity.

The lack of an ability to prove who you are on the internet is a long-recognized but seemingly intractable problem. When identity proofing is needed online, almost all websites rely on the tried-and-failed method of validating historical information about you. With your address, your phone number, your date of birth, and your Social Security number, you can file your tax return. So can anyone else with that information, leading to almost six hundred thousand cases of fraud in 2017.

The same goes for insurance fraud, new account fraud, and a host of other cybercrimes that deprive the government of tax revenue, drive up the price of insurance, and cost the economy billions. Despite these losses, it's a problem that the market just cannot seem to fix. That is where, typically, government should step in.

Getting Identity Unstuck

One of the first initiatives launched by the Obama administration to address our cyber insecurities was the National Strategy for Trusted Identities in Cyberspace (NSTIC). As the administration's first senior director for cybersecurity, Sameer Bhalotra spearheaded the effort. He was joined by Jeremy Grant, who ran the NSTIC program office from its inception in 2011 until he left in 2015.

Oftentimes, government bureaucrats are charged with a failure of imagination and with a lack of ambition. Those charges do not apply to the team that put together the NSTIC strategy. The document is visionary. It literally contains little vignettes to get you to "Envision It!" in which Mary, or another fictitious person, uses her new online credential to do the kinds of transactions we can't easily do today online, such as close a mortgage. Always wary of government overreach, particularly on issues of individual privacy, the Obama team did not propose the obvious answer of a government-issued ID card with a digital chip. Anyone who remembers the fight over REAL ID, a Bush administration effort to get states to issue secure driver's licenses, should be able to imagine why. Americans have a reflexive distrust of federal requirements for identification. Nothing is more un-American than restricting movement, as the Soviets did with their ubiquitous requests for "Papers, please."

Instead of going with a national ID card, the NSTIC team took a market-based approach that would give consumers choices about whom they used to obtain a trusted digital identity for use online. The strategy envisioned a host of potential providers, companies that ranged from banks to ISPs to independent identity providers. Despite a solid strategy, there were two problems that the NSTIC team could not solve: initial validation of users through an in-person proofing event and getting companies to pay to use the new identities.

The NSTIC team tried to sell the Postal Service on doing the identity proofing. There are 4,800 post offices throughout the country that already process passport applications, including the necessary in-person proofing. Bhalotra met with the Postmaster General and tried to sell him on the idea. He thought it was a no-brainer, because the post office is already performing this service for passports and is desperate to find new sources of revenue given the decline in traditional mail brought about by the digital economy. He figured this was an easy sell. It wasn't. The prospects were too remote and the mission too far from the core Postal Service mission of delivering the mail.

The second challenge was getting anyone to adopt the use of the new secure identities and mandate that their employees or customers use them. Bhalotra thought that the banks would be natural allies as they already need to authenticate customers for account opening and spend tremendous amounts battling fraud. It was a hard sell there as well. He tried to stimulate demand by getting federal agencies to be the early adopters. Unfortunately, he got no takers from the IRS, State, DHS, or HHS, the major agencies that interact with citizens in ways that require identity proofing. Going direct to consumers also was a nonstarter, because no one in the venture-capital community thought people wanted to pay for this service.

None of this, of course, means the approach was wrong. Particularly in government, there is no force more powerful than an idea whose time has come. In 2011, the technologies were insufficiently mature and the need for the solution was less apparent. In 2019, when almost every American has been made a victim of identity theft, it is well past time to put in place the solutions that the NSTIC developed and piloted.

For his part, Jeremy Grant has not given up. Now a member of the technology consulting team at a law firm, he is actively pursuing many of the concepts he helped to develop in government from his position in the private sector. Grant has helped bring together JPMorgan, Bank of America, Wells Fargo, and Citibank, among others, to form the Better Identity Coalition. Their idea is to create a public-public-private partnership building on the states' divisions of motor vehicles (DMV) driver's-license databases and the Social Security Administration's files.

The banks recognize that the DMVs do a pretty good job of in-person interviews and requiring multiple forms of proof of identity. True, there are counterfeit driver's licenses, but when you check DMV databases, you can usually tell that the license was never issued by the DMV. Social Security, for all of the faults associated with its number and card system, is pretty good at registering when someone dies, as is the Department of Veterans Affairs. Because a common criminal technique is to assume the identity of someone who has passed away, access to death records would help identify fraudulent identity activity.

One problem, however, is that most state DMV agencies do not have the highest level of cybersecurity on their own networks. If criminals and intelligence officers can hack into the DMV database and alter it, using the DMV as a source of verification may not be a good idea. Thus, the banks are seeking federal grants to help the states improve their cybersecurity. Until that happens, the DMVs may not be the solution. At best, they are a surrogate for a national ID card system, something that has proven politically unpalatable on both the right and left in the United States for decades. Yet we have been able to find workable solutions that address privacy and civil-liberties concerns while improving identity with a simple concept: letting people opt in.

Nobody has to fly, but it does make work and personal travel a lot easier. After 9/11, it got harder. Americans wanted to be sure that the other people on the plane with them were trustworthy, not terrorists. So there was not a lot of complaining when the government stepped in and put federal employees at the airports, asking to see your identification. Not any identification would do. It had to be a government-issued document that was hard to counterfeit. State governments were told what security standards they had to incorporate into their driver's licenses, and after some grumbling, they almost all complied.

This system, however, created long lines. So two innovations occurred, one public and one a public-private partnership. The TSA created TSA Pre-Check for people who were willing to fill out forms, go through a background check, have their biometrics registered, be photographed, and be entered into a federal database. TSA also authorized a private company, CLEAR, to manage a parallel system of authenticating travelers with a combination of your boarding pass, an iris scan or fingerprints, and a picture of you.

When you use CLEAR, you engage in multifactor authentication. You have used things you know to get the boarding pass. Then that boarding pass becomes things you have. Finally, your biometrics and photograph are things you are. No one has forced you to use CLEAR. In fact, you had to pay for it. A similar incentive system exists with E-ZPass toll-paying devices on cars.

Americans have accepted these systems, which can serve as valuable models for incentivizing the implementation of stronger authentication systems in other industries. We can use similar principles in creating secure online identities. We can use a certain degree of government compulsion. We can partner with private-sector companies. People who choose not to participate in optional additional background checks and identification would still be served, but they would be subject to more examination and given slower service.

A New Authentication Proposal: ReallyU

Building on the lessons from NSTIC and how identity is handled in other industries, we propose a new authentication system to ensure a higher degree of identity protection and replace outdated identifiers like Social Security numbers. Because it would require a combination of nudges and shoves, ReallyU would have to be authorized by Congress. Yes, Republicans and Democrats would have to play nicely together, at least on this one law.

The law would authorize private companies that met certain standards to issue ReallyU identities for use in online interactions with both the government and corporations. On an opt-in basis, you could choose from any number of approved companies to serve as your identity service provider. You would then go through an identity-proofing process that included being interviewed on-site, presenting valid government identification, giving biometric data, and being photographed. You could also provide an email address, mobile phone number, and credit card or other banking information if you chose to do so.

Then, the ReallyU provider would do a background check to verify that you are who you say you are. In that process, they would have access to some government databases. Maybe your provider would be Google (they know everything about you anyway); maybe Apple (if they make your phone); maybe Verizon (or whoever your costly cell provider is); maybe Mastercard or Visa through your bank (you get the idea). These providers would then be paid each time they validated your identity to a third party to, say, open a bank account or access your IRS record.

Each ReallyU provider could create their own federated identity network, much like Mastercard and Visa have created their own parallel payment networks that include a heavy dose of identity checking. Government agencies should be made by law to accept any one of the approved federated identity networks for online transactions. Companies doing online commerce could choose which ReallyU providers they wanted to honor.

Something along these lines would give us a system of online identification that would not be the equivalent of a national ID card because it would not be managed by the federal government and it would be voluntary, not required. Beyond a light touch of regulation, the government's main role would be to help create the market by making federal agencies that require proof of identity accept it and provide various kinds of preferential service to ReallyU members.

Once you had a ReallyU identity, you could use it to identify yourself to any company or government agency that was part of the federated network. The government agencies involved would include the IRS, Social Security, Medicare, Veterans Affairs, and federal employee retirement systems. They could also continue to accept their previously existing systems.

If you used the ReallyU system, each company and government agency could interrogate a federated database to learn about you when you logged in to use it. They could then require you to prove your identity in any number of different ways, based on a variety of two-factor or multifactor systems, including face identification (via a smartphone or camera on your laptop), fingerprint, iris scan, or one-time message sent to your mobile phone or email. In the background, the system would be checking your location, the device you were using, and other observables, the same way ThreatMetrix does now for many banks and other financial institutions.

As a consumer, you could switch identity providers whenever you want. You might pick based on security or reputation or a preexisting relationship. You might opt to pay for the service and gain more control or choose a service that is free (and possibly ad-supported), though we think a better answer is a small per-transaction fee charged to the companies that are requesting an identity-proofing or authentication event. The process for changing providers might need some degree of government regulation, as was necessary to create the phone-number porting system we use today. A light-touch regulatory approach run out of somewhere like the Commerce Department (not a national security agency) would set the right tone.

What would happen to the Social Security number? We could keep it, but only as an identifier, like your name, not as proof of anything. As former DHS cyber official Phil Reitinger tweeted, "An SSN is a fine identifier and an awful authenticator." The assumption that you, and only you, know your Social Security number is no longer a tenable proposition. Every SSN has probably already been compromised.

So, what do we need the Congress to agree on for all of this to work? We have a short list.

First, Congress needs to direct the U.S. Postal Service and the TSA to offer in-person identity-proofing services, no matter how reluctant the current Postmaster General is. Just as the USPS has competitors in FedEx and UPS, this action won't give government a monopoly but should stimulate competition. The law should require the Postal Service to partner with private companies to issue and manage the IDs, the IT/tech part of the solution. That is what the private sector, particularly Silicon Valley tech firms and their VC partners, are good at. What they are not good at, managing brick-and-mortar buildings where identity proofing is done by actual people, is what the USPS already does.

Second, Congress needs to direct the Commerce Department's standards office, NIST, to develop whatever standards they think are necessary for the seamless transfer of identity-proofing data and credential exchange, beyond, if necessary, existing standards.

Third, Congress needs to mandate that key agencies, including the IRS, accept the ReallyU system. (No more e-filing a tax return by answering challenge questions about your last tax return.)

As we have sought to make clear, what we propose is not a novel concept. It builds on ideas and programs that others have developed. We believe we are at a point at which the technology is sufficiently developed and the benefits are now clear. Identity masquerading is necessary for both financial theft by cyber criminals and all sorts of malicious activity inside government and corporate networks by foreign intelligence and military hackers.

The theft of personally identifiable information (PII) is one of the most common cybercrimes, and costs companies billions of dollars to prevent. We can greatly reduce all of that by adopting a voluntary system of federated, multifactor identification for online activities. Most criminal uses of PII would no longer work to access credit cards or other financial activities, thus greatly reducing the incentive to steal it.

While all of this would require a new law and some federal standards and support, it would not be a government ID system. It would be an identity system used by companies and individuals who want to protect their identities while benefiting from the digital economy. It is more analogous to our current credit-card system. All of this could be done today with existing technologies, piecing together bits from here and there that have already been proven to work. We just need leadership, will, and people of good faith playing nicely together, including Congress for a quick minute or two.

Chapter 9

FIXING THE PEOPLE PROBLEM

A burglar, a spy, a fugitive, a delinquent, a hacker, and a piano teacher . . . and these are the good guys.

—TAGLINE FROM *SNEAKERS* (1992 FILM)

Frank DiGiovanni is no cyber warrior. He is a real warrior. An ex-fighter pilot in the Air Force, he now works in the Navy as a civilian. The walls of his Pentagon office are adorned with the memorabilia collected over a lifetime defending the country: military decorations, photos of the teams he has been on, tactical knives, and innumerable challenge coins given out by military units in appreciation of his service. DiGiovanni has served as the director of Force Training in the Office of the Assistant Secretary of Defense for Readiness, as well as the assistant deputy chief of Naval Operations for Manpower, Personnel, Training and Education, and he is now the Deputy Director for Expeditionary Warfare. In all these roles, DiGiovanni has been charged with thinking about how the U.S. military trains to fight in cyberspace. He has come to some brutal conclusions about a field that many would agree is broken.

Breaking Through the Hype

The cybersecurity community is beset with hand-wringing about the field's workforce crisis. To match every story about the cyber-expert gap, there is one about new programs to combat it. "The cybersecurity workforce is an industrial crisis!" declares Brian NeSmith, the CEO of a well-respected managed security service provider. And indeed, there certainly are a series of problems that we need to solve to get the workforce the nation requires. The first one, though, is to put an end to the hype. Breathless headlines declare workforce shortages of a million or more people. NeSmith quotes an often-used figure of 3.5 million unfilled positions by 2021, but the denominator is important. That figure is global, for the entire planet of 195 countries and 7.6 billion people.

There's an unholy trinity of forces that have an interest in hyping the crisis. The first are companies that don't like the high salaries that cybersecurity professionals demand. Attracting more people to the field, creating a slack in demand, and driving down costs would be of interest. Every time the issue of immigration reform comes up in Congress, the tech companies, in the hopes of expanding the H-1B visa program for technical workers, cite the cybersecurity workforce crisis as one of the main drivers.

The second player in this trinity is the cybersecurity industry itself, which does not necessarily want more workers in the field. They want their customers to buy more products and services from them, including managed security services that will outsource the work, automation of workflow, and AI that will replace the workers. The message is effective: You can't hire the people you need. Spend your way out.

The last group pushing the workforce crisis are the security training programs springing up at every university and community college and competing against private training programs. All have a vested interest in making the problem seem out of hand, but what do the numbers really say?

The Cyber Census

When the good folks at NIST got tasked to help solve the cybersecurity workforce crisis, one of the first things they did was to get an accurate count of the existing workforce and the open jobs, down to a level of detail that would be useful. Then NIST created an online census of the cybersecurity workforce and job openings called Cyberseek, which brings real numbers to the workforce problem. What the numbers show is a far more nuanced story than what the tech companies, the toolmakers, and the training programs might have you believe.

NIST calculates the total cyber workforce in the United States at 768,096 people, and it identified 301,873 job openings in a one-year period. NIST then helpfully calculated that for every 2.5 people employed in cybersecurity, there is one additional opening. Nationally, across all career fields, there are 6.5 people for every one opening, so the cybersecurity talent market is most definitely tight. Where things get interesting is the data on certifications. NIST took the job postings and pulled out the certifications the postings requested. Then NIST compared them with the number of members of the workforce who have those certifications. What these numbers suggest is that the training programs endeavoring to get people into the field are solving the wrong problem.

Both of us regularly receive emails or are approached at conferences by people trying to break into the field. Many times, these individuals have no idea where to begin and are more interested in the policy aspects of cybersecurity. We generally give them the same advice. First, gain a technical grounding. Learn to work from the command line in Linux, learn the programming language Python, then take a penetration testing course. Increasingly, the people we talk to have taken several courses and obtained a series of entry-level certifications. They are applying to dozens of jobs. They are never getting a callback.

The reason for that appears to be that the demand is not at the entry level. The market wants more midcareer, experienced professionals. Looking at the data bears this out, as does talking to hiring managers. At any given company, the person in charge of cybersecurity first has to fight for money. When they get money, they have to fight for head count. Companies are often willing to spend big dollars on cybersecurity, but will fight to keep their teams as small as possible or even smaller than possible. If a director of security can staff up, the last thing they want to do is hire someone new to the field whom they will have to train for a year or two before getting any value out of them.

The data from Cyberseek bears this out: 167,776 people hold the CompTIA Security+ certification, an entry-level certification, against only 33,529 job openings that require it, for a ratio of 5 holders for every opening. If there are 6.5 workers for every opening in the overall economy, entry-level cyber isn't in much higher demand than, say, retail workers.

Go further up the stack and the ratios start to shift dramatically in the other direction. Global Information Assurance Certification (GIAC) programs tend toward higher-level skills, with a historical connection to the NSA. There are 45,527 GIAC holders and 33,239 openings that request some of the GIAC certifications. It's safe to assume that almost all of these GIAC holders already have jobs. For certified information systems security professionals (CISSP), certified information system auditors (CISA), and certified information security managers (CISM), there are more job openings than there are people with those certifications. Interestingly, for those who believe the skill shortage is only technical, auditors (CISA) and managers (CISM) are the two most in demand.

If the real shortage in the cybersecurity workforce is not at the entry level but at the level of experienced professionals, it is a much harder problem to solve. Pulling thousands of new people to the field, in many cases paying high tuition costs, will likely lead to a lot of people spending money on basic training and not being able to get jobs if new career pathways aren't created.

The Cyber Workforce Market Failure

It is tempting to conclude that the cyber workforce problem will solve itself over time. After all, to move from an entry-level information-security analyst with a CompTIA Security+ certification to a CISO takes years. As more and more core societal functions go online and as companies either go out of business or make the leap to digital-first organizations, the scary headlines probably have some truth to them: the workforce gap is still growing and market forces alone are not fixing it. In almost all cases, we think that when markets fail, governments need to intervene. While sometimes government intervention means good, old-fashioned regulation, in this case there is probably no way to regulate our way out of the crisis. While cybersecurity is a twenty-first-century problem, we can look to two unlikely historical episodes for lessons: twentieth-century military challenges and the guilds of the Middle Ages.

When DiGiovanni got the task of figuring out how the military could train more (and more effective) cyber warriors, he first looked at how current military training programs in the field worked.

He came to a stark conclusion: the Department of Defense did not know who they were looking for and how to train a cyber warrior. "We were repurposing people from the comms community and the intel community rather than taking people who were born into the cyber community," says DiGiovanni. "The military services were taking the easy way out by repurposing troops in similar areas rather than saying, what do I need to do this job, what are the attributes of the people who can do it, and what do I need to do to train them?"

As to identifying the people with the capability to become, in his words, efficacious cyber warriors, DiGiovanni quickly concluded that the basic military aptitude tests were missing the mark. "The tests we are giving people that simply measure intelligence are missing a big part of what it takes to be successful."

DiGiovanni identified a series of core attributes he was looking for, based on interviews he conducted with those who were successful in the field at doing the work he needed to train his recruits to do, i.e., hard-core hackers. He talked to dozens of them. He now knew he was looking for people who had the ability to be self-taught, who learned better on their own than in classrooms. He was looking for people who became easily obsessed and would dig deep into a new subject ("It could be anything—coffee, brewing beer, cars—they just need to be passionately curious"), people who had the tenacity to work forever, to be the kind of people who will never give up on a problem until they have solved it.

They also had to be "prestige seeking." They could be "breakers" in one sense of the term "hacker," or "builders" in another sense of the same term, but they had to want to do things that others could not. They also had to be process oriented, creative but within constraints. Finally, they had to exhibit that most hackerlike trait, a willingness to constantly challenge the status quo, something the military's culture does not exactly encourage.

DiGiovanni looked for candidates who fit these attributes within the military and the Pentagon's civilian workforce. When he found them, he did not stick them in a standard classroom. He does not believe that most real-world skills are best learned by sitting in a chair, reading a book, listening to a lecture, and taking exams. For cybersecurity, he thinks these old-school learning models are hopeless, and yet it is how the U.S. military still trains most of its recruits to serve in cybersecurity missions. It's also how most universities are approaching the problem. DiGiovanni, on the other hand, is a proponent of experiential and guided "autodidactic" learning. What that means is that he thinks cybersecurity is best learned by doing and is mostly about working on your own with some gentle guidance.

It may be that the best way to learn cybersecurity is to beat your head against a computer monitor for a decade in your parents' basement, but the nation can't wait that long. Thus, finding a way to identify students with the right innate abilities and then to move them swiftly along through a hands-on learning program may be a far better approach. With that insight, DiGiovanni created the Cyber Operations Academy Course. His first step was to hire a bunch of ex-NSA TAO guys.

TAO, for Tailored Access Operations, is the NSA's legendary elite hacking team. They carry out focused operations against the world's most hardened targets (other nation-states). They are the very definition of an advanced persistent threat and they hire their fair share of computer prodigies right out of high school and recruit heavily from the University of Maryland, MIT, and Stanford, with a compelling pitch: Come break into live computer systems legally, in the service of your country.

DiGiovanni came across a small company, Point3 Security, founded by an ex-TAO operator named Evan Dornbush and other ex-government colleagues, that was struggling to get its new endpoint system to the market. He gave them a simple pitch: Design me a course, and sit in the lab as a resource for students. Give them hints when they are stuck, but otherwise feel free to code away on your security application. And so they did, developing a series of progressively harder challenges for students to work on. There were no multiple-choice tests, no lectures.

When students got stuck, they could go to the instructors, who would mostly give them a simple piece of advice: "Google it." They left coding manuals and trade publications around the lab as a resource as well, but the most valuable resource typically was other students in the class. The first year of the class was rough. Many of the students, drawn from across the DoD, military, and civilian workforces, dropped out and returned to their previous assignments. Some got the bug for cybersecurity and gained enough knowledge that they now have thriving careers in the military, federal government, and, in some cases, the private sector. What really made the program successful was that the Pentagon provided jobs for those who succeeded.

For their part, the Point3 guys did get their endpoint detection technology, Odile, finished and on the market. They've white-labeled it to a few vendors and are happy with what they built. Most of their time is now spent commercializing the course they built for the Pentagon. They created Escalate, a series of progressively more difficult challenges that students can take online. The first three are free. Beyond that, students, or the companies they work for, pay three thousand dollars a year for access to the program. As with the in-person course, mentors are available when students get stuck.

Dornbush, both as a trainer and a hiring manager, has seen the value of the approach that DiGiovanni pitched him. Point3 is rapidly expanding and he has a lot of slots to fill. "People come with all their certificates like CISSP," says Dornbush. He gives them a challenge on Escalate and they sit there having no idea how to analyze the piece of malware he has dropped on them. They know what malware analysis is and probably aced all the questions on the CISSP about it, but they don't know how to do it. "You want me to hire you to be a malware analyst; I gave you a piece of malware and you can't analyze it?"

Point3 is, of course, not the only company with an online offering like this. Immersive Labs, a U.K. company, is taking a similar approach and has multiple customers at the large financial institutions. It's a better and cheaper approach than in-person classes and can be used to assess the competence of current workforces, as well as provide them with additional training. This is probably not an approach that can, in a short period, turn out all of the highly skilled professionals the market is demanding. For that, students taking these type of courses evenings and weekends also need the opportunity to work on real-world problems by day.

Here is where the approach that the military took to new technical fields in the twentieth century is instructive. When Admiral Hyman Rickover created the nuclear Navy, he recognized that the program would never succeed unless he could guarantee that there would be no nuclear incidents as a result. Being a control freak, Rickover personally selected every officer who joined his program and decided that the Navy would train all its nuclear engineers in-house.

To this day, having an undergraduate degree or even a PhD in nuclear engineering would not help you get into the Navy's nuclear training program. The only prerequisite for officers is to have taken calculus. Enlisted personnel are chosen based on how well they do on the Armed Services Vocational Aptitude Battery, which measures capabilities, not specialized knowledge. Similarly, taking private flying lessons is neither a requirement nor an advantage to becoming a military aviator.

For both aviation and the nuclear Navy, the military very quickly grew a large and capable workforce. That workforce, in turn, provided these trained individuals to the civilian workforce once they completed their service requirements. Go to any nuclear plant or talk to any civilian pilot and there is a good chance you will find someone who first received training and experience in the military. As DiGiovanni points out, when World War II began in Europe in 1939, the Army Air Corps could field only 1,500 aircraft. By 1944, the successor Army Air Forces had 80,000 aircraft and 2.5 million men and women under service. At the end of the war, as many of the pilots left service, the burgeoning civilian aviation market gobbled them up.

Today, U.S. Cyber Command has about eight thousand personnel. If there are over three hundred thousand job openings, U.S. military personnel leaving the services are far from being a main source of talent to fill that gap. Cyber Command doubtless needs to grow, but if we continue down a path where the private sector is responsible for its own security, there will never be enough skilled veterans for the civilian workforce. Instead, the approach of "recruit, train, deploy, and retrain" needs to be adopted by both the civilian government and the private sector.

Many in the Pentagon and civilian agencies will lament that as soon as they train up someone, the private sector will swoop in as fast as possible to hire them. Bobbie Stempfley, a former leader at the Department of Homeland Security's Office of Cybersecurity and Communications, has often quipped that if the government is so bad at cybersecurity, then why did they constantly poach her staff? Yet instead of lamenting this churn, we should encourage it. There may be no better or more direct way for the government to support the private sector than by recruiting and training a cybersecurity workforce that private companies will eagerly hire. Creating this program in a civilian government agency like DHS would likely draw a different and possibly larger pool of candidates who are not inclined toward military service. After completing training, participants would have a multiyear obligation of service to pay back the costs, though private-sector employers should be allowed to buy them out of those obligations.

Cyber Guilds

Replicating a similar program in the private sector may be more difficult. Training new personnel from scratch is typically not something shareholders will find in their interest. To illustrate, let's draw up a composite character from real people we know. She's the CISO of a midmarket company. The company does $3 billion a year in business. It has eight thousand employees. She reports to the CIO, who oversees a one-hundred-person IT department. Three years ago she was the director of IT security and had no one reporting to her. Now, as CISO, she has two direct reports. Her board and CEO are all over cybersecurity and have upped her budget every year for the last three years. She can buy just about any tool she wants. What she can't do is hire anyone.

Her CFO is tightly controlling head count. Employees are expensive.

Employees introduce liability. Hiring a handful of junior people and training them is a nonstarter. If she gets approval for another person, she wants a "ninja" or a "wizard," someone in the middle of their career who has experience across all the areas of cyber operations. A junior person would gain valuable experience working on the problems this company has, and could apply what they learn in an online program like Escalate at night each day (or by day each night, as they will probably get stuck on the graveyard shift). Here is where the guilds of yesteryear come in.

Learning by doing is, of course, not a new idea. Training programs in the form of hands-on apprenticeships were formalized in the Middle Ages, but they have largely fallen out of favor in the United States except in a few specialized trades (plumbing, carpenters, and electricians often still hire and train apprentices). When a presidentially appointed commission looked at the workforce problem at the end of the Obama administration, it concluded that the next President should create a national cybersecurity apprenticeship program with the goal of training fifty thousand new cybersecurity practitioners by 2020. The Trump administration has not moved this initiative forward.

Luckily, some of the private-sector leaders President Obama appointed to the task force have realized that the program need not be led by the government. Ajay Banga, the CEO of Mastercard, pushed leadership at Microsoft and Workday to join him in establishing the Cybersecurity Talent Initiative. Under the program, students who pursue a cybersecurity-related undergraduate or advanced degree will then do a two-year tour of duty in full-time cybersecurity roles at federal agencies such as the DoD, FBI, CIA, DHS, Treasury, and the Small Business Administration. They will then transition to positions with participating corporate sponsors. At the end of the program, the corporate sponsors will pay off outstanding student loan debt up to seventy-five thousand dollars. More than forty-five universities have committed to the program, from Harvard and MIT to a series of historically black colleges and universities. The founding partners committed to taking on a minimum of five program participants per year.

Of course, if only the founding companies join and only make their initial commitments to hire five a year, the initiative won't do much to close the workforce gap. Alex Niejelow, senior vice president at Mastercard (and a former White House colleague of Rob Knake's), who helped shape the initiative with Banga, hopes the program will grow rapidly. "We have three massive technology-enabled companies that are leading this initiative. We expect the rest of the market will follow," says Niejelow. "Every company is facing this crisis."

We applaud private sector efforts like this, but ultimately believe that government is likely to need to do two things. First, it needs to nudge the market away from requiring undergraduate degrees to get into the field and instead create pathways for professionals later in their careers. Today, many if not most of the best people we know working in even the most technical areas of cybersecurity do not have undergraduate degrees in computer science. If the national security of the United States requires college freshmen to make good decisions about their career prospects, we are likely doomed. Thus, we think an intensive boot-camp program like what DiGiovanni pioneered is likely a better pathway into the field than emphasizing formal education. Second, government may need to subsidize private companies to provide apprenticeships, as the federal government alone is not likely to be able to provide enough meaningful initial positions.

Of course, risk is inherent to the approach that we have outlined. We might train hundreds of thousands of people in cybersecurity only to have them replaced by robots. Artificial intelligence is making gains in automating some of the entry-level tasks that Tier 1 analysts do, like being "the eyes on the glass" in the Security Operations Center (SOC). Indeed, it's possible that in a decade or two, the cybersecurity workforce may actually shrink. Given that Apple, Google, and Amazon have invested billions of dollars in digital home assistants that still can't compose a grocery list, we think the point at which trained cybersecurity professionals are going to be looking for jobs is pretty far off.

Chapter 10

\|\|\|\|\|\|\|\|\|\|

POWER GRIDS AND POWER PLAYS

> This is the largest blackout in U.S. history. If that is not a signal
> that we have got a problem that needs to be fixed, I don't know
> what is.
>
> —JENNIFER GRANHOLM, THEN GOVERNOR OF MICHIGAN,
> *AMERICAN MORNING*, CNN, AUGUST 18, 2003

New York is down." It was 2003 and many people were still jumpy
from the 9/11 attack that had occurred less than two years earlier.
Just before 5:00 P.M. on August 14, a frantic news producer found
ABC News's Ted Koppel in a corridor and told him that the ABC television
network had lost contact with the mothership, Network Control in Manhattan. "We're running the entire national network from here in Washington
now." ABC had automatically instituted its disaster recovery plan and devolved control to D.C. "You have to go on," the producer told Ted. "Now. Live."

Although most Washingtonians had fled the city in the annual August
evacuation to the beach, Ted Koppel was still there. For more than twenty
years, Koppel had done a network television newsmagazine show, *Nightline*.
Weekday nights the show went on the air at 11:30 P.M. East Coast time, but

he taped much of it during the afternoon at ABC News's Washington bureau. He had just completed taping that night's show. It would never be seen.

The producer told Koppel there had been a major power blackout. New
York was in the dark and so were Cleveland, Pittsburgh, and a huge swath of
the Northeast. With little more information than that, Koppel sat on a stool
in front of a camera and tried to explain to the rest of the country what was
going on. The problem was, he didn't know. No one did. Koppel was vamp-
ing, but, being a pro at live television, he exuded calm to an anxious audience.

Dick Clarke, then an ABC News "talking head," had also been in the
D.C. bureau when control of the national network shifted to the little building on a side street in downtown Washington. The front desk guard stopped
him from leaving the building and redirected him to the studio. In a few
minutes, he was sitting next to Koppel explaining to the audience how there
were three isolated electric power grids (known as Interconnects) in the
United States: East, West, and, well, Texas, and within them there were
subregions, such as the mid-Atlantic area, known as PJM (the Pennsylvania–
New Jersey–Maryland area). "It looks like the folks at PJM acted just in
time to unplug us, otherwise Washington would have gone down too," Dick
suggested.

"But there is no way that this could have been terrorism, right, Dick?"
Koppel asked, seeking to further assure people.

Dick paused. He knew more than he could say publicly about the fragil-
ity of the power grid in the face of a cyberattack. As the nation's first Cyber
Czar, he had pushed for meaningful cybersecurity regulation of power generation and distribution companies. The electric power lobby had pushed
back hard and, largely, won. Nonetheless, President George W. Bush's 2003
National Strategy to Secure Cyberspace that Dick had released six months
before the blackout had stressed the need to increase protection of the
power grid cyber controls.

Answering Koppel within the first hour of the blackout, Dick suggested
that there was no way to know just then if the grid had been attacked, but it
was possible, he insisted, for malicious activity to bring down the grid. Koppel downplayed the idea.

If a Tree Fell in a Forest

A U.S.–Canadian investigation completed a year later placed the blame on a tree. To be fair, it had been a really big tree, in Ohio, and it had fallen on a sagging, overloaded transmission line. Buried in the study was an observation that an internet worm running rampant that day may have slowed down the control network, possibly contributing to the cascading failures that tripped circuits providing power to 50 million people. Still, no one wanted to say that the power grid could be brought down by malicious internet activity. In retrospect, the 2003 disaster was not a cyber incident, but what Dick and others knew then was that such a catastrophe could be caused by a cyberattack.

A dozen years later, Ted Koppel was convinced too. He wrote a book called *Lights Out*, about the threat of a cyberattack plunging the nation into darkness not for hours, but for months. Koppel wrote that cyberattacks could cause large transformers and generators to become so damaged that they would be irreparable, and he noted that there are few spares lying around. It takes months, and electric power, to make new ones.

Even in 2015, however, some critics found *Lights Out* to be hyperbolic, exaggerated, or alarmist. By then, however, there should have been less doubt. In 2007, a generator was attacked and destroyed from the internet in a controlled experiment at Idaho National Laboratory. In 2015, Russian hackers plunged much of Ukraine into darkness by taking remote control of a power grid control room, making the controls reflect normal activity, and then opening breakers throughout the subgrid. A year later, they did it again, although to another part of Ukraine.

By then film, television, and thriller writers had totally accepted the idea of hackers taking down the grid. It was the premise of Bruce Willis's *Live Free or Die Hard*, and the television series *Madam Secretary* showed an American President retaliating against Russia by plunging Moscow into darkness in winter. (By 2017, the idea of the President ever standing up to Russia seemed more fictional than any cyberattack on the grid.)

Is Self-Regulation Enough?

The electric power industry, however, continued to deny that there was much of a problem. The industry's self-regulatory body, the North American Electric Reliability Council (NERC), was satisfied that its rules for critical infrastructure protection (known to all in the business as "nerk sip") were adequate to protect the grid from hackers. The government's regulatory body, the Federal Energy Regulatory Commission (FERC), tended to defer to the industry. (By 2019, however, FERC was more assertive and fined Duke Energy ten million dollars for cybersecurity lapses.)

Indeed, so powerful were the industry's lobbyists that only part of the grid was subject to any federal regulation at all. FERC has its oversight limited to the "bulk" power system. Even then, the industry group managed to exempt 90 percent of the grid by declaring it "low impact" or noncritical.

The "last few miles" distribution systems are beyond the reach of the federal government regulators. State governments, which have shown little interest or ability in regulating the cybersecurity of power grids, have legal authority over it. Power companies have noted that the state governments, which do regulate the price for electric power, are really reluctant to authorize increases in electric rates. So really, you see, there is no way that the companies could come up with the money to pay for more extensive cybersecurity even if they wanted to, or so they say.

The FERC, however, did require power grid companies to report cyber incidents on the parts of the grid for which it has authority. In 2015 and 2016, no one did. That strained the credulity of even the FERC and the NERC, both of which began a process in 2018 to lower the threshold of incident reporting. FERC even suggested the radical notion (one commentator called it a "sea change") that portable devices that connect to the grid, such as laptops and tablets, should meet cybersecurity standards. FERC's newfound courage, however, may have been both too little and too late.

By the fall of 2017, the Department of Homeland Security was quietly informing power grid companies that there was good reason to believe that potential adversary nations were attempting to penetrate the controls of the

U.S. power grid. For some on the receiving end of that information, it was hardly news. Some companies had been monitoring attempts to penetrate their networks for years. Others, however, seemed as if they would rather not know. They continued to repeat the mantra that they were "nerk sip" compliant, that their controls were not connected to the internet, that they could not afford to do anything more, and that it was really the government's job to save them from foreign armies.

Blinking Red Lights

In the summer of 2018, by which time most of the nation had accepted the fact that Russia had actually meddled in the 2016 election and was hacking into anything it could in the United States, the head of the U.S. intelligence community publicly warned that the power grid had in fact already been successfully penetrated by Russia. DHS's chief of industrial control system analysis, Jonathan Homer, specified, "They [the Russian group Dragonfly] have had access to the button, but they haven't pushed it." Dan Coats, the Director of National Intelligence and a former Republican Senator, described the Russian attacks on the U.S. electrical grid as being so severe that, figuratively, "the warning lights are blinking red."

In background briefings that followed Coats's statement, government officials explained that the Russians had "jumped the air gap," which the power grid companies contended they had created between their internet-connected systems and the actual controls of the power networks. In point of fact, few companies had actually isolated their controls. There was almost always a path from the internet to the company's intranet, and another path from there to the grid controls. The connections among and between the company's internal networks were usually segmented by firewalls, but firewalls seldom stop sophisticated hackers.

By 2019, Coats and the heads of all seventeen U.S. intelligence agencies were getting more explicit. In their annual threat assessment to Congress, the agency heads wrote that Russia had the ability to disrupt the U.S. power grid and that China had the capability to disrupt the U.S. natural gas pipeline system (upon which much of the power grid relies). These were not theoretical capabilities, the agencies made clear. These were swords of Damocles hanging above America, swords that could be dropped at any time.

Russia's hackers had allegedly gone after the companies that supply parts to or do maintenance on the grid control side of the air gap. By compromising those systems, the attackers could gain the log-in credentials of people authorized to have access to the control network. Often that access would be remote, over virtual private networks (VPNs) running on top of the internet. The Russians could then plug into the grid's control. Then they could move into the systems that display the state of the grid on big monitors in control rooms and send instructions to the thousands of devices in the field.

If all of that sounds a little familiar to you, maybe you read speculation about how the United States had attacked the Iranian controls for the nuclear centrifuges at Natanz. The Iranians had basked confidently in the assurance that their control network was also "air gapped" from the internet. Not satisfied with the security provided by firewalls, the Iranians had sought to protect the plant from U.S. or Israeli cyberattack by having no internet connection anywhere in the complex. The United States attacked, according to some experts, by infiltrating the Stuxnet software into devices brought into the building by contractors, perhaps on laptops or printers.

Thus, the United States now faced the specter that people in American power control rooms could someday look up at "the big board," the giant monitors on the wall, and see everything blinking green for good, while the reality was that the system was malfunctioning.

Even if you had known for years that it could happen, having the head of U.S. intelligence say that it had taken place was enough to cause shock and high levels of concern in much of official Washington. President Trump, however, did not talk publicly about the Russian presence inside the U.S. power grid controls. He could barely admit they had tried to influence his election, and that only on alternate days. Thus, there was no presidential directive, no ten-point action plan, no public threat to Moscow whatsoever.

Left on their own to devise a reaction, the Washington policy chattering classes suggested a variety of approaches to the problem of having a potential adversary possess the ability to throw much of the nation back into a nineteenth-century preelectric age, only worse, because this time we would be without manual devices. Keith Alexander suggested that it was the military's job to defend the grid. He did not say how it would do that. Some commentators suggested that improved information sharing by the government would help the companies do a better job finding the Russians on their networks.

Taking a page from Special Counsel Robert Mueller's playbook, others proposed that the United States should indict the individual Russian military and intelligence officers who had done the hacks. In addition, maybe we could seize their assets in the United States and ask Interpol to issue international arrest warrants for them.

The more robust-sounding responses came from those who believed in deterrence. If we were in the Russian power grid controls, then maybe we could scare the Russians into inaction, they said. Just like the U.S. President on that *Madam Secretary* episode, we could throw Moscow into wintry darkness if they tried to shut off the power in Washington, or mess with the Eastern Interconnect (everything east of the Mississippi, including Ontario).

All of those reactions struck us as pathetic and, were this not a serious business that could lead to death and war, even laughable. Russia doesn't care if we sanction their intelligence officers, and none of them have assets in the United States anyway. They do not travel abroad under their real names, and they are never going to be caught because of an Interpol notice. Russia will not be deterred by the threat of the United States turning off their lights. If they are going to attack us, they will already have calculated that it will result in some risks and costs. Moreover, will you really feel better as you freeze on a dark night, eating cold tuna fish from a can and figuring out how to break into an ATM, knowing that your Russian counterpart is also in the dark? At least *they* have plenty of vodka.

The reason the Russians are in the controls of the U.S. power grid is because it is easy to be, and very useful to be. Whether or not they could actually bring the country to its knees without firing a shot, no one knows. And that is the point.

We have to admit that it's a hard problem. The power grid is a crazy quilt of hundreds of disparate electric power companies of very different sizes and competencies. Each company has tens of thousands, if not hundreds of thousands, of devices connected to it, many of them sitting out in the open, unguarded.

We got here by ignoring the warnings that have been issued by government experts for almost twenty-five years that the power grid was becoming vulnerable to cyberattacks. Those warnings were ignored because such an attack had never happened before, what Dick, in the 2017 book *Warnings*, called the Initial Occurrence Syndrome bias.

Taking the warnings seriously would have been an inconvenience to grid owners and operators. It would also have meant spending money, which would have had the effect of raising electricity rates and/or lowering company profits.

Moreover, because self-regulation usually results in minimal regulation, really addressing the problem would have meant having serious, mandatory government regulations and compulsory compliance enforcement. Business leaders tend to resist any government regulation. They resist new regulation of any kind like white blood cells attacking a disease. "How would government know what to do? They can't even protect their own networks."

We have placed the national security task of creating cybersecurity for most of the power grid into the hands of fifty state-level electric-rate-setting regulators, some of whom just might be subject to the blandishments of big utility companies and their lobbyists.

Five Not-So-Easy Pieces

The more important question which you are now asking yourself is, How do we get out of this mess? Well, we begin by admitting we have a problem, a big one. There is no need here to once again paint the picture of what could happen. By now, you can imagine it. If we have a big problem, it may require a willingness to engage in bold solutions. Half measures are not recommended. We have tried that already and they have failed. So . . .

First, put someone in charge and give them real authority. We suggest that this someone be a senior official in Homeland Security. If you feel better with someone from the Energy Department, fine. If you think the military should do it, read chapter 12 on the military and realize that they are busy enough trying to defend themselves.

Real authority means federal-level mandatory and compulsory regulatory directive capability, unencumbered by prolonged legal review processes. It means authority over the cybersecurity of every aspect of the power grid: big power companies, little cooperatives, bulk power, generation, distribution, and last-mile access. It means the authority to raise rates and to direct spending. Did someone tell you security was cheap? Would you rather buy everyone an emergency generator and months of fuel?

Second, launch a major program using the best private-sector threat hunter firms to find and remove foreign implants, backdoors, and remote access to the industrial control systems (ICS) and supervisory control and data acquisition systems (SCADA) on the grid. This will not be easy. Ask the U.S. Navy how easy it was to get the Iranians out of their network (and by the way, the Russians are better).

Third, put in place that combination of state-of-the-art cybersecurity best practices that have achieved success in America's most secure corporations. Private-sector expert panels can design the essential set of controls, but they are likely to include permanent threat hunting software and teams, continuous monitoring applications, privileged access management controls, microsegmentation, endpoint detection, remediation systems, limited remote access, and vendor/supply-chain controls. Private, third-party teams, incentivized to find vulnerabilities, must then be used on a near constant basis to monitor compliance. A pattern of noncompliance would result in severe fines, or forfeiture of the property.

Fourth, prepare better for the worst. We also need to be discussing how to maintain society once the grid goes down for a long time. There needs to be a contingency plan that helps to mitigate the most severe effects of such a worst-case scenario.

It may not be possible to stop the lights from going out from an attack that essentially flips breakers, but it should be possible to put better controls on transformers and generators to prevent a hacker from overriding their limits and causing physical destruction. In the event that fails, there should be replacement systems stockpiled, or many more generators on standby than are currently used day to day. Those spares should not, however, be used on peak days. They would be dedicated to respond to hostile attack situations to bring the grid back up in isolated subgrids.

Fifth, you want to hack into the Russian power grid's controls and publicly threaten them with retaliation? Sure, okay, but we may already have tried that, and if so, it has not deterred them. Maybe we could say we are serious this time. And maybe deterrence will work, and maybe we can secure the existing grid with retrofits, but it would be nice to have a plan B in case deterrence fails and we cannot get all of the power companies to secure their networks.

We don't really have a plan B today, and that contributes to crisis instability. There is probably greater uncertainty on our part about what destruction they can do to us than there is uncertainty on their part about that same question. As Dr. Strangelove might have said, "Vee need to close the uncertainty gap." We can do that by stepping up our cyber defenses on the power grid and causing the Russians and others to be uncertain what the effect would be if they tried a major attack.

What would a plan B look like? It would be a secure, segmented, diverse-source microgrid (SSDM) program, with some microgrids completely federally funded and some built with incentives from the federal government. To build a bipartisan coalition for the program, it would be justified by both national security and climate change concerns. What we are suggesting for a plan B is:

- Thousands of heterogeneous sources of electricity generation and storage that would not be tied to any of the three big national Interconnects, or even the regional subnetworks
- Power generation facilities that would have guaranteed access to fuel, with on-site or near-site storage, or would use alternative fuels
- Alternative fuel sources that would include hydrogen cells, wind, solar, hydrothermal, and new-design compact nuclear reactors
- New innovative methods of storing power at every building, such as new high-capacity battery packs, or pumped-storage hydroelectricity

- Microdistribution networks that would carry the power on new lines, ideally underground, to key facilities that must have continuous power, including military bases, hospitals, and national-level infrastructure
- The location of power generators on the premises of critical facilities, such as military bases, to the greatest extent possible.

Our SSDM proposal is at once evolutionary and revolutionary. The evolutionary aspects include the construction of large alternative-energy plants. There already are large solar and wind plants built by the private sector. Hydrogen fuel-cell plants are being built, including a 20-megawatt generator we were briefed on that would use an abandoned factory in New Britain, Connecticut.

The DoD has already built large-scale solar and geothermal plants on its bases, such as a 16-megawatt solar plant at Davis-Monthan Air Force Base outside Tucson, a 14-megawatt solar plant at Nellis Air Force Base outside Las Vegas, and a 170-megawatt geothermal plant at China Lake Naval Air Weapons Station in California.

The revolutionary parts of the SSDM proposal are threefold. First, it would be the building of a new, second national power grid on a crash basis as a major government initiative, with significant private-sector involvement. Second, the new grid would not be interconnected, but would instead consist of thousands of energy sources intended only for specific facilities. Not being interconnected, or connected in any way to the internet, it could not be taken out by a single or even a handful of cyberattacks. Third, and most important, perhaps, it would be designed with cybersecurity in mind, rather than as a grudgingly added retrofit and afterthought.

Yes, it would be expensive, but think of it as a weapons system. Without a system like SSDM, the nation will be defenseless against a nation-state actor, somebody like the Russian GRU, engaging in a cyberattack that would technologically revert us to the nineteenth century, but without all the equipment that people in the nineteenth century had to deal with life in a society without electricity.

We spent $201 billion to fund the DoD Missile Defense Agency between 1985 and 2017. In 2018 alone, Congress approved $11.5 billion for missile defense. Yet no defense expert we talked to thinks that the United States could stop a Russian missile attack on America. By saturating the defenses with multiple, simultaneous launches and scattering decoys, Russia or China could easily defeat the missile defense system. Nonetheless, we spend because we just don't like the idea of Russia or some other nation being able to attack our territory and knock the legs out from under our society and economy. Now, remember earlier in the chapter when we quoted the Director of National Intelligence saying the Russians were hacking into the controls of our power grid?

We've spent enough time between us in the Executive Office of the President to know how that game is played, so we have a pay-for. If you don't care for ours, get your own. Ours is the Air Force program to replace the Minuteman intercontinental ballistic missile (ICBM). They are planning to spend upwards of $140 billion to do that, and you just know there will be a cost overrun. We do not need to have ICBMs, land-based nuclear missiles sitting in holes on farms in Wyoming with about four hundred nuclear warheads. They are a relic of an age when we thought seriously about engaging in the kind of thermonuclear war that would kill off the population, all of it. For that purpose, we also have five times as many nuclear warheads on missiles on submarines. There are also bombers and cruise missiles.

Which kind of Russian attack is more likely: one that crashes our power grid (the power grid they have already penetrated) and causes our society to effectively cease functioning for months, or one that uses nuclear weapons and risks our nuclear retaliation and the end of all human life? Don't struggle with the answer. It was a rhetorical question.

We are not saying abandon all efforts to secure the existing grid. We are saying that probably won't work too well and we need a plan B, soon. A plan B that gives us another grid that the Russians could only have low confidence in damaging significantly, a second grid that would keep some of our most essential systems able to operate even if the Russians take down our Interconnects.

Some of you may be thinking that the government should not be regulating cybersecurity because it can't even secure itself. You would be half right, as we see next.

Chapter 11

....

SECURING THE FEDS

Agencies do not understand and do not have the resources to combat the current threat environment.

—WHITE HOUSE OFFICE OF MANAGEMENT AND BUDGET,
"FEDERAL CYBERSECURITY RISK DETERMINATION
REPORT AND ACTION PLAN," MAY 2018

S hit, it's snowing," the lanky, blond guy said aloud, looking out from
the lobby of the Business School. Overhearing him, a friendly,
white-haired professor standing nearby asked, "Is that a problem for
you?" The professor, Corey Schou, was one of the founders of cybersecurity
education in America. "It snows a lot here. After all," he said, "it is Idaho."

"I know, but it's hard to practice pole-vaulting in the snow," the student,
Connor Pate, explained. Pate was a senior at Idaho State, recruited from his
Reno, Nevada, high school because he was among the top pole-vaulters in
the country. Unable to practice that day, he accepted Professor Schou's offer
to tour the cyber lab. The professor recalls liking a student who was mad
because he could not train. He was also impressed by the undergrad's knowledge of game theory, something they discussed on the lab tour.

A week later Connor Pate was filling out an application to join Cyber-Corps, a little-known federal scholarship program that has been helping to provide cyber-defense personnel for the U.S. government for almost two decades. The next year Pate was in the MBA program at Idaho State, specializing in cybersecurity as a member of CyberCorps and paying no tuition.

He did, however, have mandatory Saturday classes and had to be part of a team creating a cyber range on which to practice attacking and defending, staff a security operations center, participate in a multiuniversity cyber competition, and provide an oral defense of a written thesis. All of that and more were in addition to the core work required for the MBA. "At Idaho State," Pate told us, "CyberCorps is elite and tough." Professor Schou admits, "We allow only about a dozen students at a time, combining both years of the two-year program here."

CyberCorps is a Scholarship for Service program funded by the National Science Foundation, administered by the infamous Office of Personnel Management, and advised by the NSA and DHS. Created by President Clinton in 1999, the program first existed at only a handful of schools, including from the start Cory Schou and Idaho State. Now it offers full scholarships at more than seventy undergraduate colleges, graduate schools, and, recently, community colleges.

When CyberCorps was created, its originators, chiefly Janet Reno and Dick Clarke, were not very hopeful that it would be a long-term solution to the human resources needs of federal cybersecurity offices. At least, however, it would give the government some highly trained people for a few years at a time, introduce the latest state of the art to other federal cyber employees, and increase the number of people in the nation's overall cyber-skilled workforce. The results have been better than expected, in part because many of the faculty involved, people like Corey Schou, instilled a sense of public service in their students.

Schou had been teaching cybersecurity for almost fifteen years before CyberCorps came into existence, as well as helping the government to create security standards for its national security–related networks. He had been a leader in national efforts to create certification requirements for cybersecurity professionals. It was only natural that he would help to create the first standards for colleges to qualify as CyberCorps's National Centers of Academic Excellence in Cyber Education. He was also on the first panel of academic experts to determine which schools actually made it. (He recused himself when it came to Idaho State, but his school became one of the original seven approved for the program.)

The leaders in cyber education in America in 1999 were not the universities that you might have assumed would be pioneers in the field, like MIT or Stanford. Places such as Idaho State and Tulsa University were among the early leaders and the best at producing cybersecurity practitioners at the undergraduate and graduate levels. Meanwhile, MIT was still handing out SM degrees in computer science without requiring a recipient to take even a single semester-long course in cybersecurity.

Each one of the National Centers of Academic Excellence in Cyber Education can organize a unique program, but the curriculum and faculty must meet the national standards. Cory Schou's program is not in the computer science department. It's in the business school, because Schou thinks cybersecurity experts need to understand risk management and how cyber decisions fit into overall business decisions. When admitting students to the elite program, Schou looks for diverse backgrounds, not computer jockeys. He limits his two-year program to a few students at a time to "create Bentleys, not Cadillacs."

Not only do the CyberCorps students get free tuition for two years, they are also paid thirty-five thousand dollars a year for room, board, books, and equipment. In return, they promise one year of service in a government agency's cybersecurity office (federal, state, local, or tribal government agencies qualify) for every year of scholarship, up to two years.

The government also pays to fly the CyberCorps students to Washington, D.C., usually twice. One time they go to a job fair to land a summer intern assignment. Connor Pate found a summer internship at NASA's Glenn Research Center in Ohio. The second year they go back to the fair looking for an entry job. There is no lack of openings. The starting salary, however, is usually a little shy of sixty thousand dollars. In many cities in America, the starting salary in a corporation for someone with the same skills would be at least twenty-five thousand dollars higher.

"But then, I don't have any student loan debt," Connor Pate told us. "And I am getting to learn so much more than I ever would have in an entry-level job in some company." Pate landed a position in 2018 as a civilian cybersecurity expert in the U.S. Army and is working his way through a two-year series of assignments around the Army, from operations to research to procurement.

Will he stay on as a government employee defending a federal network after his two-year obligation is up? Right now his answer is: "Definitely. It was weird at first going to work at a fort, like Fort Belvoir, or hearing artillery going off and shaking my building up at Aberdeen [Aberdeen Proving Ground, an Army research center]," Pate recalled. "But you get to work with some amazing people on really cutting-edge problems. The Army is always under a cyberattack and they are doing and spending a lot to defend themselves." He hopes the promotions will come quickly so that his government salary doesn't fall further behind what he could be making in the private sector.

The motivating quality of public service, the great challenge, and, in some agencies, the resources available have been enough to keep many of the CyberCorps graduates in federal service after their two-year obligation. Some, like Idaho State alum Steve Hernandez, have moved rapidly up into leadership positions. Hernandez moved over in 2017 from Health and Human Services to be the chief information security officer at the U.S. Department of Education. Another Idaho State alum, Alma Cole, was the CISO at Customs and Border Protection (CBP) in 2018.

Even with the CyberCorps Scholarship for Service program, it is still difficult for the government, and some other organizations, to beat the competition from corporations offering bigger salaries, signing bonuses, and other perks. Often, those recruited by the private-sector companies end up working for the federal government, but in ways that prove to be more costly and create less institutional memory or loyalty. That happens because the government uses contractor corporations such as Booz Allen Hamilton, ManTech, and General Dynamics to provide "butts in seats," corporate employees sitting in government buildings doing what you might have assumed a government employee would be doing.

The contractors are not incentivized to create secure networks. If they do, they may work themselves out of jobs. They also have few real disincentives for failing to secure a network. Few federal contractors ever pay penalties or have their contracts canceled because they have failed to secure an agency's network.

Contract employees have no loyalty to the federal agency they are assigned to and are often moved around from one agency to another. Butts in seats do not often get to understand the culture or mission of an agency. For-profit corporate employees have also proven to be a security risk in the handling of sensitive, classified information. While it is true that the cost of the actual butt-in-seat staffer may be in the same range as the current all-in cost of a federal employee, the compensation of the corporate leaders of federal contract firms is often three, four, five, or six times higher than that of the Senior Executive Service (SES) federal employees who hire their firms.

What has prevented the federal government from having its own large, strong cadre of cybersecurity personnel is the overly rigid civil service system. That system makes it difficult for government employers to dismiss employees when they are dissatisfied with their performance or when the job for which they were needed is completed. The rules have been there since the late nineteenth century to prevent political parties from firing professional employees and replacing them with partisan supporters. In the twenty-first century that is still a concern, especially given Trump's treatment of career officials. The rules do, however, need to be modified to suit the new nature of work and the new needs of government.

As 2018 came to an end, Congress agreed on something. It came as a shock to cynics who thought the partisan gridlock had made a bipartisan approach to any subject impossible. What the two parties and the two houses of Congress agreed upon was cybersecurity, or at least a new agency to deal with it. The Cybersecurity and Infrastructure Security Agency (CISA) was authorized to come into existence within the Department of Homeland Security, on a par with other agencies in the department such as the Secret Service, Coast Guard, and Federal Emergency Management Agency (FEMA).

Actually, CISA is really just a reorganization of things that were already in DHS and not an increase of resources, but the new agency's mandate is to help the other civilian federal departments and agencies protect their cyber-space. CISA is also to work with the private sector to encourage and assist corporations and other organizations. While not the proverbial silver bullet, the creation of CISA was a good step. Many other steps are needed to secure the federal departments and key agencies such as the National Weather Service, the Centers for Disease Control and Prevention, the Food and Drug Adminis-tration, and other civil service organizations that keep us safe and healthy.

There are scores of ideas about how to improve federal department and agency cybersecurity, suggested in numerous task forces and review com-missions. Given how difficult it is to get anything done in a time of hyper-partisan politics in Congress, we think that starting with a small number of nonpartisan ideas is more practical than trying to solve all of the government's IT security problems at once. Therefore, we propose just two additional steps for consideration: creating a professional cadre of federal cybersecurity offi-cers and centralizing some federal IT operations.

First, the professional cadre: Today CyberCorps is a program to fund college study, recruit entry-level employees, and help place them in their first jobs in the departments. We would like to see it become more than just an entry-level system, but rather a government-wide cadre of highly skilled employees who could be deployed in federal agencies and departments as needed. In our vision they would all belong to a central organization such as DHS's new agency, CISA.

CyberCorps could centrally hire cyber experts at all levels of skill, pro-vide them specialized training beyond what they learned in school or on the job, create a continuing education program, establish grades or ranks requir-ing advanced certification and experience, compensate them differently from the rest of the federal civil service, reward them with significant incentive bonuses, and be able to dismiss them more easily. CyberCorps could then al-locate personnel to departments and agencies for shorter- or longer-term as-signments, while retaining central personnel management authority.

CyberCorps officers could also work in state and local governments and some critical infrastructure corporations on limited project-based assign-ments. Over time, the chief information security officers of the departments and agencies would be selected from and by CyberCorps.

This professional cadre of federal IT security experts would have ranks from entry level to a Senior Cyber Service, modeled on the Senior Foreign Service (at the State Department), the Senior Intelligence Service (at the CIA), and the Senior Executive Service elsewhere in government. These existing Senior Service ranks are now the equivalent of general and admiral ranks in the military. To advance through the ranks of the Senior Cyber Service, professionals would have to continually qualify with work experience, tests, and continuing education programs similar to the National War College (a prerequisite for becoming an Army general or Navy admiral). Homeland would, in our plan, run a National Cyber College for members of the Senior Cyber Service.

The civil service laws would have to be changed to allow the creation of that kind of expanded CyberCorps. In addition, the current Scholarship for Service program might have to be changed, to recruit, train, and place more cyber experts in the new federal service. Specifically, the existing scholarship program might need expanded funding for more scholarships, faculty training, equipment such as cyber ranges for realistic training, paid internships, hiring bonuses, and moving expenses.

CyberCorps may also be one place where some of the security clearance problems associated with hiring into the federal government could be addressed. Your two authors have both taught graduate courses at a couple of universities and have noticed that all too often our students have to hang around for many months after graduation before starting work in the federal government. They wait with no pay for their security clearances to be completed. For our Idaho State cyber scholar Connor Pate, it took nine months from the time he graduated with his MBA and a federal job offer to when he could start work and be paid. Connor waited. Others do not. They take that attractive private-sector offer. CyberCorps could begin the clearance process for students as soon as they joined up, while in school. The Corps could also give them a starting job that would not require a top-secret clearance while they were waiting for a full vetting to be completed.

It's good that the military has its Cyber Command to defend military networks. The other half of the federal government, however, needs its cyber defenders too. We need a new CyberCorps.

Learning from State Governments:
Not Everyone Can Do IT

We would also centralize IT service in the civilian agencies of the federal government. People like to justify the existence of fifty state governments in this country with the phrase "the states are laboratories for innovation." The system of fifty fiefdoms also gives you a better-than-even chance of living in a state that has poor education and health systems, but we digress. One thing that several states have done successfully and that could serve as a model for the federal government is to create information technology departments. We have had the pleasure, as unpaid advisers, to work with the IT departments in both New York and Virginia.

The idea is simple enough. No state agency (or in the case of Virginia, no commonwealth agency, because "commonwealth" just sounds classier) or department is likely to have the ability to recruit enough quality IT professionals to run the agency's own network effectively and securely. Moreover, the leadership of, let's say, the Fish and Game Department is probably not really likely to be a great set of supervisors for a bunch of computer geeks running the agency's network. Nothing against Fish and Game people, you understand.

The solution is to make all, repeat all, IT functions into services that state agencies buy from the one state agency that specializes in computer science, network management, data storage, and, oh yeah, cybersecurity. Rather than just issuing cybersecurity guidelines and rules and hoping that the other agencies think the rules are important enough to spend money implementing, the IT department is responsible for securing everything.

The statewide IT departments often contract out to one or more IT services companies, which actually run parts of the network day to day. The IT department specifies the deliverables, the standards, the security features that will appear in the contract. The state employees in the IT department do contract monitoring, oversight, and quality control. Expecting each of forty or fifty separate state-level agencies and departments to be able to do that kind of contract management is unrealistic. Many states have figured that out and have centralized IT.

Why don't we take the results of this successful experiment in "the laboratories" that are the state governments and try it out at the federal level? Today, there are scores of independent federal departments and agencies, each with the authority to decide whether they are going to run their own IT network or let some other department do it. If they do run their own, and they almost all do, they must live up to security standards issued by the White House's Office of Management and Budget in association with Homeland Security. Most departments and agencies, however, get away with flouting the security standards.

You can't really blame a Cabinet secretary for wanting to spend money on, say, a shiny new embassy complex in London, rather than a state-of-the-art endpoint detection and response (EDR) software application. After all, you can cut a ribbon and throw a hell of a party at a big new embassy. Besides, what diplomat even knows what an EDR is anyway?

The Government Accountability Office (GAO) gives the federal departments and agencies grades, but there is no real cost to the people who run the departments if they get a bad grade. The Secretary of State, for example, is not held back and denied promotion to the next grade. So, of course, most of the departments and agencies do poorly in the cybersecurity grading and continue to underfund security. If there is no cost for poor performance in things that agency leaders do not want to do and do not really understand, then there will always be poor performance. Although usually there is no cost for failure or mediocrity in federal cybersecurity, there are exceptions.

The GAO doesn't usually give out F grades, but for all practical purposes, Katherine Archuleta got an F and flunked out. Yet in a way, it wasn't really her fault. Nonetheless, we are still kind of mad about the whole thing. Both of your authors held top-secret and "code-word" security clearances. Before the government deemed we were worthy, it spent hundreds of thousands of dollars vetting us. Security investigators went around the country talking to our high school teachers, college roommates, drinking buddies, coworkers, landlords, and cranky neighbors asking them to tell embarrassing stories and provide derogatory information about us. Somehow, nonetheless, we both got clearances.

All of those interviews, along with bank and tax records, medical files, college transcripts, credit scores, and other documents, went into the databases at the Office of Personnel Management (OPM). Then the Chinese People's Liberation Army downloaded it all and sent it to Beijing. Almost a year after the OPM figured that out (because somebody told them), they sent us notices telling us that they had a little problem. The OPM suggested we click on a link to get free credit-score monitoring. Neither one of us was terribly inclined to click on a link, especially one suggested by the OPM. Talk about a privacy breach. Do we still sound bitter?

Well, Katherine Archuleta was the head of the OPM at the time, and after a lot of other bitter people demanded it, she was forced to resign. It was a rare occurrence of executive accountability in government. From her perspective, though, was she really supposed to win a fight with the Chinese army? She was a teacher from Denver, who had become a school administrator and then a political activist. We are sure that when the Obama White House people offered her the OPM job, no one said there might be a cyber battle with a foreign army. She thought she was just going to run the federal government's highest-level human resources (HR) office. That would have been challenge enough for anyone.

In the great tradition of the government closing the barn door after the Chinese have run off with all the horses, when the smoke cleared, the job of handling all that sensitive security background investigation material was given to the Pentagon. It's a common punt in Washington to make the military do something hard. Of course, as we know and will discuss later, the military are not exactly stellar examples of secure network operators either.

What we think makes more sense than asking all the little agencies like the OPM to defend against the Chinese army is to create a federal IT Services Agency (sure, call it ITSA) to own and operate the computer networks of all civilian agencies. The DoD and the intelligence community could keep control of their networks, not because they are perfect at cybersecurity but because they would use all their influence to kill any proposal to take away part of their empires.

There could also be a few exceptions granted to some civilian agencies, of course, like the state police who have an exception in Virginia. Maybe there would be an exception for the Energy Department's programs for managing nuclear bombs, okay, but almost every other civilian agency ought to be using a series of federal networks and cloud services run by our proposed ITSA.

There have been baby steps in this direction. Departments and agencies can now ask some bigger department to run their network for them, but few do. Maybe it's a prestige thing for everyone to run their own network, similar to the status requirement that seems to force every Cabinet secretary to have their own security personnel and black Chevy Suburban with blinking blue lights. (Are there really that many people who want to kill the head of the Environmental Protection Agency or the Department of Education? Probably not, but having that security detail cuts down on the commuting time in traffic and they also get you really good tables at D.C. restaurants and walk you around TSA lines.)

The Obama administration did create new titles for people in the White House, such as chief information officer and chief technology officer. After seven years, President Obama even got around to appointing a federal chief information security officer when there were less than four months left in his presidential term. What we have in mind is something more ambitious.

Civilian federal departments and agencies would specify their IT needs and then buy them from a federal IT Services Agency. That agency would only deliver the services with high levels of security designed and built in by the CyberCorps experts over in DHS's new CISA. As the state governments do now, the IT agency could contract out to private IT services companies to provide support, but the IT agency and CISA would specify the requirements and the standards and then ensure they are met.

By forcing most civilian federal agencies and departments to buy IT as a service from one federal agency, there could be cost efficiencies, higher standards, better management, and continuous modernization. Some may object that security is better achieved by diversity. Actually, that is not true when the diversity results in a lot of nonsecure networks. Moreover, an IT services agency could design in diversity, redundancy, and a heterogeneous system that would increase the complexity for an attacker and make recovery easier.

How would we pay for ITSA? It would not need to cost more than we now spend. In fact, it would undoubtedly cost less by achieving economies of scale and other efficiencies. Each department and agency would pay for IT as a service from their existing budgets. ITSA would be phased in over several years, but eventually it would own all the hardware, software, clouds, networks, and security systems used by civilian federal agencies. We would be more secure.

Continue the Bipartisanship: Two Simple Suggestions

Building on the creation of CISA in 2018, we would be delighted if Congress would in 2019 or 2020 go on to make all of the cybersecurity staff in the civilian federal agencies and departments members of a new, expanded Cyber-Corps, and thus employees of CISA. CyberCorps would be led by the top federal CISO, who would also be the head of CISA. It would be a professional cadre, with ranks, cross-departmental assignments, continuing education, and testing. The top-level members of the Corps would constitute a Senior Cyber Service.

ITSA would provide software and networks as a service to federal agencies, and CISA, through its new version of CyberCorps, would make the security decisions and run the cybersecurity operations for the civilian federal agencies. Not everybody can manage IT or achieve adequate cybersecurity. We should stop pretending that every federal agency can.

:::::::::::::: **PART IV** ::::::::::::::

WARRIORS, DIPLOMATS, AND CANDIDATES

Chapter 12

THE MILITARY, DOMAINS,
AND DOMINANCE

After land, sea, air and space, warfare has entered the fifth domain: cyberspace.

—MATT MURPHY, *THE ECONOMIST*, JULY 1, 2010

Patrick Shanahan is the man who manages the giant corporation that
is the Pentagon. In that building and in U.S. military units around
the world, the former Boeing executive, known in the airplane company as "Mr. Fix-it," was in 2018 known as DEPSECDEF, the Deputy Secretary of Defense, until he became Acting Secretary late in 2018. In May
2018, he announced the Trump administration's intentions toward the fifth
domain: "The Department of Defense will ensure our military is ready to
fight and win against any adversary, dominating the cyber domain."

Dominate the domain, that is how the Pentagon thinks about cyberspace. Four months after Shanahan offered that simple guidance, the Defense
Department elaborated in the 2018 DoD Cyber Strategy:

The Department must take action in cyberspace during day-to-day
competition to preserve U.S. military advantages and to defend U.S.

interests. Our focus will be on the States that can pose strategic threats to U.S. prosperity and security, particularly China and Russia. . . . We will defend forward to disrupt or halt malicious cyber activity at its source, including activity that falls below the level of armed conflict.

That statement followed the release a few days earlier of the White House's National Cyber Strategy (the first since that rather good one issued in 2003), and National Security Presidential Memorandum (NSPM) 13, a classified directive that devolved decision making on cyber operations to the Pentagon. (President Obama had reined in cyber operations in the wake of Stuxnet by issuing PPD 20, which reportedly required the President to approve significant cyber-offensive actions.)

Critics of the new Pentagon plan to dominate the domain predicted that it made conflict in cyberspace more likely by suggesting that the U.S. military would be taking action on a daily basis to disrupt cyber activity without an armed conflict serving as justification for doing so. Pentagon officials countered that the strategy simply recognized the reality that there is already a daily competition in cyberspace with Russia, China, and others, even in the absence of a declared war. By engaging more vigorously against Russian and Chinese cyber units, the Pentagon believes it can eventually create stability in cyberspace.

Defense or Domination?

Can an organization designed for war contribute to the lowering of tensions and a reduction in the likelihood of conflict? That is the question this chapter addresses. More specifically, we ask: How can the U.S. military contribute to limiting or preventing cyber war? How can the military reduce the possibility of crisis instability and rapid escalation of fighting? Some of what it needs to do may seem counterintuitive. It needs to get better at cyber war, both defensive and offensive.

The nuclear forces of the United States and the Soviet Union (later Russia) helped to prevent those two countries from engaging in direct military conflict for more than seven decades. The mere existence of those nuclear weapons did not prevent the third world war. It was the way in which those weapons were combined with diplomacy, strategy, and arms control.

Despite leaders calling for the elimination of nuclear weapons for decades, the arms continue to exist in the thousands. So too, however, does a form of global peace. It is a peace filled with tensions, competitions, and low-level conflict that may not seem like a desirable condition. Yet compared to the world wars of the twentieth century, the way in which arms control, strategy, and diplomacy were combined to prevent global conflict was a success. Now that long absence of global war among superpowers is threatened by the emergence of a new kind of weapon in a new domain, cyberspace.

Mishandled, cyber weapons could trigger a larger conflict of the kind we have successfully struggled to avoid. Indeed, the current level of U.S. cyber-defensive and cyber-offensive capabilities combined with those of potential opponents is creating a situation of high risk, of instability. America's weak cyber defenses may invite a potential adversary to engage in cyber-attacks, and America's response to that may spin tensions out of control into a wider war.

Thus far, military strategists and diplomats have failed to develop the combination of weapons, policies, and arms-control measures to deal with the threat to global stability created by cyber weapons. In this and the next chapter, we suggest the ways they might do so. This chapter addresses what the military should do to contribute to cyber stability, or cyber peace.

Pentagon officials had traditionally talked in terms of four domains, or spheres of potential combat: ground, sea, air, and outer space. Over a decade ago, with the advent of U.S. Cyber Command, defense officials added a fifth domain of potential combat to their list: cyberspace. U.S. Cyber Command is a joint organization, meaning it is composed of Army, Navy, Air Force, and Marine components. Their mission, in the language of the Pentagon, is to achieve dominance in that domain.

Dominance in cyberspace is not, according to the Pentagon, something that occurs only in a war. If U.S. cyber capabilities, both offensive and defensive, are obviously adequate and, indeed, superior to any threat, dominance can occur in peacetime. That, at least, is the theory and the goal the U.S. military has set out for itself. So far, the U.S. has not achieved dominance in the fifth domain. Indeed, it is far from it, and that, arguably, increases instability. Instability can lead to war.

How, specifically, can the U.S. military lower tensions, avoid crisis instability, and deter or prevent a major cyber war? In the most basic terms, we think the U.S. military should be capable of defending itself so well in cyberspace that it could perform its conventional (or, in the extreme case, nuclear) military operations without significant degradation from cyberattacks, and thereby deter enemy activity. It should combine that defensive cyber capability with the ability to achieve rapid dominance over an enemy, in part by using cyber weapons in the early stages of conflict to limit and bring a quick end to fighting.

The Pentagon's To-Do List

While that all sounds good as a goal, it has proven difficult to achieve. The Pentagon's 2018 strategy has five stated objectives (see endnote on page 325). We would slightly reformulate them into five distinct missions: 1) defending the military's own networks; 2) protecting the corporations that make our weapons and that form the defense industrial base (DIB); 3) ensuring the integrity of U.S. weapons once they are deployed; 4) guarding the private-sector infrastructure that the military needs to do its job; and 5) being ready to go on the offensive to degrade potential enemies' militaries in part through cyber operations.

How is the U.S. military doing at those five missions today? We have found in our teaching and in our consulting that often the best way to drive home a message is to have people envision and "live" a near-future situation that tests them and their systems. This technique is similar to a new boss asking his organization, "How well would we really do today if this happened?" The "this" for our purposes is a political-military crisis leading to a regional war. The best way to think about how the DoD and Cyber Command are doing at cybersecurity is to ask how they would do if excrement hit that ceiling fan right now.

Borrowing a phrase from the military, we call these imagined scenario developments tabletop exercises (TTXs). We have run these learning simulations for graduate students, corporate CEOs, and for U.S. national security Cabinet members. Let's answer the question about how well the U.S. military is doing on its five primary cyber missions by envisioning a near-term political-military crisis.

Envision the Near Future

Perhaps the most likely international crisis that might erupt this year or next is a conflict between Iran and Israel. What follows is a scenario of how such a crisis could evolve and our assessment of how the U.S. military's current cyber capabilities might perform.

TEL AVIV, 10 NOVEMBER 2019

The air-raid sirens sounded at 0200. Israelis awoke and ran to bomb shelters throughout the country. The hundreds of rockets and missiles that hit the country were launched from hidden sites in both Lebanon and Syria. The strikes hit air bases, Ben Gurion Airport, the Defense Ministry complex in Tel Aviv, electric power stations, and the ports of Haifa and Ashdod. Although Israel's antimissile defenses intercepted scores of incoming warheads, because of the high number of simultaneous attacks, many rockets and missiles got through to their targets. The damage was significant.

The attack launched by Iran and its allied militias in Lebanon and Syria were themselves retaliation for a large-scale Israeli airstrike on pro-Iranian forces in Syria three days earlier. A second wave of rockets and missiles hit Israel at 0400. The Israeli Air Force reported to the Defense Minister that it was having difficulty launching fighters to hunt down the mobile missile launchers. Damage levels at some air bases were critical, with squadrons of F-16s incapacitated. Drones launched from Lebanon and Syria had dived into Israeli missile defense radars, blinding some of the Arrow, Iron Dome, and Patriot antimissile batteries.

As dawn rose over Jerusalem, the Israeli Prime Minister called the U.S. President. Reluctantly, he asked for immediate U.S. assistance. Specifically, he asked for an airlift of critical weapons and key components to replace some of the inventory that had been destroyed. He also requested that U.S. Navy antimissile destroyers be deployed off Israel's coast to augment the nation's overwhelmed defenses, and U.S. F-35 fighter-bombers be deployed for joint strikes on the mobile rocket and missile launchers. The President agreed immediately and directed the Pentagon to assist. He also ordered a cyberattack on the missile launchers and their command-and-control system, including mobile missile launchers in Iran that had not yet been used to attack Israel.

Within an hour of the Prime Minister's call, two U.S. Navy Aegis destroyers near Spain swung about and moved at flank speed east through the Mediterranean. At Defense Logistics Agency (DLA) supply depots throughout the eastern seaboard of the United States, train cars were filled with pallets and prepared to move cargo to U.S. air bases. C-17 aircraft were being readied for a massive airlift reminiscent of the U.S. operation to support Israel in the 1973 Arab-Israeli War. The long protective arm of the United States was once again getting ready to reach out to shield a beleaguered Israel that had surprisingly found itself overwhelmed.

WASHINGTON, 12 NOVEMBER 2019

The President was furious. His wrath was like an energy wave flowing down the video-conference line from the White House Situation Room to the Pentagon's National Military Command Center. Rockets and missiles continued to pound Israel. The Chairman of the Joint Chiefs of Staff had just told the President over the video link that the two Aegis destroyers were still disabled, their propulsion systems off-line and damaged. Tugs were en route to tow them to port in Italy. Norfolk Southern Railroad derailments in Virginia and South Carolina were still preventing trains with critical cargoes from reaching air bases. Power blackouts in the mid-Atlantic states had plunged McGuire Air Force Base in New Jersey and Dover Air Force Base in Delaware into darkness.

Back-up generators at the bases did not work. The DLA reported that its attempts at mounting backup databases had failed, following the wiper attack on its inventory supply system.

A few U.S. Air Force F-35s had landed in Israel, but on their first combat sorties from Ramat David Air Force Base, all four U.S. aircraft had sustained radar system failures and returned to base, landing amid a hail of incoming missiles. In Huntsville, Alabama, the Raytheon Corporation was assessing the damage from an explosion and fire that had engulfed its Patriot missile production line. It was unable to ship spare parts. On the offensive side, U.S. Cyber Command reported that it believed it could penetrate and disrupt the missile force in Iran in a week to ten days. It had never studied how to penetrate the Iranian-controlled launchers in Syria and Lebanon. That would take longer.

It had been fifty-five critical hours since the President had ordered the Pentagon to help Israel and almost no assistance had arrived. Turning red in the face and sputtering at the large flat-screen showing the Pentagon leadership, the President demanded to know why.

From another screen on the wall of the Situation Room teleconference facility, the Director of National Intelligence spoke up, filling the silence coming from the Defense Department. "Sir, we assess that Iran has launched cyberattacks to degrade our operations in support of Israel." Sitting next to the President in the Situation Room, the National Security Adviser mumbled, "No shit, Sherlock."

"Well," the President said, turning on his adviser, "what do you suggest we do now?"

"It's very clear, Mr. President. Iran has stymied our assistance to Israel with cyberattacks. We must now escalate. Commence conventional attacks on Iran. B-2 bombers and the aircraft carriers must strike them tonight."

Without a moment's thought, the President turned to the Secretary of Defense. "Do it. Begin bombing Iran."

Incredible fiction? We think not. We believe that were there a "kinetic," or conventional, war today in which U.S. forces were opposed by Iran, Russia, China, or even to some extent North Korea, the Defense Department would be hampered in the execution of its operations and largely unable to conduct significant offensive cyber operations against enemy military targets.

In this scenario, the United States faced off against Iran and lost, at least in the first round. In the real world, Iran does have significant offensive cyber capabilities. The barrier to entry to having a meaningful cyber-war offensive force is low. Countries that could never defeat the United States in a purely conventional military battle can pose significant asymmetric risks to us in cyberspace. To see why we make that claim, let's look at each of the five cyber missions we think the Pentagon should undertake and see what a mid-tier power like Iran could do to us.

In our scenario, the DoD failed in its first cyber mission, to protect its own network. Hackers penetrated the Defense Logistics Agency's unclassified network and erased all software, including the contents of a backup file, using a wiper hack that turns computers into useless pieces of metal by eliminating all of the data on them. In the real world, Iran did penetrate the U.S. Navy's unclassified computer network in 2013 and was able to remain there for years even after its presence was discovered, despite intense efforts to eject the Iranian presence. Iran has also successfully used wiper hacks, including an attack against the world's largest oil company, Saudi Aramco.

Cybersecurity experts have been warning companies that hackers are placing ransomware in database backups, so that when network operators attempt to activate their business continuity systems, they will find that the backup is inoperable too. Those same techniques could be used for a wiper program, which would activate on the backup database once that system was used, destroying all files, operating systems, and applications on a network.

It is not just the DoD's unclassified networks that are at risk. Russia was able in 2008 to gain access to the Pentagon's secret-level SIPRNet system. North Korea succeeded in 2016 in stealing from a classified network the U.S.–South Korean combined operations plan to attack the North and kill its leadership.

American military officials operate today on the assumption that their unclassified and secret-level systems have been compromised and may not be available to them or be reliable in a crisis. They hope that the top-secret-level Joint Worldwide Intelligence Communications System (JWICS) network is secure, but know that it is a high-priority target of many nations' hackers.

As we noted in chapter 2, even the National Security Agency, which is part of the Defense Department, has been unable to protect its own network. Its top-secret files have been stolen by and from employees of NSA contractors such as Booz Allen Hamilton. If the NSA, the home of U.S. government cybersecurity expertise, has its information systems compromised, it is highly likely that the same or worse is happening elsewhere in the DoD.

In our scenario, the DoD was also unable to perform its cyber mission of protecting its own weapons systems. The engines of the two disabled U.S. Navy antimissile destroyers became casualties as a result of a cyberattack on the ships' propulsion system controls.

The reality may actually be worse than our scenario. In October 2018, the Government Accountability Office issued a scathing report on the cybersecurity of U.S. weapons systems, claiming that an enemy could easily hack into and disable (or take control of) many of the country's newest weapons. Although a distinguished Defense Science Board review panel had sounded a loud alarm about this precise problem in 2013, five years later the GAO concluded that the "DoD is in the early stage of trying to understand how to apply cyber-security to weapon systems." Note that the conclusion was not that the DoD was in the early stage of fixing the problem, but in the early stage of "trying to understand how to . . ."

In the scenario, U.S. Navy ships were hacked. In the real world, too, U.S. Navy ships are completely networked. The General Electric gas turbine systems on Aegis destroyers are well known and similar to engines used in civilian systems. Could a nation-state get into a ship's system and give disabling orders to a key system? The Navy thinks so. It reported that its new USS *Freedom*-class combatants are vulnerable to hacking.

In 2018, classified data about highly sensitive Navy programs was stolen from a contractor who worked for the Naval Undersea Warfare Center in Rhode Island. Separately, a Navy technician was discovered to be a criminal hacker. There is widespread belief in the Pentagon that the repeated collisions of U.S. Navy destroyers in the Pacific in 2017 were a result of cyberattacks, although the DoD officially denies it. The Navy still uses the outdated and insecure Windows XP operating system throughout the force.

In our scenario, protection of the DIB was also a problem. A key corporate facility, a Raytheon plant that makes parts for antimissile systems, caught fire and blew up, preventing shipment of components to Israel. We have no reason to believe that this specific facility or company is any less secure, or any more secure, than other parts of the DIB, but we do know that defense contractors have regularly been hacked by foreign adversaries.

Among the weapons systems compromised are the Extended Area Protection and Survivability System (EAPS), a system designed to counter rocket, artillery, and mortar fire in flight, and the Patriot, THAAD, and Aegis antimissile systems. Also hacked were databases containing data on the F-35 fighter-bomber. And these are just the systems listed in one report by the Defense Science Board, a group of outside advisers to the Pentagon.

When foreign adversaries are able to hack into computer networks at private-sector corporations making things for the Defense Department, the risk is threefold. They can steal the weapon designs, potentially allowing them to reproduce similar weapons. That is what most of the hacking of the DIB companies has been used for to date. They could, however, once inside a corporate network, covertly place code in the operating systems of the weapons, allowing them to take control of the weapons if and when they encounter them in combat. Finally, hackers could do things to the controls of a factory, product line, or support systems to sabotage facility operations.

The fourth cyber mission some people think the DoD ought to be doing is to protect other corporations, not those making weapons, but those supplying the DoD itself with essential services such as electricity or rail transportation. We said "some people" in the last sentence because the exact role the Pentagon should have in defending critical infrastructure companies is a bit controversial. In our scenario, there were electric power blackouts in New Jersey and Delaware, forcing the key airlift bases at Dover and Mc-Guire onto frequently unreliable backup generators. Trains in our fictional scenario bringing spare parts and weapons to air bases and maritime ports were derailed, preventing much of the needed resupply to Israel.

In the real world today, the DoD would fail to protect those power grids and rail-control systems because it has no legal authority to do so and, thus, no program at work to secure the off-base civilian systems on which the bases depend. The responsibility to assist corporations providing "critical infrastructure" such as electric power and rail is that of DHS. While DHS does share information with some critical infrastructure companies, it does not act to monitor or to defend their information networks. Russia, meanwhile, has reportedly been able to penetrate U.S. power grid control systems, as we discussed in chapter 10.

Iran, the potential enemy in our scenario, has already successfully attacked the U.S. financial sector infrastructure in 2011 and 2012, using a simple but powerful DDoS attack, a type of flood technique, to overwhelm the publicly facing networks of the largest U.S. banks.

The division of labor between the DoD and DHS frustrates some in the Defense Department who believe that DHS and the corporations involved will never be able to do enough to secure the critical infrastructure upon which the Pentagon, and the country as a whole, depend. One of the many problems with making the DoD responsible for defending critical infrastructure, however, is deciding where to draw the line. DHS defines seventeen industries as part of "critical infrastructure," including even the retail sector (e.g., Walmart, Costco, Home Depot).

Not only does the DoD not have the authority to defend such networks, it is not entirely clear that many of the corporations involved want the military poking around their networks. One of the critical infrastructure corporations most often targeted is the megabank JPMorgan Chase. When some of its cybersecurity personnel began discussing the possibility of a pilot program involving the DoD protecting its network, our sources informed us that CEO Jamie Dimon and other top bank officials quickly shut down the idea.

Finally, we posited that the fifth mission of the U.S. military in cyberspace should be to have the ability to attack enemy military systems using cyber techniques. Most observers take for granted that Cyber Command can at least do that well. The truth has been otherwise. Bureaucratic and legal impediments have prevented America's cyber warriors from being a real offensive threat for almost all of Cyber Command's first decade of existence.

In our scenario, the President, upon request of the Israeli Prime Minister, ordered cyberattacks on the command-and-control systems supporting the Iranian missile launchers, the similar systems of the Iranian-backed Hezbollah militia, and on the missiles themselves. Cyber Command responded that it might be able to have some initial capability to do that in two weeks' time. Of course, by then Iran and its militia allies could have emptied their missile inventories onto Israel. Were we unfair to Cyber Command's offensive capabilities in this simulation? We think not.

Surprise: Cyber Comm Wasn't Offensive Enough

Ten years ago, we argued in the book *Cyber War* that the U.S. military seemed to be too fixated on developing offensive cyber capabilities and insufficiently focused on defense. As is often the case in Washington, the pendulum then swung to the opposite extreme. For most of the second decade of the century, Cyber Command did what we had advised (no doubt it was coincidence and not because they were actually aware of and agreed with what we had written). They focused on defense, but they did so to an excessive degree, forgoing much of what was needed to be in a position to launch a major offensive operation if called upon to do so by the President. Although U.S. intelligence agencies were conducting covert operations in cyberspace, the U.S. military was, to our admitted surprise, insufficiently offensive in its cyber war preparations. Although preparations can themselves be destabilizing, it is also true that if a potential enemy knows that you have little offensive capability, then deterrence is diminished.

Getting inside a potential adversary's military command-and-control systems, or its weapons systems, is not something that can be achieved within days of a President ordering it to happen. It can take months or even years to mount covert programs to penetrate such systems. Once access has been achieved, it is then a difficult operation to maintain an undetected presence capable of being activated remotely upon command. Even an adversary's simple software update can completely destroy a backdoor that took years to develop.

Despite the fact that the terrorist group ISIS was the major adversary with which the U.S. military was engaged in combat in the Obama administration, few if any cyberattacks had been mounted against them. Toward the end of the administration, Secretary of Defense Ash Carter directed Cyber Command to mount Operation Glowing Symphony to "drop virtual bombs" on ISIS. Later, Secretary Carter testified to Congress that he was "largely disappointed" in that operation's ability to degrade the terrorist group.

Secretary Carter was not the only one in the Obama administration to have been disappointed by cyberattacks. Obama himself was, as were many of his top advisers. They were disappointed with the first major U.S. cyberwar attack, the now infamous Stuxnet program. Officially known as Operation Olympic Games in the intelligence community, the operation seemed at first to have been a marvel of both covert action and cyber intrusion. (The attack is now the subject of many books and even a movie, *Zero Days*, directed by Alex Gibney.) Upon further examination, however, it had failed on several important criteria.

The attack was supposed to remain covert. The Stuxnet attack software was discovered by the Iranians. How it worked was supposed to remain secret. European and American cyber experts decompiled it and publicly discussed its design. The attack was supposed to be limited to the plant. The attack software got out of Natanz and took on a life of its own, exploring the world, and was captured and copied by cyber criminals and other nation-states throughout its journey. The covert cyber assault was supposed to do significant damage to the enrichment program. Although it did cause eight hundred centrifuges to be repaired or replaced, Iran then built twenty thousand centrifuges. Finally, the fact that the United States was the first (or among the first) nation to destroy infrastructure with a cyberattack was never supposed to be known.

As we've seen, after the Stuxnet experience, some would say "fiasco," Obama issued orders that prevented any further major covert operations without his personal approval. It had a somewhat chilling effect. In a White

House dominated by lawyers, an interagency debate arose about which U.S. government agencies could do what in the realm of offensive cyberattacks. Pentagon, CIA, and Justice Department lawyers engaged in what some policy makers saw as Talmudic sophistry. Stripping away the mystery and jargon, let's try to understand the debate.

The military's Cyber Command had not done the Stuxnet attack. The CIA and the NSA did. They did so under the authority of Title 50 of the U.S. Code, the set of laws that govern the U.S. intelligence community. Under those laws, U.S. intelligence agencies can covertly collect information abroad. They can also take actions to damage or destroy things abroad, even in peacetime, when the President issues a specific "finding" that it is in the national security interest of the United States to do so. The issuance of a finding is a highly secret, ritualistic, arcane, and usually time-consuming process involving thousands of hours of government lawyers' time, including time spent in consultation with a select bipartisan group of Members of Congress. Even once a finding is issued, every time a significant action is about to be undertaken pursuant to the authorization, the process is repeated to issue a Memorandum of Notification (MoN) about that new action.

Despite their off-putting experience with the outcome of Stuxnet, the Obama administration apparently did not give up on the idea of using cyber weapons against Iran. As the so-called P5+1 talks with Iran about nuclear weapons dragged on, the Obama administration reportedly authorized a contingency plan, code-named Nitro Zeus, to destroy or damage key parts of Iran's infrastructure if the talks failed. That cyberattack allegedly would have been an accompaniment to a conventional attack and would have been, at least in part, implemented under military authority. In general, however, Cyber Command was not authorized to go after enemy weapons systems.

Cyber Command and the military in general are covered by a different section of law than that which was used to authorize Stuxnet. The military is authorized by Title 10 of the U.S. Code. Lawyers in the Obama administration argued that the military could not violate international boundaries by penetrating other nations' computer networks in peacetime for the purpose of causing damage or destruction without a specific order from the President (or the Secretary of Defense). Military intelligence units could collect information about other nations' systems, but that would be under the intelligence authorities, and could not be conducted with the intent to destroy things. Some in the military wanted to "prepare the battlefield" by lacing the weapons systems of possible future enemies with "logic bombs" that could be triggered to destroy the enemy network or weapon in a conflict. They were not given that authority until 2018.

Thus, Cyber Command and its component military units spent almost all of its time since its inception trying to fend off other nations that were trying to infiltrate our military networks and weapons. Given how many such attacks were going on and how successful they were, spending most of the time on defense was likely the right thing to do, but having little or no offensive cyber capability against enemy militaries created a weakness.

In the 2018 Department of Defense Cyber Strategy, Secretary of Defense James Mattis had ordered Cyber Command to "defend forward" by joining with the intelligence community in attempting to identify potential enemy cyber systems, penetrate them, and in some cases, stop incoming attacks. What some U.S. war-fighters wanted, however, was more. If they were ever ordered to bomb Russia or China, for example, they wanted to be able to make the "enemy" air defense radars show no incoming U.S. attack. They wanted the opponents' air defense missiles to blow up on the launchpad when they were fired against U.S. aircraft. (Media reporting suggests that U.S. intelligence may have penetrated both Iranian and North Korean ballistic missile tests and caused several of them to blow up on the launchpad. Apparently, however, the North Koreans later developed missiles that did not include that particular feature.) The U.S. war-fighters wanted to send erroneous commands on the other nations' military communication systems. After all, they argued, that was what Russia and China were apparently trying to do to us and, for all we know, they may be in position to do that right now. We were not, at least not as much as most observers assumed, and it was in part because of the arcane legal battles.

The fiscal year 2019 National Defense Authorization Act (NDAA), known as the John McCain Act, added language to make clear that the military, specifically Cyber Command and its regional and service components (such as Army Cyber Command), may take measures in peacetime against potential adversaries' systems, so that they will be able to degrade their military operations quickly in the event of combat, defining such actions as "traditional military activity."

Despite the controversy about the open-ended law that Congress passed after 9/11, the Authorization for Use of Military Force (AUMF), the McCain Act also preauthorizes the use of military force. Although little noticed publicly, the law gave the Secretary of Defense and Cyber Command specific authority to engage in cyberattacks against four nations (Russia, China, Iran, and North Korea) if any of those countries are found to be "conducting an active, systematic, and ongoing campaign of attacks against the Government or people of the United States in cyberspace, including attempting to influence American elections and democratic political processes." Cyber Command is also specifically authorized to share information with private-sector companies, including those in social media.

Trump then signed National Security Presidential Memorandum 13, a directive seen by many as taking off the leash that has held back the U.S. military from "preparation of the battlefield." That authority was described in the NDAA as falling within the ambit of "traditional military activities," but what it authorizes is anything but traditional. Following the Congressional action, the White House delegated day-to-day cyberattack decision-making authority to the Department of Defense.

Having U.S. military units penetrating potential enemy weapons in peacetime is seen by some observers as destabilizing. The argument is that such U.S. action might lead to peacetime "attacks" by both sides, or all sides, that could accidentally cause a highly destructive incident and lead to an escalatory process and open combat among the world's great militaries. That concern has merit, and even if the White House has devolved authority to the Pentagon, there is a real need for interagency review (including White House staff) of planned DoD cyber operations to prevent miscalculation. One way of reducing the likelihood of general war may be to enhance uncertainty.

Traditionally, military strategists argue for greater certainty in political-military affairs. Certainty equals stability, they contend. That was, and is, the case with the prospect of major nuclear war. The certainty of mutual destruction creates deterrence. We have been taught that for the last fifty years. With cyber war, however, uncertainty may deter significant military action.

For uncertainty to promote deterrence in the context of cyber war, a potential enemy needs to be uncertain of two things. First, the potential enemy must be uncertain about how well its own conventional weapons will work. Second, the potential enemy must be uncertain about how well our cyber defenses will work. Creating those two kinds of uncertainty will increase U.S. security and deterrence.

If potential enemy leaders think there is a real possibility that their conventional weapons will malfunction because we have hacked them and that the U.S. military would quickly overwhelm them, they may be deterred from initiating hostilities. Similarly, potential enemy leaders must be made to disbelieve their own military and intelligence commanders' claims that they can defeat the U.S. military and badly damage U.S. infrastructure through cyberattacks. Cyber Command could contribute greatly to creating those two kinds of uncertainty. It has not.

The blame does not belong on Cyber Command. The U.S. government as a whole has lacked a clear strategy, adequate funding, the needed laws and regulations, and, most important, the organizational structure and leadership to create the combination of defensive and offensive capabilities required to increase cyber stability and to deter cyber war.

As we discussed earlier in this chapter, key U.S. government networks have already been penetrated. The networks of companies making U.S. weapons have been compromised. Some U.S. weapons may have "kill switches" or backdoors inserted by potential enemies. The civilian infrastructure the U.S. military needs to go to war can be successfully attacked by cyber weapons right now. The U.S. military lacks the ability to degrade significantly the military operations of potential enemies.

If the U.S. military cannot degrade an enemy using cyber weapons during a growing crisis that has already seen limited combat, if it cannot defend itself or our allies from disabling cyberattacks, then it will quickly escalate to a larger conventional war. We just saw that happen in our fictional scenario. That is crisis instability, the inability to control escalation. That is likely where we would be today were a crisis to occur with Russia, China, Iran, or even North Korea.

Seven Steps for Stability

How do we fix that sad and unstable state of affairs? We suggest these seven measures:

Unity of Command

It is a major tenet of military operations that there needs to be a single, clearly defined commander for a military operation. Everyone necessary for the success of the battle must be under the control of that one commander. For Alexander the Great, that meant both the hoplite infantry and the cavalry did what he told them in battle. For Dick's late friend General Norm Schwarzkopf, it meant in the First Gulf War that Norm controlled the air strikes, the armor units, and the aircraft carriers. In the creation of the U.S. nuclear Navy, it meant that the design, build, and operation of the reactor-powered ships were all subject to Admiral Hyman Rickover's direction, for decades.

Today in the Pentagon, policy, direction, and oversight on some things cyber resides in a Deputy Assistant Secretary of Defense (DASD) in the policy chain, with little or no responsibility for research, development, or procurement. As our friend Eric Rosenbach, who once had that DASD job, told us, "It's not always obvious to a four-star general, like one running Cyber Command, that they take direction from a DASD."

There needs to be one very senior civilian in the DoD whose only job is to have clear policy and operations authority over not only U.S. Cyber Command, but also both the Pentagon's intranet run by the Defense Information Systems Agency (DISA) and its own internal counterintelligence force for cyberattacks, the Defense Cyber Crime Center (DC3). Such an official must have authority and cyber responsibility over existing U.S. weapon and support systems, procurement of new systems from defense industrial companies, and the contracting for critical infrastructure support from civilian providers.

Clarity of Mission

The 2018 DoD strategy envisions some Pentagon role in defending the power grid and other critical infrastructure essential for DoD Mission Support. Many of the owners and operators of such networks are not pleased at the prospect of the military tramping around in their systems. Moreover, it is not clear that the Pentagon has either a plan or the legal authority to do so. Because of the interconnected nature of the power grid, gas pipelines, and telephony networks, it is hard to define or defend the parts that just support the DoD. Moreover, prior laws and executive orders have given the Department of Homeland Security the role to defend critical infrastructure.

We think that it is urgent that the debate about the DoD's cyber role must end soon with a new law. The DoD, working with Homeland, must be able to demand and enforce high standards on its vendor supply chain, including the specific power and transportation systems it relies upon. They can do that through a combination of regulatory power and contractual language. Such authority should supersede any other federal or state regulation, and it should permit the DoD to continuously monitor the state of cybersecurity of the corporations involved.

The DoD and the intelligence community should look for incoming attacks on the power grid, and a handful of other critical infrastructure sectors. They should have procedures and authorities to block such attacks working with infrastructure companies. The concerned industries, working with Homeland and the DoD, should develop and operate continuous monitoring systems to find vulnerabilities and malicious actors within the infrastructure control planes and supply chain. Finally, industry, state-level emergency management agencies and the National Guard, DHS, and DoD should have detailed plans and capabilities to restore operations quickly in the event of a successful cyberattack on key infrastructure.

Clarity of mission also requires that the Pentagon and the intelligence community effectively deconflict their operations. They should not both be trying to infiltrate the controls of Moscow's power grid, but, until we achieve a diplomatic understanding with Russia and others about the laws of cyber war, one of them should definitely be doing it. Someone needs to ensure that missions like that do not fall between the cracks.

Crash Program to Secure U.S. Arsenal

We cannot wait for a real shooting war to discover that a weapon will not work because a potential adversary has been able to take control of our navigation, communications, guidance, or other systems.

In *Cyber War*, we painted a picture of the U.S. trotting out its expensive new weapons to go to war in the near future with some near-peer nation-state enemy only to have the enemy figuratively flip a switch to shut off the U.S. weapons and then attack the American "sitting ducks." Five years after we painted that scary scene, the Pentagon's Defense Science Board wrote an alarming report with the same conclusion. In 2018, the GAO concluded that little had been done to secure U.S. weapons from enemy hacking. If true, this is a crisis of extraordinary proportions, for it would mean that after spending trillions of dollars on defense, we may be defenseless.

The Secretary of Defense should have no higher priority than determining the extent of the cyber vulnerabilities of U.S. weapons systems, and fixing them and the supporting infrastructure with the greatest possible speed. That may require, at the least, an unprecedented diversion of resources within the Pentagon's annual $700 billion budget to test for and remediate existing weapons.

After the initial review-and-repair project, the Pentagon must constantly engage in large-scale testing and continuous monitoring of networks and weapons for cyber vulnerabilities, on both DoD and contractor networks. When mistakes are discovered, DoD or corporate staff should be penalized and fines levied on the contractor. The commanders of the U.S. Navy Seventh Fleet warships that were involved in the suspicious collisions with civilian vessels were punished, as were their superiors. Yet when civilian contractors' employees compromise the NSA's most valuable secrets, the companies involved continue to receive valuable contracts and their leadership continues to take home enormous paychecks. As Admiral Rickover knew when it came to establishing a culture of safety for Navy nuclear reactor systems, there must be severe consequences for nonperformance. So, too, in cyberspace the culture of security can be created only by establishing a fault-intolerant system.

Resource Adequacy

The DoD budget is too big. It has risen consistently, even without taking into account the cost of the Long War operations against Iraq, the Taliban, al-Qaeda, and ISIS. Within the DoD budget, resources for cyber missions have grown disproportionately to other missions. Nonetheless, doing the kind of major security-assurance operation we believe is necessary on the DoD's own networks, corporate networks, and weapons systems will require greater efforts. That means more money.

In fiscal year 2019, the Defense Department will spend more than $700 billion. Of that immense amount of money, the DoD is programming slightly less than 1 percent for offensive and defensive cyber programs. We admit that how you define what is in that category is arbitrary, and some definitions would result in the percentage being higher, but however you define it, the funding is inadequate to replace current DoD systems with a highly defensible and resilient set of capabilities anytime soon.

Information systems technology does not always reduce the cost of doing business, as some people believed in the 1990s. IT system dependence and the need to secure those systems can actually increase the cost of the systems you buy, capital expenditure (CapEx), and the financial burden of running them, operating expenses (OpEx). Because the DoD, more than most large organizations in the world, is IT dependent, it needs to spend a huge percentage of its CapEx and OpEx on IT systems and their cybersecurity. Those resources can come from only one place: elsewhere in the DoD budget, even if that means reducing the size of the conventional force structure. It will do us no good, for example, to have ten aircraft carriers if none of them are combat effective due to cyber vulnerabilities. It would be better to have six that worked even under cyberattack.

System Failure Capabilities

Every corporation in America knows it needs to spend money on disaster recovery and business continuity. That's without there being an enemy nation-state actively attacking and sabotaging their systems (although for some companies that could be the problem someday). Even if the DoD leadership embraced everything we recommend in this chapter and embarked on an accelerated program to implement it, America's military would still have cyber-vulnerable weapons and support infrastructure for years to come.

Thus, part of the immediate task before the Pentagon is to develop and deploy the ability to fight in a degraded environment. Forces need to be able to communicate without the internet (or NIPRNet, SIPRNet, or JWICS), and need to be able to coordinate when frequencies are jammed by an enemy. Weapons must work even if the Global Positioning System does not. Senior U.S. military commanders know this, but that has not yet translated into a real ability to perform the DoD's missions in a world in which cyber-attacks have brought our forces back to a preinternet era. Getting there will, as mentioned in the point above, mean more money, not for shining new objects, but for boring old tech.

Escalation Dominance

One way to control when and how escalation occurs is to quickly jump a few rungs up the escalatory ladder and combine that demonstration of strength with both an offer to cease fire and a threat to do even more damage if that offer is ignored. To do that, the United States has to be able to execute devastating cyberattacks against both infrastructure and military targets, while being relatively impervious to attempts to do similar things to us. We are a very long way from having those capabilities today, but we can and should have a road map to achieve them.

Supporting Diplomatic Arrangements

One way to judge who the good military commanders are is by examining the importance they place on their "POLADs," the diplomats and civil service experts that the State Department provides to them. When fighting breaks out, the system has failed. Peace and stability are achieved and maintained by combining strong offensive and defensive military capabilities with smart and active diplomacy. Today there is no real ongoing diplomacy with regard to cyberspace and cyber war.

In the Obama administration, a high-level advisory group recommended to the President that cyber war diplomacy be elevated by creating an Assistant Secretary of State for Cyberspace. Similar global threats such as terrorism and illegal narcotics have had Assistant Secretary–led bureaus in State for years, to give focus and ensure the issues are placed on the department's list of top diplomatic initiatives. Obama rejected the recommendation for an Assistant Secretary for Cybersecurity Policy. Trump went one step further and eliminated the State Department office and senior adviser of cyberspace. The Trump administration then eliminated the position in the National Security Council staff that coordinated cyber-diplomatic efforts.

Reducing tensions in cyberspace, enhancing stability, and avoiding wars (accidental or intentional) requires combining strong military capabilities (offensive and defensive) with a diplomatic architecture. Diplomacy helps to define what acceptable and unacceptable activity is in peacetime, and in the event of conflict. A diplomatic architecture creates international systems for avoiding misunderstandings, dealing with misbehavior without combat, and designing stable systems and institutions. It is how to achieve that diplomatic system that we turn to in the next chapter.

Chapter 13

••••••••••••

A SCHENGEN ACCORD
FOR THE INTERNET

Cyberspace is not borderless; rather, everyone lives on the border.

—MICHAEL DANIEL, FORMER WHITE HOUSE
CYBERSECURITY COORDINATOR

Eric Schmidt thinks the internet will split in two. At a private dinner event in San Francisco in the fall of 2018, the chairman of Google and longtime tech luminary told the audience that in ten years there would be one internet dominated by the United States and its tech giants and one dominated by the Chinese and its tech giants. The rest of the world would need to pick sides. Not to be outdone in the gloom-and-doom prognostications, the *New York Times* editorial board then upped the ante, predicting that the internet would not be split in two but into three, adding in a future that included a separate European internet. These are but recent examples of a long-held concern in the cybersecurity community that the internet would "splinter" or "balkanize" into national internets, ending the vision of what the Obama administration described as an "open, interoperable, secure, and reliable" internet in its 2011 International Strategy for Cyberspace.

Rumors of the coming disintegration of the internet are likely exaggerated. While Russia announced plans to create an "independent internet" by August of 2018, as of the spring of 2019 it had yet to conduct a planned test of disconnecting its network. As the internet has evolved from its humble beginnings, it will continue to evolve and change in response to new technologies, new markets, and new government requirements. Ten years ago, the internet had barely begun to connect mobile devices. Cloud was viewed as an untrusted and unproven technology. Ten years from now, we are likely to see similar evolutionary changes. It's fair to predict that some of those changes will include the spread of the Chinese model of internet control and censorship to other countries. The fight for the future of the internet will likely take place in Africa, where China has invested heavily to shape the networks it is helping to build in its own image. Unfortunately, it seems likely that internet freedom will be degraded in much of the world. No matter what, we will still be plagued with many of the problems we face today on the international stage, like cyber-criminal safe havens, poor international cooperation on investigations, and unclear rules for cross-border cyber actions involving third-party states. Unless, of course, the United States and its like-minded allies manage to adopt a new approach to global cyber leadership.

Instead of waiting for the internet to disintegrate around us, an alternative strategy would be to exclude those nations that do not respect freedom of expression or privacy rights, that engage in disruptive activity, provide safe havens to criminals, and are not responsive to law-enforcement requests for assistance. In turn, those nations who buy into the vision of an open, interoperable, secure, and reliable internet would maintain and extend the benefits of being connected. What might that look like? A real-world corollary is the European Union's model of open borders within the Schengen zone.

The Schengen Accord created a bloc of countries within Europe where people and goods could travel freely without going through customs and immigration control. It's why you can drive through countries from Germany to Spain without getting your passport stamped along the way. Once you are in the Schengen Area through one country's border-security apparatus, you can freely access any other country. Negotiating the Schengen

Accord was a monumental undertaking, because control over borders has defined state sovereignty for the last three hundred years. A Schengen Accord for the internet would allow the free flow of data across borders, harmonizing national laws so that all data that can be legally accessed in one country can also be legally accessed in other member states. To allow for that to take place, stronger mechanisms for handling the bad that comes with the good of open borders in cyberspace must be built.

A few years back, such an idea would have been hard to implement. Today, as the European Union looks to be on the verge of getting smaller and U.S.–EU cooperation reaches a new low, it looks all but impossible. Yet the problems that it solves for both commerce and criminal response remain. The idea of a Schengen Accord for the internet might just be crazy enough to work.

Barlow Was Wrong

The internet is not what its founders thought they were building or what the early adopters of the technology envisioned. What began as a project to connect mainframes at research universities and morphed into the freewheeling global network of the 1990s is now being split up into smaller national and corporate networks. At the highest level, however, the internet operates much as it did thirty years ago and uses the same (somewhat archaic) protocols to do it. There is, at least for now, still a single global Domain Name System and data can still flow, if not entirely freely, from one country to another. As the internet has gone from being the place you go to visit bulletin boards on esoteric topics to undergirding all of modern existence, the early vision for cyberspace as a domain beyond the reach of the state now seems hopelessly naïve.

The internet pioneer John Perry Barlow is often held up as the embodiment of this "techno-utopian" vision for the internet. The founder of the Electronic Frontier Foundation (EFF), Barlow is a fascinating character. Steven Levy described him as a "cowboy, poet, romantic, family man, philosopher, and ultimately, the bard of the digital revolution." When he died in early 2018, *Rolling Stone* titled his obituary "John Perry Barlow, Grateful

Dead Lyricist, Dead at 70." Barlow wrote such classics as "Mexicali Blues" with band member Bob Weir. On his death, Weir said that Barlow would live on in the songs they wrote together. Barlow's work at EFF could have a longer-lasting legacy. EFF has probably done more than any other organization to help protect freedom of expression and the right to privacy online. It helped win court rulings that made intercepting electronic communications a violation of the Wiretap Act.

While William Gibson coined the word "cyberspace," it was Barlow who popularized its use to capture a realm separate and apart from the physical world, in which people could be freed from the limitations imposed on them by their bodies and the body politic in what he called "meatspace." There are not too many people in the world who have had both a backstage pass to every Dead concert and an open invitation to the World Economic Forum, but Barlow did, and in Davos in 1996 he tapped out his now famous "A Declaration of the Independence of Cyberspace." In it he exhorts governments to leave the denizens of cyberspace alone, declaring, "You have no sovereignty where we gather."

Of course, that wasn't true. As Tim Wu and Jack Goldsmith document in their excellent 2006 book *Who Controls the Internet?*, it didn't take long for governments to impose their sovereignty on the internet. Barlow declared, "Your legal concepts of property, expression, identity, movement, and context do not apply to us. They are all based on matter, and there is no matter here." The reality is that the 1s and 0s of computer code and the packets of internet traffic are all reliant on physical systems and are used by people in sovereign jurisdictions. That means that states could manipulate and control cyberspace the same way they can manipulate and control matter and matters in their physical domains.

The trend toward government control over the internet that Wu and Goldsmith examined over a decade ago has only accelerated in that time. China, Russia, Iran, Syria, Burma, and many other states have created national networks where communication within their countries stays within their countries and where there is at least the potential to inspect, filter out, or cut off communication with the outside world. Meanwhile, corporate players are busy dividing up the internet into commercial enclaves where users log in to a contained world that is curated for them, probably by Facebook or Google. Real names are increasingly mandatory. Even business communications, once the domain of email and its open standard, are moving into proprietary channels such as Slack and Skype.

For a brief period, the corporate world did battle with governments. The corporations lost. Early internet companies tried to convince bureaucrats that the internet was an open, flat network and was therefore a "take-it-or-leave-it" proposition. Countries such as France and Germany were told that they could either opt in to the global internet or opt out. What they could not do was try to change it. This ruse worked for a short while, but government bureaucrats are rarely as dumb as technologists assume they are. When Yahoo told France that it could not possibly filter out search results for copies of *Mein Kampf*, France told Yahoo that it would put its executives in jail the next time they landed at Charles de Gaulle. Very quickly, Yahoo and other companies learned how to do geolocation on their users and not serve up illegal content to those users in prohibited locations.

Like all border-control efforts, these early pushes to force content providers to abide by laws in different nations were only partially effective. The dedicated and technically savvy could easily circumvent these controls. Leave Germany through a virtual private network, get a U.S. IP address, and Google will serve up neo-Nazi websites to your heart's content. Silicon Valley quickly realized there was far more money to be made by adapting their vision to the wider world than trying to force the wider world to adopt the vision of an internet where free speech reigned supreme. Barlow's vision of cyberspace as a space unfettered by states has slowly been dying ever since.

Barlow Was Right

Barlow may have been naïve, but he was not hopelessly so. Rather, he was hopefully so. "A good way to invent the future is to predict it," said Barlow. "So I predicted Utopia, hoping to give Liberty a running start before the laws of Moore and Metcalfe delivered up what Ed Snowden now correctly calls 'turn-key totalitarianism.'"

What Barlow saw, and captured in his elegant turn of phrase, was that the growth of processing power (Moore's Law) together with the growth in value of a connected network (Metcalfe's Law) would inevitably mean that the internet would be used as a surveillance tool rather than as a space where people were, in fact, more free. Yet what Barlow recognized was what many in the military community have also recognized: cyberspace is the only changeable, man-made domain. While the laws of physics do apply in cyberspace, they are guideposts. As long as you stay within them, the domain can be altered, on the one hand, to create a surveillance state, or, on the other, to promote freedom of expression.

The Obama administration put no small amount of energy into the preservation and extension of the U.S. vision of a global open internet. David Edelman crafted the International Strategy for Cyberspace, enshrining that concept. Chris Painter at the State Department racked up a million frequent-flier miles promoting that vision around the globe. Michele Markoff, another State Department official, has spent the last decade trying to persuade the Russians and other counterparts in the UN's Group of Governmental Experts to get on board with that vision. That vision is no longer tenable because it is no longer true. The internet was always a "network of networks," an *inter*connected *net*work (get it?), but whereas in the early days those networks were all open and packets of data flowed across them based on the optimal route, now many of those networks have erected barriers around themselves.

Still holding it all together is the United States. Most global internet traffic still travels through the United States. An email going from, say, Budapest to Hanoi would head across the Atlantic through undersea cables, traverse the Lower 48 states, and plunge into the Pacific before hitting Japan and being dispersed in the direction of Vietnam. The United States continues to be the loudest voice in the various internet forums for maintaining the global internet. ICANN, the Internet Corporation for Assigned Names and Numbers, which manages the global Domain Name System, is still very much a U.S. entity (though it is no longer controlled by the U.S. government) and it promotes the original U.S. view of the internet.

The problem is that this view of the internet is fundamentally incompatible with the direction Russia, China, and other authoritarian regimes wish to take it. As they carve off their chunk of the internet and continue to expand the controls they place on their citizens and on companies doing business within their country, they are also pressing to remake the global internet in their image. That image would put states in charge, ending the multi-stakeholder model that would allow companies and users a voice in how the internet operates. Meanwhile, by controlling the internet and the systems and information that are accessible to it in their own countries, nations led by authoritarian regimes are using our own relative openness against us, siphoning up our intellectual property, manipulating our elections, and generally using the internet to wage a low-grade war against us. These countries act as safe havens to cyber criminals or, in the case of North Korea, actively use cybercrime to support the regime.

It does not have to be this way. Instead of working to preserve a global internet that is open, interoperable, secure, and reliable (something that was always more fiction than reality), we could choose to structure the balkanization. We will never persuade the Chinese and the Russians to accept our vision of the internet until we persuade them to accept our vision of an open and tolerant democratic society that respects the rights of the individual. The ability of the internet to shape societies was always overstated, at least in comparison with the ability of societies to shape the internet. Thus, instead of begging and pleading with authoritarian states to play by our rules, we should set the terms under which they get to have unfettered access to the unfettered internet and, in the meantime, as it were, fetter their access.

Why a Schengen Model Just Might Work

It's an odd time to be basing anything on what some are now calling the "European experiment," particularly its immigration and border policy. The United Kingdom has been having paroxysms over its exit from the EU and fully one third of "leave" voters said that exiting the EU "offered the best chance for the UK to regain control over immigration and its own borders." More strikingly, almost half of leave voters said their vote was about sovereignty, believing that membership in the EU broadly meant that the U.K. had simply given up too much of its authority to the bureaucrats in

Brussels. As Britons were getting cold feet about exiting, post-Brexit arrangements on borders and immigration were looking like they may stay largely the same. That's because for all the ills that being connected to Europe seemingly (to many) brought to the U.K., the benefits far outweigh the losses (the best we can hope for in public policy).

At first, only five of the ten member states of the European Economic Community agreed to sign the Schengen Accord, then a limited agreement to harmonize visa policy and reduce border checkpoints. The goal was to let border communities cross freely to work and shop. Five years later, the agreement was extended to completely eliminate all internal borders and to establish a unified visa policy. Four hundred million people live within the Schengen Area and can roam freely over all its 4.3 million square kilometers. The agreement became part of EU law in 1999, excepting only the U.K. and Ireland from the area, at their request, and Bulgaria, Croatia, and Cyprus, because their external controls were deemed insufficient. To the north, the non-EU states of Iceland, Norway, Switzerland, and Liechtenstein have chosen to join the Schengen Area.

Joining the Schengen Area comes with three requirements. First, nations must issue uniform Schengen visas and demonstrate strong security on their external borders. Second, they must show that they have the capacity to coordinate with law enforcement in other Schengen countries. Finally, they must connect to and use the Schengen Information System, a system for tracking entries and exits into the Schengen Area and for law-enforcement coordination. The rules include how cross-border surveillance can be conducted and the conditions under which "hot pursuit" across borders is allowed. They also allow for faster extradition of criminals between the states.

Unlike efforts to tackle cybercrime alone, the Schengen Accord has a clear quid pro quo, a give-something, get-something model built in. Want your citizens to have the right to live, work, and travel anywhere in the EU? Then enforce your borders, issue common visas, and cooperate in the investigation of cross-state crimes. To date, all efforts to bring the international community together to address cybercrime, economic espionage, and other ills of the internet age lack such an incentive structure.

The most successful of these efforts, the Council of Europe Convention on Cybercrime (also known as the Budapest Convention), sets out all the reasonable actions that states should undertake to combat cybercrime. It provides model laws, requires extradition, and offers some nominal coordination requirements. Sixty-one countries have ratified the treaty. Yet it is hard to find defenders of the Budapest Convention for the simple reason that it hasn't worked. The convention has failed to make any meaningful progress on the problem of cross-border cybercrime.

Damningly narrow in scope, the Budapest Convention needs to be replaced with an accord that provides real benefits to join and real consequences for failing to live up to obligations. A Schengen Accord for the internet would abandon the conventional wisdom that the United States, its allies, and like-minded countries need to continue to press for a single, global, open internet. Instead, these countries would work toward harmonizing not only laws that deal with cybercrime, but also laws that define legal activity on the internet and promote digital trade. The most effective way to pull countries into the accord is to deny them some or all of the benefits of connecting to the internet of Amazon, Google, Facebook, and Microsoft, not to mention the wallets of the 700 million consumers in Europe and the United States. Indeed, the United States has had the most success combating moves toward data localization when it's tied the issue to trade. The attempt to jettison NAFTA, the United States–Mexico–Canada Agreement (USMCA), includes a chapter on digital trade that, among other things, bans the three countries from requiring data localization and has requirements for all three countries to have rules to address things like spam and consumer protections online. What it fails to do is provide the necessary levels of specificity and to set up sufficient mechanisms for cross-border cooperation on cybercrime. As Michael Geist at the University of Ottawa points out, maintaining things like antispam laws is useless without specific requirements and mechanisms for ensuring accountability.

A hypothetical accord should provide common rules for how data is stored and how it can be accessed by law enforcement in the country where it is stored, the country where it is owned, and by third-party countries. By harmonizing these rules, member states would be making it easier for companies to compete across national boundaries. Companies would need to institute mechanisms to coordinate on law enforcement. The CLOUD Act, passed by the U.S. Congress in 2018, laid much of the groundwork, allowing the President to enter into agreements for the facilitation of cross-border access to electronic information by foreign law enforcement. A multilateral agreement could provide far stronger and better mechanisms to deal with the downsides of open borders in cyberspace. Such an agreement would need to include a commitment to allow the free flow of internet traffic across national borders. This commitment would not mean that countries are giving up sovereignty but simply, as with the Schengen Accord, that they will not exercise that sovereignty on their borders. Germany could still, for instance, make transmitting the text of *Mein Kampf* a crime within Germany, but it would not attempt to filter out files that match its hash when they enter Germany.

As we have noted, we are not fans of borders in cyberspace. The ability to meaningfully filter out malicious traffic on a national level is beyond the capability of technology today. Moreover, doing so would require that governments have the ability to decrypt traffic, which would do more to harm security than it would to help (to say nothing of privacy and civil liberties). Thus, we would not, at least initially, suggest that a Digital Schengen Accord would involve "hardening" external borders. Instead, we would focus on promotion of the benefits of being within the accord and development of the mechanisms to address the drawbacks (such as law-enforcement coordination). We would, however, have ISPs institute what some are already calling "Schengen routing," in which they keep all traffic internal to member countries within those member countries or create massive, encrypted tunnels when doing so is not possible.

Eventually, as the attractiveness of being part of this new Digital Schengen Accord grows, the ability of its members to exclude countries from it or limit their connectivity to it could be used to shape behavior of problematic countries. Together with traditional sanctions, dropping or limiting traffic from nuclear proliferators or unrepentant havens of cybercrime could prove a powerful tool for reforming bad actors. Before that can happen, though, states within the accord would need to clean up their own acts.

It's no secret the United States typically ranks up with China as the country where most malicious cyber activity occurs. That is, in large part, because there are more computers that are more powerful and connected at higher rates of bandwidth in the United States than anywhere else in the world. Rather than waste time compromising networks of home machines to build a botnet, cyber criminals are now doing what fledgling start-ups are doing and buying computing power from Amazon's cloud (the only difference is that they use stolen credit cards to make the purchase). The United States lacks strong mechanisms for limiting misuse of its infrastructure. American internet service providers do not have the kinds of systems for notifying and quarantining owners of infected systems that German and Scandinavian ISPs do. Because of that, most DDoS attacks and all manner of other cybercrime originate in the United States.

On the other side of the pond, European countries have been in a pro-tracted battle over protection of their citizens' data when it is stored by U.S. companies and for access to it when a crime has been committed. The pro-cess to access data in a foreign country for a criminal matter is still governed by agreements between individual countries, known as mutual legal assis-tance treaties (MLATs), that are typically decades old and do not provide for rapid responses. The CLOUD Act has partially addressed this problem, but a broader solution is still required. What might that look like?

First, the Digital Schengen Accord would need to require a broader harmonization of law and a clear process for handling differences. Respect-ing Western values, it should set freedom of expression on the internet as the common denominator, and layer in exceptions on a case-by-case basis. For instance, the United States would not be forced to accept European re-strictions on free speech but instead, like today, accept that U.S. companies would need to take reasonable efforts not to sell or display banned content in those countries. While this approach would, in many ways, enshrine the status quo, it's essential protection against the vision that China and other countries are now demanding for the internet as a whole: that foreign coun-tries must meet their standards for what they term "information security" in its full Orwellian meaning.

Second, we would need to establish a mechanism for monitoring adher-ence to the Digital Schengen Accord. Countries would need to be evaluated on whether their laws are meeting the requirements of the accord and whether their law-enforcement agencies are implementing those laws. A model for this kind of mutual evaluation can be found in the Financial Action Task Force (FATF), which has effectively instituted measures to address money laundering.

The FATF was created by the Group of 7 countries in 1989, together with the European Commission. Its first effort was to simply create a set of forty policies that countries should adopt to combat money laundering. Its thirty-seven member countries account for much of the world's financial transactions. FATF monitors compliance with its standards and helps countries implement them. Instead of a heavy-handed centralized effort, monitoring is done on a mutual basis, with teams of countries reviewing the efforts of one another and making recommendations.

FATF has also supported the creation of what the organization dubs FATF-style regional bodies. These FSRBs adopt FATF standards and work to implement them on a regional basis. A FATF-like organization at the center of a new treaty on cross-border data flows would provide what the Budapest Convention never could, a mechanism for assisting in and evaluating adherence to agreed-upon policies.

Third, the Digital Schengen Accord would then need mechanisms for monitoring and responding to malicious activity. In this case, the arena of public health offers a valuable model: a World Health Organization at the top, national equivalents to the Centers for Disease Control and Prevention, and teams that provide international assistance. The WHO-like organization would be responsible for organizing efforts to reduce vulnerable systems (the equivalent to vaccinations), identifying and responding to emerging malware families and botnets to stem them before they cause widespread harm (the equivalent to outbreak monitoring), and coordinating takedown and remediation efforts when prevention fails (crisis response). National CERTs would be responsible for contributing to the central organization and for leading efforts in these areas in their own countries. Under a new law passed in Europe, national CSIRTs (computer security incident response teams) are meant to fill this national role.

Finally, the Digital Schengen Accord would need much stronger law-enforcement coordination mechanisms than exist today. Almost a decade ago, the U.S. Department of Justice set up a 24/7 pager network among like-minded countries. There are still DOJ employees handing off a single pager around the clock. Suffice it to say, in 2019, the cyber problem requires a 24/7 law-enforcement coordination capability. Interpol has also made efforts in this direction but remains well understaffed and without sufficient authority. What is needed is a central capability to receive and mediate requests for law-enforcement assistance.

The organization needs to have the capacity to coordinate requests among all member states, and, when warranted, nonmember states. It will also need to be authorized to call balls and strikes when unlawful requests are made. Maintaining and publicizing real-time metrics on the responsiveness of countries can be a powerful naming-and-shaming function. With this kind of system in place, the United States and other countries that are part of this internet Schengen zone would be much better positioned to push nonmember states to be responsible actors in cyberspace. At present, U.S. pressure on China to curtail cybercrime is often met with a somewhat fair "you first" response.

Under a Schengen-like system with stronger abuse reporting, stream-lined takedown requests, and rapid law-enforcement cooperation, member countries would have a ready answer to such charges of hypocrisy. More-over, the difficult questions of when offensive cyber operations can be em-ployed against third-party countries would be answered. Such offensive operations would not be permitted, because reliable means of achieving the desired outcome (shutting down of command-and-control servers or elimi-nation of bots in a botnet) would be established by the agreement and exe-cuted swiftly by the mechanisms it establishes. Of course, those countries that are outside the zone and do not have similar cooperative mechanisms or fail to use them would be fair game for offensive cyber operations.

Throughout this book we have been making the case that much of the responsibility for addressing cyber threats falls to the owners and operators of those systems. We've argued that the view that offense has the advantage today is overstated and that we can take steps to reduce that advantage further. We are also painfully aware that there are threats that companies cannot address on their own, and that government has a role to play. That role is most clear in the international arena, where state power is most relevant. The ad hoc approach we have taken as a government to diplomacy, law enforcement, sanctions, and norms development has not produced the outcomes that many in the field believe are necessary.

The Schengen Accord began with only five members agreeing to a limited harmonization on visa policy. It was then expanded over a fifteen-year period until the agreement gave us the Schengen Area we have today. To replicate this model for a new internet accord, the United States and its like-minded allies should continue to harmonize relevant laws through digital trade chapters in trade agreements and begin to establish or strengthen the necessary mechanisms to handle malicious cross-border cyber activity. As these digital trade chapters grow, it will then make sense to harmonize them into a multilateral treaty that would establish common rules across all member countries. Eventually, such an approach could yield a single shared network with harmonized laws that reflect Western values and have the mechanisms in place to deal with the harms that a free and open internet will necessarily allow. While we fully endorse the vision of an open, interoperable, secure, and reliable internet, we are no longer convinced that version of the internet will also be global. It is likely time to take a new approach. Perhaps that new international approach should also address the use of cyberattacks and influence ops on our democratic processes. That's next.

Chapter 14

·····

DEMOCRACY'S SHIELD

Defending Electoral Systems from Cyber Risk

Brush your teeth. Eat your spinach. Audit your elections.

—POORVI VORA, PROFESSOR OF COMPUTER SCIENCE,
GEORGE WASHINGTON UNIVERSITY

Adrian Chen pulled back the curtain, figuratively and literally. He was sitting in a restaurant on Savushkina Street in Primorsky, a neighborhood in St. Petersburg, Russia, peering out from behind a drapery at the nondescript office building across the street, a building where people were busy making things up.

Chen revealed his findings in a prescient article in *The New York Times Magazine* in June 2015. We read it that Sunday and then reread it on Monday. That it was important seemed clear to us, but why it was important we could not then guess. In hindsight, of course, it seems obvious.

The Clue on Savushkina

The building on Savushkina was home to the Internet Research Agency, an allegedly private Russian organization that was busy creating very professional-looking videos and social media posts about what seemed to be purely random and completely fictitious stories. The one that was most striking was a highly developed, multimedia effort to convince readers that a particular chemical plant in Louisiana had blown up. It hadn't. What was the point of saying it had?

We asked reporters and ex–intelligence officers back then, in 2015, that very question. Most shrugged. When we pressed them, the answers we got were things like "trial run" and "rehearsal." But for what? No one could guess.

Well, now we know. The Russians were experimenting, trying to see if American social media would stop them from creating fiction and promoting it as real. They were also learning how gullible Americans on social media might be. They were perfecting the skills of Russians living in St. Petersburg pretending they were Americans living in Louisiana, among other places. They did it all in plain sight and, for the most part, no one noticed.

Even if American authorities had thought it was a problem that Russians were pretending to be Americans online, it was not clear that any laws were being broken. Even had American authorities focused on the "troll factory," they would not have known that the Internet Research Agency's activities were only one small part of a multifaceted assault on our democracy. Nor would the reason for the activity have been obvious.

By 2018, what the Internet Research Agency was doing was so obvious that U.S. Cyber Command reportedly attacked the organization's computer network, perhaps not coincidentally on Election Day. It was a rare if not unprecedented event, the U.S. military attacking a Russian organization, and it gave great satisfaction to Dick Clarke, who had called for just such an attack in a series of television appearances.

The Russian government of Vladimir Putin has for years been involved in an undeclared "hybrid war" with the United States and the West in general. Cyber tools have been his most commonly used weapons. Unable to significantly increase the military or economic power of his country, he wants to pull down other countries, so that the gaps between them and Russia are narrowed. He wants to reduce the power of the United States and the Western alliance relative to Russia. His strategy is simple: divide.

He seeks to divide Americans from one another, to divide Britain from the European Union, to divide Turkey from NATO, to divide Catalonia from the rest of Spain, to divide parts of Ukraine from the rest of the country, etc. Hybrid war includes cyber war, of every sort. It also includes classical intelligence operations to buy influence, paramilitary activity, and diplomacy. It is everything short of major armed conflict. We, however, are going to focus on the cyber-war components.

When the potential for cyber war began to emerge in the 1990s, the U.S. military called it "information warfare." The problem with that was that they had already called the massive propaganda operations of the Cold War "information warfare" too. It was confusing, the Pentagon labeling two different things with the same phrase. Eventually, the computer network operations were labeled "cyber," in part due to the Clinton administration, to the eternal frustration of language purists.

The Russians, however, never saw cyber war and propaganda as separate. From before the Russian Revolution, they had been masters at spying, deception, and disinformation. They had Russian words and phrases for their tools, such as *maskirovka, disinformatia*, and *kompromat*. It was literally part of their military's checklist. The advent of computer networks just gave them another place to practice spying, deception, and disinformation when permitted by civilian authorities. Putin not only permitted, he ordered.

In the words of Alex Stamos, Facebook's former CSO, "Their [U.S. adversaries'] dream is when most Americans say [about the election], 'I don't have a choice in this.'" Putin ordered an attack to undermine America by heightening its internal divisions and undermining its citizens' confidence in their democracy. He unleashed hybrid war against a score or more of countries of the former Soviet Union and Europe, but the campaign against the United States was specifically tailored to take advantage of our own vulnerabilities. It is on his cyber-enabled attack on U.S. democracy that we will focus in this chapter.

Defenders of Democracy

Laura Rosenberger and Eric Rosenbach not only share similar last names, but also both served as Obama administration officials, one at State and one

at Defense, and are now separately spending their days trying to counteract
Russian efforts to subvert U.S. democracy.

Like so many other Americans of her generation, Laura Rosenberger
saw her life change in 2001, on 9/11.

A senior in college and thinking of what should come next, she was
thrust into a state of shock, as was all of America, on that day. The day after,
however, she knew: "I need to dedicate my career to do my small part to
make sure this never happens again." After graduate school in government
and a brief stint with an international peace organization in Kosovo, Rosenberger entered the State Department as a Presidential Management Fellow
during the George W. Bush administration. That program is undoubtedly
the most valuable way in which the U.S. government recruits its future leaders. Rosenberger quickly proved she may be one of them.

After a tour on the Korea desk, she moved to the National Security
Council staff for a rotation and eventually ended up in the West Wing, helping to make the Deputies Committee work. It is the Deputies Committee,
the number two officials or chief operating officers of the national security
departments and agencies, that meets almost daily to make and implement
policy in response to the ever-changing global situation. Staffing the "DC,"
as it's called inside the Beltway, Rosenberger saw it all, including Putin's
hybrid war and military invasion of Ukraine. The U.S. response, however,
was less than optimum, in large part because the United States did not fully
recognize what a hybrid war was at the time.

"We weren't seeing the whole picture, given the kinds of tools the Russians were using," she told us. "Connecting how the hacks related to the
Little Green Men (the Russian troops pretending to be local militia or civilian volunteers), related to the *disinformatia*, related to the financial manipulation." Putin, the career intelligence officer, had orchestrated the use of all
of the tools available to the Russian state to invade and occupy a large and
valuable chunk of the neighboring country, but had done so in ways that did
not look like a traditional war and, therefore, never quite triggered a full-
throated U.S. and NATO response. It worked.

"So I had that experience around Ukraine, and then fast-forward to the

[2016] election and I am watching from inside the campaign and I see the same things happening again." Rosenberger had left the White House in 2016 to work as a national security adviser to candidate Hillary Clinton. "We were trying to raise alarm bells right and left, but people thought we were crazy or alarmist or doing it for political purposes."

Like many who worked in the Clinton campaign, Rosenberger thought then, and even more so now, that the Obama administration should have done more to say what the U.S. government knew about Russian interference before the American people voted. Clinton herself has tried to understand why there were few alarms sounding, and has written about Initial Occurrence Syndrome, citing Dick Clarke's 2017 book *Warnings*. The first time a phenomenon occurs, there is a cognitive bias against believing it is true, or as significant as the data indicates.

For Rosenberger, as for us, the day after the election gave her a very brief insight into what clinical depression might feel like. "I don't even know how to describe what recovery was like. I was trying to fall off the face of the earth for a while." Then, when it was less raw, she looked back at what had happened and realized that before the vote neither the Clinton campaign nor even the U.S. intelligence community were fully aware of some of the hybrid war tools that were being used.

"There were a lot of things we did not know were happening," she told us. "The social media stuff, all of that, was a postelection realization." Then, as she had on 9/12, she asked herself what she could personally do about it. The result was the Alliance for Securing Democracy (ASD), a new, bipartisan, transatlantic, nongovernmental organization dedicated to exposing the continued Russian subversion and explaining its corrosion of Western democracies.

Sitting in the German Marshall Fund building in downtown D.C., Rosenberger codirects the ASD in the United States and Europe with Jamie Fly, a former national security adviser to Republican Marco Rubio. "I knew from the beginning it had to be truly bipartisan. Putin's strategy is to divide us, so if you respond from a divided perspective, you really play into his hands." Together, along with a team on both sides of the Atlantic, they created the Policy Blueprint for Countering Authoritarian Interference in Democracies, an action plan for defending against hybrid war.

The ASD is transatlantic because the Russian cyber and disinformation operations haven't just been directed at the United States. In fact, they had tested them extensively in Europe before bringing them to America. "Our European friends had been sounding the alarm for a long time and maybe, we thought, we should start listening to them in ways that we hadn't been."

Two of the key recommendations in the Policy Blueprint are closing known cyber and information vulnerabilities, and exposing ongoing activities. What frustrates Rosenberger is that many of the vulnerabilities remain. "Our house was robbed, so at least let's lock the door," she vented to us. The problem is that there are many doors in the United States. There are more than three thousand county governments, each of which has some modicum of sovereignty over how it manages and secures, or doesn't secure, the election process.

Exposing the ongoing activities is necessary because, according to Rosenberger, "the Russians are much more brazen. What they used to hide, they now do out in the open." The same phony Russian Twitter personas that were thumping for Trump in 2016 are now pretending to support far-left candidates and progressive causes in the United States, with the goal of stoking division in the Democratic Party and in the United States more broadly. ASD tracks the tweets, Facebook posts, and other social media content in real time on its Hamilton 68 website. It looks like the big screen inside a corporation's security operations center, spotting and calling out the Russian activity for the world to see.

While the Alliance for Securing Democracy has done good work, Rosenberger sees a need for government to step up. "We have to break down the silos of cyber and info ops, money laundering . . . and civil society subversion . . . and understand them as part of a tool kit," the tool kit that Putin uses. To do that, she calls for a multifaceted, coordinated U.S. government effort, orchestrated from the National Security Council staff. For complex, emerging problems, having an "orchestra director" in the White House has always seemed to us the sine qua non of effective government response.

Captain Eric Rosenbach was a young U.S. Army officer in Europe during the Bosnian and Kosovo wars, using cyber operations and signal intercepts to provide real-time intelligence to U.S. and NATO forces in the Balkans. It was the 1990s, and techniques to wage cyber war were only just being conceptualized. Upon leaving the Army, Eric stayed in Europe and married a German lawyer. While she practiced law, he worked on cybersecurity for a European internet provider and learned just how insecure corporations and private users typically were online.

After graduating from Harvard's Kennedy School of Government in 2004, Rosenbach went to Washington and earned a coveted staff position with the Senate Select Committee on Intelligence, working for Republican Senator Chuck Hagel. Later, he moved to the Pentagon to fill a new slot, Deputy Assistant Secretary of Defense for Cyber. Not long thereafter he was promoted to Assistant Secretary, and then in 2015, when his former Kennedy School professor Ash Carter became the SECDEF, Rosenbach became his Chief of Staff. In that job he saw almost everything that went on in the vast Defense Department bureaucracy. With the end of the Obama administration, Rosenbach and Secretary Carter returned to the Kennedy School to codirect the storied Belfer Center for Science and International Affairs.

Back on the banks of the Charles in February 2017, Rosenbach didn't have to think hard about how to keep the Belfer Center relevant. "When I was in the Pentagon I saw in near real time what the Russians were doing to mess with our election. We didn't do enough," he admitted. "The administration made a huge mistake. It was burning in my gut." Rosenbach decided he would build a program to help state and local governments defend against another wave of attacks. The resulting Defending Digital Democracy Project is something that Eric, still addicted to Pentagon-style acronyms, calls D3P.

By a year later he would have state and county election officials from forty-two states in the Kennedy School quad, making the problem real for them by making them play the kind of stress test that the war gamers in the Pentagon called a tabletop exercise, or TTX.

In the TTX, Rosenbach and his team put the election officials through their paces by demonstrating the numerous ways in which a Russian, or other attacker, could try to interfere with the election ecosystem. The D3P director, Caitlin Conley, an active-duty U.S. Army Major and Kennedy School graduate,

knew how to run an effective TTX. She divided the officials into four fictitious states and then compressed months of cyberattacks and hybrid war
operations against the states' election infrastructure into a three-hour
game. No one left the game thinking the problem we face is anything but
significant.

D3P did more than play war games or restrict its activities to Harvard
Square. The project invited students from Carnegie Mellon, Tufts, Georgia
Tech, Georgetown, and other top universities to develop tools to help defend
democracy. In a 2018 hackathon, teams from these schools competed for a
cash prize for the most valuable contribution to the defense.

Rosenbach's team went on to write a playbook for defending candidates,
campaigns, and state and local election operations. Among other recommendations, the playbook spells out five primary measures, simple things
such as using two-factor authentication, which gets you 90 percent of the
way to being secure, Rosenbach contends.

While Rosenbach is more sanguine than we are about the skills and
intentions of the thousands of county-level election officials, he agrees that
"no election official should be required to defend against the pointy end of
the spear of Russian military cyberattacks." At heart, Rosenbach thinks
about the problem through the lens of systems analysis. He told us, "It's
important to think about the election infrastructure as a system of systems,
all interconnected, and any of which can have vulnerabilities that the Russians can exploit."

The Election Ecosystem

In the United States, the election ecosystem has seven major components:
1) the candidates, their personal devices, and their emails; 2) the campaigns,
pop-up organizations with a short life span and almost never enough money
to conduct even traditional voter drives; 3) the two major political parties,
with their national, statewide, and local offices; 4) the state government and
county government, which run voter registries, databases that say who can
vote and where they have to go to do so; 5) the voting machines on which
votes are cast and recorded; 6) the devices and networks that send the ma-

chines' total to statewide election officials for tallying; and 7) the social media platforms that people, the media, parties, and candidates use to discuss the election and political issues. All seven can and have been targeted by the Russian military.

We are not going to rehash here the stories of the Russian attacks in 2016, or their continuing role in the 2018 election as the electoral battlefield is being shaped for 2020. There are plenty of good accounts of what happened and what is ongoing. We want to focus on solutions. Before we do, let's examine the "security through diversity" and constitutional arguments that some state-level election officials have used to contend that there is no need for, or legal basis for, federal action to defend the election system.

The security through diversity theory is that the great strength of the U.S. electoral ecosystem lies in the fact that each state (and to some degree, each county) gets to design its election infrastructure and, therefore, the theory goes, every state's system would require a unique approach to attack. Proponents of this theory postulate that so many disparate systems would mean that the Russians could never figure out how to compromise any significant number of them. Well, think again. What infrastructure diversity actually does is create a tier of bottom crawlers whose security is so bad it invites attack.

Moreover, the Russians do not have to attack every machine or precinct. They just need to affect enough of the "right" districts to tip the election. American elections are often close, and it is usually very easy to figure out in advance which precincts are going to go heavy for one candidate, and which will be toss-ups. With that knowledge, you could construct a limited series of attacks that could change the outcome.

An attacker could crash a few voting machines to make lines long at polling places where the candidate they want to defeat is expected to do well. Alternatively, they could drop voters from the registry database, preventing certain swaths of citizens from voting entirely, or change their designated voting precinct, resulting in long conversations and arguments at the check-in desks. Many voters, confronted with long lines at the end of the day, would give up and go home without voting, something we saw happen in 2004 in Ohio. Many John Kerry supporters thought the long lines at pro-Kerry precincts were intentionally created by the Republican election officials and may have cost him the state. Had Kerry won Ohio, he would have defeated George W. Bush in his bid for reelection.

Could the Russians do that? Almost certainly. We know because the U.S. government admits that the Russians attempted to break into more than half the states' voting registries. Did they succeed? The state election officials say no, but how would we ever really know? None of the states have the sophisticated threat-hunting capabilities that major U.S. banks possess. After all, "state IT officials did not sign up to go against Chinese or Russian colonels," as Alex Stamos said. We cannot expect our state-level bureaucrats to fend off military-grade attacks.

We know that nation-state-sponsored hackers regularly penetrate government and corporate systems. Three quarters of all corporations that have been successfully attacked did not discover that fact themselves, but were told later by somebody else, often law enforcement.

If nation-states regularly penetrate networks without being noticed, why would we believe that state electoral organizations, with tiny cybersecurity budgets and limited cybersecurity expertise, would detect an attack that altered the voter registration data? Furthermore, few states have done sophisticated audits to look for penetrations or alterations. What is that old saying? "The absence of evidence is not the evidence of absence."

As for the argument that the Constitution says the states should decide the "time, place, and manner" of Congressional elections, yes it does. The same sentence then has the word "but" and another clause that says Congress may pass laws regulating the time and manner of Congressional elections. Congress could, using authority granted by the Constitution, establish minimum cybersecurity standards for voting devices, databases, and networks. Incredibly, even after the 2016 debacle, it has not.

Congress did not act in part because it had been controlled by Republicans who have found a variety of reasons to justify not doing more to defend the state systems. Republicans blocked additional funds for the states to enhance election security. Perhaps some Republicans think that if Russian meddling happened, it might have helped the party achieve its 2016 electoral victory. A more powerful reason for inaction has been the opposition of state and local election officials, who see Washington's help as an inconvenience, a condescending allegation of their failure to secure the vote, and an arrogation of local government powers. Many local election officials are in a state of denial rivaled only by climate-change deniers for their damaging effects on our country.

Election Security Solution Sets

Because the election ecosystem has numerous components, there is no single, all-encompassing solution. We see four discrete solution sets.

The first solution set outlines minimum essential cybersecurity standards for federal elections set by law, combined with federal funding to achieve those standards. We are not suggesting a particular network architecture or a list of specific products, but we do think there are some procedures that at a minimum should (or should not) be used, and some types of products that ought to be mandated.

Today, only a handful of vendors produce voting machines. Time and time again they have refused to allow government officials to examine their software for vulnerabilities that could lead to exploits. That is simply outrageous and has to stop. While we would not dictate which voting machines in particular should be chosen, we would insist that all hardware or software required to conduct an election be certified as secure by one of a handful of approved and impartial expert labs. Think "Underwriters Lab" approval for toasters and other household appliances, but instead, for election infrastructure.

We envision minimum essential security standards for voter registration databases, for voting machines, for devices and networks that report results up the tape, and for pre- and postelection audits of devices, databases, and results. Among those requirements would be continuous monitoring software, vulnerability detection software, endpoint protection, code analysis, intrusion prevention software, data loss prevention software, multifactor authentication of users, and support from a managed security service provider (MSSP), all performed by certified firms using software and devices that have gone through the same certification process that the Defense

Department requires of its cyber vendors. It will not produce perfect results, but it sure will be better than the target-rich and insecure environment we have today.

Then there are obvious dos and don'ts. Do use a paper ballot backup that can be audited. Without a paper trail, it's impossible to know if the results (as reported by the largely insecure voting machines) are accurate. Do not use internet voting, even for overseas military voters. The risks of internet voting far outweigh the benefit of the small amount of time saved by not having to deal with paper ballots or tabulation machines.

When Terry McAuliffe was running for Governor of the Commonwealth of Virginia in 2013, he entered the voting booth, ready to cast a vote for himself. He touched his name on the screen, but nothing happened. Then he tried again. And again. "It took the third time, I think," he told us. With or without his own vote, he won, but he never forgot the experience he had, and always wondered how many voters never caught the glitch in the machine. As Governor in 2014, when he tried voting for Mark Warner in the U.S. Senate race, his Republican opponent Ed Gillespie's name lit up on the WINVote machine instead.

He had had it. McAuliffe put $1.6 million in his budget to have the state, instead of the local government, pay to replace the three different types of direct-recording electronic (DRE) machines still in use in some counties of the Commonwealth, machines with no paper backup that could be audited. Between the curious politicization of the issue and the influence of voting-machine manufacturers, the bill did not pass the legislature. "Some thought the state shouldn't be doing what is a local issue," he remembered. And there was a lot of lobbying by the voting-machine companies. "A summer vacation paid for, a trip, maybe this, maybe that."

After the Russian interference of 2016, McAuliffe's patience with the legislative process had run out. He ordered examination of all DRE machines in the Commonwealth. "Counties didn't want to turn them over. They were afraid we would easily hack them and they would be embarrassed." It turns out their fears were not unfounded. "We were able to hack into all of them."

"At that point," McAuliffe said, "I had the Board of Elections, which I appointed, vote to decertify all DREs two months before the election of 2017." This time the counties had to pay to replace them immediately. There was no state money. The counties had missed their chance. "Now every machine in use has a paper audit trail. It's what's needed throughout America." But as in Virginia, there are local election administrators who resent the intrusion into their realm, there are voting-machine company lobbyists who see their clients' business threatened, there are politicians who are more than willing to accept gifts and campaign contributions to look the other way, and there are easily hacked voting machines despite what the local officials tell you.

The second solution set is extending federal election campaign advertising rules and adding other controls to social media. We agree with Laura Rosenberger that "if our work is focused on protecting democracy, let's not undermine the First Amendment in the name of [it]." Knowing who said something, if they were a real person or a bot, if they were in Moscow or Cincinnati, is another matter. Similarly, disclosing who paid for a political advertisement is a well-established norm of American politics that could and should be ported from television and radio to the internet.

After the Congressional hearings of 2017–2018, Facebook, Twitter, and other social media companies have faced mounting public pressure to spend time and money trying to identify bots and fake identity trolls on their platforms. It turns out, identifying these sorts of users is doable and they could have been doing it all along, but purging accounts would have made their user numbers smaller and, in turn, would have modestly decreased their advertising revenue. Simon Rosenberg and his colleagues at the Democratic Congressional Campaign Committee ("the D-trip," the organization supporting Democratic candidates for the House of Representatives) got Facebook and Twitter to do just that in the 2018 election.

Using open-source software developed at the University of Indiana, the D-trip group found Russian bots and trolls. On their first run with it, they found 110 fake Russian Twitter accounts. They immediately, and privately, informed Twitter. The accounts were quickly taken down. As the campaign progressed, Rosenberg and the team were in regular contact with both Twitter and Facebook, telling the companies things that their corporate programs were not catching. Having been burned by the Congressional hearing earlier in the year, the two companies cooperated. Rosenberg told us, "Working together, we even took down one account within half an hour." Not everyone was so cooperative. YouTube, owned by Google Alphabet, did not respond to requests from Rosenberg and the D-trip team. Given their limited staff and funding, Rosenberg told us, the D-trip unit did not focus on all social media. Reddit and other platforms were not scanned. We now know, however, based on a report from the Senate Select Intelligence Committee, that in 2016, Reddit, Tumblr, Instagram, Snapchat, and a host of lesser-known social media platforms were used by the Russian manipulation campaign. Getting all of the platforms to do the right thing, especially after the public scrutiny diminishes, may require a law and regulation.

To assure a minimum level of scrutiny, Congress should by law require social media to look for and delete bots and foreign entities pretending to be Americans. The Federal Trade Commission, which has a decent record of protecting consumers online, should rise to the challenge and issue regulations governing disinformation campaigns on the internet. While they are at it, Congress should take the minimal step of requiring online political ads to disclose who paid for them, and then ban foreign money from ads supporting candidates or causes.

Simon Rosenberg would also have political parties and candidates sign a voluntary and public pledge that they will not use fake personas on social media or engage in the kind of bot and troll operations pioneered by the Russians. The pledge could also include an obligation to report publicly and to social media platforms when the candidates or their organizations become aware of such operations.

The third solution set is intelligence and law-enforcement reporting of foreign cyber and information operations in near real time. It is interesting to know now that Facebook and Twitter posts allegedly from Black Lives Matter groups saying not to vote for Clinton were actually being posted by very white people in Russia, not black people in Chicago. It would have been useful to know that before the election. The same goes for the posts telling Americans to vote for Jill Stein of the Green Party because "Hillary is going to win anyway." Whether or not you supported Clinton, you might have wanted to know that the Russians were behind these social media posts. In addition to requiring social media companies to disclose what they find, the government should be required to disclose what it uncovers.

Sometimes federal law-enforcement officials say they cannot reveal things they know because the facts have been, or might be in the future, presented to a grand jury as part of an effort to indict somebody for breaking a law. Sometimes intelligence officials say they cannot publicly reveal what they know because of the mysterious and intentionally obfuscatory phrase "sources and methods." Eric Rosenbach told us that, with regard to the decisions he participated in, the intelligence community's fear about losing valuable "sources or methods" was very often exaggerated or completely "bogus."

In 2016, the Obama administration did publicly say that there was foreign interference in the election, but not in a way that attracted a lot of voter attention or fully reflected the severity of the problem. While the government did know a lot about Russian involvement, the extent of Russian social media manipulation was not known until after the election.

In 2018, the National Security Agency and U.S. Cyber Command created the "Russia Small Group" to conduct operations to counter Russian cyber-related interference in that year's Congressional elections. General Paul Nakasone, the head of both organizations, briefed Senators behind closed doors on what the two units observed the Russians doing and on what the U.S. did to counter it. While the Senators seemed pleased, one of them, Senator Richard Blumenthal of Connecticut, noted that while the Russians know what the U.S. did to counter them, the American people do not.

To clarify what the intelligence services and law enforcement should do, Congress should by law require ongoing and unclassified reports to the public of incidents and activities involving foreign entities' attempts to masquerade as Americans to influence elections. Specifically, there should be a detailed report issued two weeks before every federal election, drawing on everything that any agency of the U.S. government knows.

The fourth solution set is to cooperate with and assist other democracies under Russian attack, or attack from other foreign cyber and information operations, aimed at undermining their democratic processes. We are not alone in being the target of Russian attempts to sow division, dissension, and doubt within democracy. Nor were we the first target. Former Soviet republics, former Warsaw Pact nations, and NATO allies across Europe have been similarly attacked.

To act on that principle of mutual defense of democracy by democracies, the United States should make gathering information about such activities a high-level intelligence collection requirement. As suggested by Laura Rosenberger, a center within the U.S. intelligence community should fuse intelligence and analysis, drawing heavily on so-called open-source (not secret) sources. Then we should share what we know with the foreign targets and with the public.

In addition to sharing intelligence, we should be part of a forum of democracies that shares best practices, other resources, and training to help one another identify, prevent, and counter foreign attempts to undermine our democratic processes and institutions. This kind of mutual aid and learning should take place both at the government-to-government level and at the political-party-to-political-party level.

That alliance of democracies should also pledge to engage in collective sanctions against the individuals, the organizations (we are talking about you, GRU), and the governments that engage in subversion of democracies. Sanctions are far more likely to have impact if they are collective, simultaneously applied, and enforced by many nations.

One of the old saws in cyber-policy discussion is whether it will take a "cyber Pearl Harbor" to get America to do the right things on cybersecurity, or whether there could ever be such a thing as a "cyber Pearl Harbor" to begin with. Well, we had one. It took place in 2016 when the Russian military engaged in cyberattacks, *disinformatia*, and other techniques to attack the most precious thing we have as a country, our democracy.

Eric Rosenbach thinks something like it, maybe even worse, could happen again. "It's not going to look like Pearl Harbor or 9/11. The big cyber-attack is going to be something that undermines our democracy in a way that leads Americans to question the viability of our system," he told us. "It's going to be something that's much quieter than explosive, but it's really going to hurt."

The attack on Pearl Harbor in 1941 really hurt, but in 1942 America came roaring back against the threat. It's time to realize that what has happened with a foreign military attacking our democracy in 2016 is just as significant, and requires the same kind of national unity and resolve in response. That unity has not happened yet, but it should, and still could.

:::::::::::: **PART V** ::::::::::::

THE (NEAR) FUTURE
IN CYBERSPACE

Chapter 15

. . . .

REAL AND ARTIFICIAL
INTELLIGENCE

Whoever becomes the leader [in AI] will become the ruler of the
world.

—VLADIMIR PUTIN

We headed for the Eiffel Tower to see the future of cyberspace. It was a hot August day in 2016, and we were not in Paris, but in the Paris Hotel and Casino, with its replica of the Eiffel Tower, in Las Vegas. After a briefing in a small white-and-gold ballroom meant to be reminiscent of eighteenth-century Versailles, we were ushered into a hall next door, a vast twenty-first-century space filled with computer racks and purple lights. We had one question in mind: Was artificial intelligence (AI) the revolutionary tool that would finally give cyber defense the advantage?

We will return to Las Vegas in a bit, but first let's put in perspective the introduction of AI into cyber-war. The ongoing low-grade cyber wars around the world are not static. Both offense and defense are forever developing tools or, as in the case of AI, entirely new classes of weapons. Having new technologies hit the battlefield during a period of conflict is not unusual.

During World War II, warring nations spent six years engaged in the most destructive campaigns in human history, killing millions and wiping out hundreds of cities. They did so with technology such as tanks and bomber aircraft that had evolved significantly since they were introduced, when the nations involved had engaged in the same kind of mass folly in Europe only twenty years earlier.

Those evolved weapons were far more destructive the second time around, but they were merely more advanced versions of the same kinds of technologies that had emerged in the Great War. While WWII was going on, however, some of the participants were engaged in frantic work back in the labs. The Germans made advances in rockets and weaponized them, creating ballistic missiles (the V-2) that were impervious to air defenses and could destroy entire city blocks. The Americans, with considerable help from immigrant European scholars, invented nuclear weapons. The Americans had been using large formations of B-29 Superfortress aircraft to drop thousands of conventional explosive bombs on Japanese cities. They then used one B-29, dropping only one bomb, to obliterate an entire city. A few days later, they did it again.

Nuclear weapons are a technology and have an outcome that is so qualitatively and quantitatively different from any weapon ever employed before that experts agreed that they created an entirely new era in war. They also created a form of peace. Almost seventy-five years after the first two nuclear weapons were used, no further nuclear combat detonations have occurred. The weapons are, however, used every day to deter and prevent certain kinds of warfare. Significant diplomatic and intelligence agency efforts have been expended trying to prevent other nations from acquiring nuclear weapons, but eight nations followed the Americans in successfully acquiring them, at considerable financial cost.

Just as nuclear weapons were developed during the war, AI and quantum cyber weapons are being developed during the present period of cyber hostilities. The more important historical similarity at work here, however, is that the qualitative and quantitative changes in cyber warfare that these two new classes of weapons can bring about could be as significant as the difference between what one conventional bomb dropped by a single B-29 aircraft could do compared with what one nuclear weapon dropped from that same aircraft actually did.

That may seem like hyperbole, especially given what AI has been used to do thus far in cybersecurity, but the use of AI in cyber war has barely started, and quantum capabilities have yet to be employed at all in the cybersecurity realm. Moreover, few analysts have begun to examine what the combination of the two new technologies could bring to the effort to secure cyberspace.

Both AI and quantum have been the subject of a lot of hype, venture-capital investment, and fearmongering about an arms race of sorts with China. So, in this and the next chapter we are going to explore these two new computer science technologies and specifically what they mean to cyber war.

The Reality of the Artificial

When Vladimir Putin told an audience of Russian students in September 2017, "Whoever becomes the leader [in AI] will become the ruler of the world," he sounded a bit like a pseudo-technologist McKinsey consultant. China's President Xi seems to agree with Putin, however, because China has set a national goal of being the dominant country in AI by 2030. These and other statements kicked off a round of punditry focused on the new "arms race in AI," and what America must do to win it.

In the nonmilitary, nonsecurity arena, America seems to be doing quite well deploying AI. It is already widely in use in fields as diverse as banking and finance, logistics, advertising, and even medicine. To see what AI means for cybersecurity, we are going to take a bit of a digression to discuss the AI field in general, beginning by defining what we mean by the term. It is often the case in the field of information technology generally, and in the subset of IT that is cybersecurity specifically, that terms are thrown around loosely and commonly utilized definitions are hard to find.

Buzzword bingo is a common parlor game in cybersecurity. At least since 2012 at cybersecurity conferences, such as the huge RSA convention, the term "AI" has been used with wanton abandon and imprecision. AI, it would seem, is like bacon: it makes everything taste better. Thus, it is now alleged to be incorporated in many cybersecurity products. The frequent use and misuse of the term "AI," and especially of the subsets of AI, can be confusing, especially to policy wonks.

Historians point to the 1956 Dartmouth Summer Research Project on Artificial Intelligence as the birthplace of AI, a meeting at which computer scientists agreed that it could be possible someday to have computational machines do things that hitherto had only been done by humans. AI was, thus, originally meant to be the simulation by machines of certain human cerebral activity. Many of the current uses of AI are still, in fact, attempts to have machines do things that humans do. What is important for us, however, is that AI has moved on to do things that no individual human could do, indeed what even groups of highly trained humans could not reliably do in any reasonable amount of time.

Using AI, machines can now have meaningful visual capacity, so-called computer vision. They can see things by translating images into code and classifying or identifying what appears in the image or video. Cars can now see other cars, view and understand certain traffic signs, and use the knowledge they gain from their visual capacity to make and implement decisions such as braking to avoid an accident. AI can "see" someone doing something on a digital video feed and recognize that the action requires an alarm: a package has been left unattended on a train platform, alert a guard. AI can "see" a face and, perhaps, recognize and associate it with a name, and maybe even correlate it with a police be-on-the-lookout (BOLO) notice. These types of facial recognition systems have been deployed in concert with CCTV systems in China on a massive scale in order to apprehend wanted persons with unparalleled speed.

Of course, many life-forms have visual capacity, so AI is not doing something uniquely human when it sees things and reacts to them, but humans were unique in their ability to engage in speech and conversation with other humans, until AI. Now machines can speak, not merely playing back recorded messages, but thinking about what it is appropriate to say in a context and then doing so. Moreover, they can then react to what is spoken back at them by a human, and sometimes, within the limits of their programming, even do so with an appropriate and humanlike response. (If you are thinking about Siri and its limitations, be assured that there are far more powerful programs working today in research labs.)

AI is also being used to allow machines to walk and perform other movements, identifying what is an obstacle and determining what to do to get around it. Machines created by Boston Dynamics have demonstrated remarkable dexterity using AI programs to guide their decision making as they traverse real-world obstacles outside the laboratory.

The field of AI gained greatest acceptance in the corporate world when it began processing the sea of data that the rest of information technology was producing. The subset of AI that is data mining proved that software could far exceed human capabilities. It could sift through great volumes of data in seconds to find what a large team of humans would have taken weeks to do. Moreover, it could read and correlate data from multiple databases, each formatted in a different way. Advanced forms of data mining could look at and pull information from both structured data, such as organized databases or Microsoft Excel spreadsheets, and unstructured data, such as a photograph, audio recording, or text document.

The smarter cousin of data mining and the most powerful type of AI is machine learning (ML). ML applications began with categorization. Computer scientists input data with labels assigning inputs to one category or another: this is a dog, this is a cat. The software "learned" what the distinctions were in the data that led to the labels, and was then able to do the sorting itself without them. This form of ML that requires training the application is called supervised learning. Other ML applications can sift through oceans of data and detect commonalities and patterns without being told what to look for. This unsupervised learning actually does somewhat simulate human learning and thought, most of which comes down to noting differences and patterns.

Within ML (got those acronyms now?) are two other subsets, deeper levels, literally, of machine learning. The first is what is called an artificial neural network. ANNs somewhat simulate in software design the way human cerebral wiring is structured, the way neurons interact with other neurons to send messages with charges of varying strength to cause thoughts within the human brain or to cause body parts to take actions. ANNs can adjust their own "wiring" and weighting based upon patterns in data, in order to improve themselves and their predictive abilities. For instance, an ANN that classifies pictures of cats or dogs will, over time, learn the distinguishing factors of the two types of animals and adjust its "wiring" so that its cat or dog predictions are more accurate. The second type of ML you will also hear about is deep learning, which is in turn a type of ANN that uses multiple layers of "neurons" to analyze data, allowing it to perform very complex analysis. Enough with the definitions. What can AI do defensively or offensively in security and warfare?

Artificially Intelligent About Security?
AI/ML for the Defense

On a large corporate network today, there are between three and six dozen separate cybersecurity software applications in use, each contributing to the security of the overall network in a specific capacity. Pity the poor chief information security officer, who has to make the best-of-breed selection for each of those dozens of tools and then integrate them. She will likely select products from more than twenty different vendor companies. In the last three years, many of those vendors have claimed that they have woven AI into their products, and in fact many have done so to one degree or another. This trend toward AI-enabled, single-function, or "one-trick" security applications is one of the reasons that the balance is shifting away from offense and toward defense.

The most widely deployed cybersecurity products incorporating AI today are endpoint protection systems. In fact, this kind of software has begun to replace the traditional antivirus software packages, which were the first cybersecurity products in widespread use beginning thirty years ago. Unlike traditional antivirus or intrusion detection systems, which check network packets against "known bad" signatures (a blacklist approach), the endpoint protection systems using AI ask whether the user is trying to do something they have never done before. Is the activity unneeded or even unauthorized for the user's role? Would the activity being attempted damage the network or security safeguards on the network? These products are learning patterns, rather than applying blacklists, and modifying their behavior as they learn. This software learns not just from what it sees on its endpoint, not just from what happens on other endpoints on the network, but, in a classic example of Metcalfe's law, they learn from every endpoint on every network on which they are deployed.

A second widespread use of AI today is in applications known as vulnerability managers. AI can intake machine-readable intelligence reports on new threats and can automatically prioritize those threats based upon what it already knows or can quickly find out about your network. For example, an AI-driven vulnerability manager could check to see whether you have already addressed the weakness the new attack exploits. Have you installed a patch from the software manufacturer, or is the newly reported exploit attacking something you have not yet fixed on your network?

A third use of AI/ML is in cybersecurity software products known as identity and access management (IAM) and privileged access management (PAM). The software determines if the user is who they claim to be by checking multiple databases simultaneously. The AI would ask: Where physically in the real world is the user? Did the user already badge out of the building? Does travel data show that the user is not in the building, but actually in London today? Is the user originating on the appropriate computer? Is the user accessing applications and databases they normally use? Is the user attempting to do something with the data that is unusual, such as encrypting it, compressing it, downloading it, or transmitting it to an inappropriate destination? Are the mouse movements and stylistic keyboard usage of the actor consistent with their previous patterns? Or is the user acting too quickly and smoothly, like a bot?

The answer to those questions is not binary; rather, each of them is likely to produce a score relative to the confidence that the AI has in each answer based upon what data is available and how accurate it has been in the past. The combination of the weighted scores from the several questions asked will result in a decision, and the user will be allowed in, kept out, permitted only to perform limited functions, asked for further proof of identity, or placed under ongoing observation.

When conventional security software does detect possible malicious activity, it sends a message to a security-monitoring console being watched by a human. Unfortunately, today in most corporate or government networks, alarm messages are coming into security monitoring systems at such a high rate that triage must be performed by the human(s) in a security operations center, or SOC.

The humans might get distracted in ways any of us do at work, eating, nodding off, visiting a bathroom, or texting with a partner. AI, however, is always on, continuously at the same level of attentiveness. AI could prioritize threats for itself, or for the humans in the SOC. If trusted and authorized by the network owner to do so, AI could take action to block malicious activity, or to delay execution of a dubious command until a responsible human can review it.

Thus, there was a lot of hope for the new companies that rushed into the market claiming to be using AI to stop cyberattacks. When NSA Director Keith Alexander retired from the military, he quickly started an AI cybersecurity firm, IronNet, and gained more than $100 million in backing. A British firm, Darktrace, claimed its ML software could learn about an attack while it was ongoing and alert network operators. Darktrace soon became a "unicorn," a company worth more than a billion dollars. Critics of IronNet and Darktrace claimed that the AI actually still needed a lot of human assistance.

Indeed, no cybersecurity firm has at this time deployed what we envision as the full promise of AI/ML, what we call the Network Master, the one AI to rule them all. A Network Master AI/ML program could correlate billions of actions on tens of thousands of machines over weeks of activity, drawing on all the data logs from the dozens of security software programs and network management systems. Within milliseconds of coming to a conclusion based on correlating scores of diverse data sources, the Network Master could quarantine suspicious activity, create honeypots, modify firewall rules, increase authentication requirements, isolate subnets, or even in an extreme emergency disconnect the corporate network from the internet. Such capacity does not yet exist.

If all of that sounds like AI could give the defender the decisive upper hand in dealing with cyberattacks, the reality is that we are not yet there.

Yes, some previously existing one-trick security applications like those mentioned above have added AI/ML techniques and are now better at some specific tasks. However, the ML that runs the network, spotting and swatting attacks that no human would detect, is not yet a reality for a variety of technical and procedural reasons.

For example, AI/ML works best when it has a lot of data to analyze, particularly when that data is in a variety of databases and formats. Then AI/ML can do what humans manifestly can't do, quickly cross-correlate billions of seemingly unrelated pieces of information to infer a conclusion. For most AI/ML programs to work well, that data all needs to be swimming in the same place, in what big corporations call their data lake. It seldom is. It's scattered. Or sometimes it is not even collected or stored, or not stored for very long, or not stored in the right format. Then it has to be converted into a usable format through what data scientists politely call "manicuring" (and behind the scenes call "data mangling") for the AI/ML engine to perform its work.

Capturing all the data and storing it for six weeks or more to catch the "low-and-slow" attacks (ones that take each step in the attack days or weeks apart so as not to be noticed) would be a very expensive proposition for any company. Only the wealthy *and* highly risk-averse corporations would do that. In our discussions with network operators at major corporations, we have found that very few have such vast and complete data lakes readily accessible.

Most network operators do not yet trust AI/ML programs to wander around their live databases. Maybe their fears are irrational, but they are real. How do they know if that semi-sentient ML program is going to morph its software and then do something it has not done before, like wipe software off a server or disconnect a key router from the network? While such nightmares have never happened, there is always a first time, and what paranoid network security officer is going to take that risk?

If, however, instead of allowing access to your live database, you only permit the database to rummage on a near real-time basis, that may mean that you have to replicate your vast data lake at considerable expense by adding many physical or cloud servers. If you do that, the AI/ML cannot really tell you about a live security event, only about something that happened before you mirrored the databases. Even then, while ML programs are learning, they are often returning so many false positive alarms themselves that they are actually making the monitoring problem worse for all the humans watching panes of glass in the SOC.

For a real Network Master to be created two conditions are necessary, beyond the enormous software challenges. First, someone or some group would have to be willing to fund the development. Most venture-capital or private-equity firms would not normally be willing to place a bet on that kind of development. It will likely require a well-heeled tech company willing to fund a "moon shot," or possibly a government agency willing to sponsor and fund it. Second, after the AI/ML had been proven on simulated networks, it would require a large network whose owner-operator was willing to be the first mover to employ it on a live network. It is difficult to imagine who that might be.

If (and as you can see it is a big IF) those problems can be overcome, AI/ML could make it very difficult for today's attackers to succeed. Meanwhile, however, today's bad guys are not standing still. They are also playing around with AI/ML. Of course they are.

Weaponizing Nonhuman Sentience?
AI/ML on the Offense

When most people think about AI, they're not thinking about cybersecurity. They're thinking about killer robots. Given all of the existing applications of AI that are in everyday use behind the scenes doing good things (such as instantly making a decision on whether a credit-card purchase made online is actually fraud), it is disappointing to data scientists that when (and if) the average citizen thinks about artificial intelligence, the Terminator comes to mind. Many people have already internalized the idea of weaponized AI, even though the kind of thing they fear does not really exist except in some experimental Russian programs.

In the field of kinetic war, the Russians, the Chinese, and the Pentagon do seem to have a fascination with semi-sentient swarms of fire-and-forget drones that could fly around, talk to one another, decide on what things look like targets, divide up which drone would go after what target, and so forth. Think of a bunch of smart, angry hornets, then give them explosives. A DoD directive bans autonomous weapons that would use AI to determine on their own if something or someone should be attacked. There still must be a human in the loop authorizing a weapon to attempt a kill. While that is mildly comforting, with a few keystrokes, autonomous killing AI software not used in peacetime might be activated on a drone or missile in wartime. In a shooting war with a near peer, it would be hard to resist such a tool, especially if the opponent were the first to use autonomous AI weapons to find, swarm, and kill.

All of those fears involve drones and kinetic kills in the physical world in the future, but for cybersecurity experts, the reality is more immediate. The same kind of defensive AI/ML software we discussed above can be used in a slightly modified way to perform a cyberattack on a network.

Cyber criminals and malicious actors are no longer, if they ever were, the archetypical acne-plagued boys alone in their parents' basement hacking for fun and profit on a Red Bull–induced, pizza-fueled jag. Malicious actors in cyberspace today can be military or intelligence officers or well-funded criminals. Both types are staffed and supported by computer science graduates with advanced degrees and AI/ML proficiency. The criminals can afford the highly qualified help because cybercrime pays, and it pays well.

Using AI/ML on the offensive is not just theoretical. In August 2016, DARPA, the Defense Department's Advanced Research Projects Agency, commissioned six teams from universities to develop attack AI programs to attempt to break into and steal information from a highly defended network, with no human in the loop after the attacks were launched. The teams convened at the Paris Hotel and Casino in Las Vegas. So, back to our visit to Vegas.

After DARPA Director Regina Dugan explained the competition to a select group of observers, and us, we all walked into a vast event space, with six stacks of servers on a stage. On signal, the competing teams launched their attack machines and then walked away. For hours there was no human participating in or overseeing their activity. The AI/ML software programs scanned the defended network for faults and defenses, learning and trying tools and techniques to break in until they succeeded, then climbing up through layers of protection software, acting on their own, until they captured the flag (the data they sought), and exfiltrated it back to their own computers.

If you had been there expecting to see something dramatic happen, the DARPA event was somewhat anticlimactic. The servers just sat there and blinked at us. Their fans whirred softly. For hours. Finally, the DARPA judges announced that the attack AI software created by the team from Carnegie Mellon University had broken through all the defenses and extracted the target data. We celebrated their win at one of the casino bars and concluded there were not many networks that could have successfully defended against that CMU attack bot. We said to each other then that we had just seen the future. Well, that future is now.

Computer scientists at Cornell University showed in a 2017 paper that one could use a "generative adversarial network" to fool other software defending against attacks (in other words, software that creates an attack AI perfectly suited to beat the defensive software it is up against). At the Black Hat cybersecurity conference in 2018, also in Las Vegas, an IBM team demonstrated an AI attack program called DeepLocker. As they described it, DeepLocker is a highly targeted and evasive malware powered by AI, which is trained to reason about its environment and is able to unleash its malicious behavior only when it recognizes its target. DeepLocker learns to recognize a specific target, concealing its attack payload in benign carrier applications until the intended target is identified.

In other words, like the fire-and-forget killer drones that would fly around until they saw something that looked like the kind of target they were supposed to blow up, DeepLocker would scan the internet looking for the kinds of networks it was supposed to attack. DeepLocker would do so in a camouflaged manner, perhaps while looking like a legitimate service used by the internet service provider. Then, DeepLocker would adaptively use multiple attack tools and techniques, learning about the defenses in use, until it got in.

It occurred to us that what IBM was showing off to the public in Vegas was probably something like what the United States and some other governments had already come up with on their own, and probably already used. Indicators of what may be happening behind closed doors often come from what cybersecurity experts not involved in classified programs are discussing publicly.

For example, an expert at the cybersecurity firm Endgame has publicly demonstrated how offensive AI can be used to "poison" defensive AI software by essentially fooling the defensive technology engaged in the learning phases of ML. Think of it this way: ML could be fooled by creating a flood of false positive alarms, which could cause the detection system to disregard a type of attack. Then the real attack, looking sufficiently like the false positive, could be launched successfully.

Alternatively, defensive systems could be attacked repeatedly and, after each time the attack was defeated, AI could alter the attack a little and try again. In that way, the attacker could persistently change its signature just enough so that it no longer matched what the defense was looking to block, but it would have sufficient functionality for the attack package to remain effective. Hackers have been doing this manually, testing their attack tools against antivirus software, but AI/ML would do this so much faster and more effectively.

Hackers have a big data problem too: lots of personally identifiable information stolen from hundreds of companies. An expert at McAfee has publicly discussed how AI could be used to plow through the troves of data that hackers have already stolen from numerous databases. Data in only one database may not be sufficient for the hacker to successfully impersonate you, but by using AI, they could scan multiple databases they had hacked and compile a sufficient amount of information to successfully impersonate your online identity. Maybe they have discovered your password on one website, and then they use the same password successfully to get into a secure network, pretending to be you, because you made the mistake of using the same password on multiple applications. You don't do that, do you?

Neglected Defensive Potential

In the next three to five years, we are likely to see continued growth in the use of AI/ML as a part of applications that will do specific defensive tasks better than they are now being done. AI/ML use will become more sophisticated in one-trick security applications doing identity and access management, privileged access management, endpoint protection, and vulnerability scanning. Some vendors will incorporate the technology into their defensive applications more successfully than others. Already companies like Illumio are beginning to apply AI/ML to assist in network management orchestration. Some network operators will buy the better products, others will fall for flawed defensive applications, and some will neglect to buy cybersecurity products incorporating AI/ML technology altogether. Many cyber vendors will claim that they have an AI/ML application that will do everything, but they will be, to put it kindly, exaggerating.

The Network Master controller AI/ML for cybersecurity is unlikely to emerge soon for the reasons we have discussed. A time frame of three to six years from now is more likely. On the other hand, AI/ML for the offense, something like the weaponization of the 2016 DARPA Grand Challenge, is probably already in use to some degree and is likely to grow steadily in its application by a small set of nation-state actors. If recent history is any guide, such technology will eventually make its way into the hands of the second-tier nations and to nonstate actors. This second tier of players may not use AI/ML attack tools in as sophisticated ways as the U.S. and Chinese governments will, but AI/ML will still make them much more capable of successful attacks than they are currently.

On balance, in the near term the growing use of AI/ML in defensive software is likely to increase the ability of the defenders, unless they are being attacked by a sophisticated and determined state actor using AI/ML offensively.

Chapter 16

●●●●●●●●●●●●

A QUANTUM OF SOLACE
FOR SECURITY

Those who are not shocked when they first come across quantum
theory cannot possibly have understood it.

—NIELS BOHR

He just wanted to keep on wrestling. Growing up on a farm in the
vast open spaces of Saskatchewan, Chad Rigetti assumed that after
high school he would be the fifth generation working the family
farm. That's what Rigettis did. Even the farms adjacent to his father's property were owned and operated by other Rigettis. With high school coming
to an end, however, Chad assumed he would no longer be on a wrestling
team. He had not even thought of going to college until he was recruited by
the wrestling coach from the University of Regina. He agreed to go to college because it meant he could continue wrestling for four years. He didn't
know that going to college also meant he would end up wrestling with qubits.

In the international race for quantum supremacy, there are at least four
major U.S. contestants. Three are well-recognized tech giants Google, IBM,
and Microsoft. The fourth company is Rigetti, a start-up based in a dingy
warehouse district in Berkeley, California.

While most Americans, and even more readers of this book, have given little to no thought to quantum physics and computing, their relevance to cybersecurity means that we would all do well to understand them better. Simply put, quantum computers will soon be able to solve complex problems that no conventional computer has ever been able to. You cannot think about the future of cyber war without understanding the momentous changes that are about to happen to computing and IT in general, as well as cybersecurity specifically, with the advent of quantum computing.

Before we went to Berkeley, we brushed up on quantum physics, and before we talk here about the effect quantum computing may have on cybersecurity, we need first to take a deep dive to understand quantum in general. It is a dive to the lowest, tiniest level of existence, the quantum level. It is the level at which, we think, particles cannot be further subdivided into smaller things.

Comprehending the Incomprehensible, and Why It Matters to Cyber

The first discussion of quantum computing and its cybersecurity implications ever held in the White House may have been the meeting Dick Clarke convened in 1999. Back then, he asked experts from the NSA and the University of Maryland to begin by explaining how a quantum computer would work. Unfortunately, they began, as many quantum physicists do, by talking about Schrödinger's cat (which is both dead and alive simultaneously). If you are new to quantum, we advise you to avoid that analogy, which we find usually confuses people more than it helps explain the quantum phenomenon.

We find it more useful to begin by cautioning the newcomer to quantum that the laws of physics that you know, or have implicitly grasped by observation, do not apply at the level of the smallest elements of matter. Once we know or are told about the way things work at the very tiny quantum level, most of us intuitively reject it. It just does not make sense.

To overcome your cognitive bias to what we are about to discuss, think about Dick's grandparents or Rob's great-grandparents, people born in the nineteenth century. If they were brought back to life with the knowledge they had as teenagers and were shown an Airbus A380, a metal object weighing six hundred tons, they would not believe for a second that it could fly. If they then saw it fly, they would think it was magic. Nothing about a six-hundred-ton metal object traveling at five hundred miles an hour seven miles up in the air would make any sense to them.

Truthfully, most of us do not really understand the physics behind what makes that A380 fly. Maybe some of us heard something about a guy named Bernoulli, but we accept that the aircraft flies. We know it is real, it happens, and it is not magic. Well, treat quantum computing the same way. A century from now it will be as broadly accepted as a real phenomenon as flight is today.

What is so mind bending about quantum physics? Well, let's focus on two properties of the really small objects at the atomic level. First, observation: Matter at the atomic level (electrons, photons) may be either a particle or a wave, but in experiments like the famous double-slit experiment (see the endnote and watch the video), which form they take (wave or particle) is dictated by whether or not they are observed in motion by a measuring system, such as a camera or a particle detector.

Does the quantum matter somehow "know" that it is being observed? Probably not. There are a variety of theoretical explanations, but the experiments do make it seem that the matter knows when it is being watched, and there is no satisfying explanation in classical physics for the behavior.

The qubit, the quantum bit, is not actually in one state, such as positive or negative. It is in all possible positions or values until it is acted upon by observation. This state of "being about to be" in one position or another is called superposition.

The second unusual phenomenon occurring at the qubit level is entanglement. When a particle, for example a photon shot by a laser through a crystal, is split in two, or in some other way two qubits are made to be related, the two quantum particles are said to be entangled. When they are thereafter modified, whatever is done to one causes the other to change in the same manner instantly. The weirdness comes in when you realize that this "change one, the other instantly changes" phenomenon occurs even when the two particles are significantly separated in distance. No one really knows how this happens, but repeated laboratory experiments over many years have demonstrated that it does. The separation distance can be quite immense, as a 2017 experiment proved.

In the experiment, Chinese scientists created two entangled photons on a satellite in space and then shot them via laser, one photon to each of two ground locations 748 miles apart. Then, once on the ground, when the polarity of one of the photons was modified, the other one simultaneously changed. In what might be called an understatement, the Chinese scientists said of their test, "The result again confirms the nonlocal feature of entanglement and excludes the models of reality that rest on the notions of locality and realism." Yeah, so much for that model of reality that rests on realism, we never liked it anyhow.

Einstein famously called entanglement "spooky action at a distance." Scientists still debate why and how it happens, but no longer argue that it does occur. Some physicists think it opens the door for new methods of communication. The more visionary, or perhaps imaginative, believe it could be the basis of a future system of teleportation, but don't plan on that happening in time to ease your commute. What it does in 2019 is open up new computing possibilities.

In standard computers, electrical signals open or close gates, making an electron into a signal or "bit" that is either a 1 or a 0. This is why it is called a binary system. It has to be in one of two states. Everything in your computer is based on that principle, lots of little 1 or 0 signals happening down in the computer chip. Because in conventional computers the electrons have only those two possible states, 1 or 0, it takes a large number of bits to encode a piece of data. For example, the letter *m* is expressed as 01101101, and the word "Hello" is 01001000 01100101 01101100 01101100 01101111. That's a lot of digits just to say hello.

Each qubit, such as those made from electrons, ions, or photons, has multiple potential values (not just 1 or 0) simultaneously, based on such characteristics as their spin or polarity. Herein lies the revolutionary advantage. With a few qubits, much more information could be encoded. Each added qubit doubles the capacity of encoded information. If one qubit encodes two values, two encodes four, three encodes eight, four encodes sixteen. By the time you have sixty-four qubits you can encode the equivalent of more than a million terabytes of classical computer data. The traditional way of explaining great volumes of data to laymen is to say that the entire U.S. Library of Congress is about fifteen terabytes, and a copy of all the books in the world would be about sixty terabytes. So, sixty-four qubits would be the equivalent of, well, a lot more books than actually exist.

Chad Rigetti is shooting for 128 qubits on his machine in 2019, and may have done so by the time you got around to reading this book. That would be a device that could encode more than all the data that moved on the internet globally in a year, and then could process that data in some desired way.

Since each qubit can have multiple values at the same time, a quantum computer exploiting that odd phenomenon can process data using all of the possible values for each of its qubits almost simultaneously. Conversely, classical computers are sequential; they proceed in serial fashion. Something a quantum computer could do in a second might take a classical computer four centuries. If you had begun crunching a hard mathematical problem when the first operational computer, ENIAC, started on the Penn campus in 1946, and if ENIAC always had the capacity of a modern scientific computer, it would still need about another 330 years to complete what a 128-qubit device could do in a second. Quantum computers with 128 qubits will soon be able to solve math problems that no conventional computer has ever been able to. That will enable them to break codes, design new materials, develop new drugs, and perhaps to simulate the human brain.

Getting the idea now? When a quantum computer works with three hundred qubits, it will have capabilities that exceed the computational requirements of any problem known today. "The most exciting applications of that kind of computing will be things we haven't even dreamed of yet," Rigetti gushed to us. Buckle up.

The Struggle to Get Quantum Working

The key words in the last paragraph were "when a quantum computer works." Consensus hasn't prevailed on whether anyone has really got one running in a practical sense yet. What experts agree on is that some people are simulating what a quantum computer would do, some people are using quantum principles in specialized devices, and others have experimental systems running. The experimental systems, however, still have a lot of problems.

The 1s and 0s of classical computing are easily generated with electrical pulses moving in silicon. Qubits are much more difficult to create. Doing so usually requires a lot of equipment to chill the quantum computer close to absolute zero. Although a lot of work is going into quantum chipsets that work at room temperature, most quantum computers, such as Google's and IBM's, still look like some sort of Rube Goldberg science fair project or a 1950s science fiction movie set in an evil genius's lab, with vats of super-cooled gases and a complete maze of pipes and wires.

The major obstacle is that qubits, even when created and maintained at absolute zero, do not last very long. They decohere; that is, they lose their superposition in mere fractions of a second. Interference and noise from the environment can easily alter the intended state of a qubit. Moreover, thus far, most experimental quantum computers generate results that are, well, wrong a lot of the time and have to be modified using classical or conventional computers. The race to make practical quantum computers today is all about these two problems: decoherence and error correction.

Jim Gable and Wil Oxford of Bra-Ket, one of the many smaller start-up companies in quantum computing, think they are on a path to solving both problems using what they call pure photonics: in other words, light, rather than the electrons and ions in other companies' approaches. Their goal is to create quantum computer chips that manipulate single particles of light on silicon, which they believe reduces the error rate, and to maintain coherence for a full second of time.

Making quantum computing chips using photonics and operating at room temperature is also the approach of Christian Weedbrook of Xanadu, a Canadian start-up. To see such a chip we went to Toronto, where Xanadu is trying to create this magic in an old textiles building. The room across the corridor still had spindles, but in the quantum lab, Weedbrook was squeezing photons into pathways on chips. We had to look really closely to see the

Xanadu quantum chip, which was the size of a child's fingernail, but it was working and at room temperature.

Xanadu and Bra-Ket are among scores of quantum start-ups. Few are as well funded as Rigetti, which has already gathered $120 million in investment. In fact, Rigetti has created what it calls an ecosystem of affiliated start-ups so that the company can eventually offer "full stack" capability, from quantum chips to cloud computing to an App Store offering quantum software to solve specific kinds of problems. Right now, however, Rigetti is focused on keeping a qubit alive long enough to be useful and creating software and hardware that will produce low error results.

The proof that someone has achieved that, at least in an experimental way, will come when they can prove that they have done something no classical computer has ever done, such as solving for a hitherto unsolvable mathematical equation. You can probably find a Vegas bookie who will take your bet on when that event, called quantum supremacy, will be achieved. In 2017, Google said it would achieve quantum supremacy in 2018. In 2018, the company said that it would do it soon, but no longer gave a date. Chad Rigetti told us, "Quantum computing will take people by surprise. We will get there very fast."

The race to quantum supremacy is primarily between the United States and China. The Chinese government has what has been reported as a billion-dollar investment in quantum computing, including a planned "Quantum Research City." In 2018, the U.S. Congress *authorized* a billion-dollar research program, though it has yet to actually *appropriate* that much money. The governments, scientists, and venture capitalists behind the new quantum industry obviously think they are on to something that will be a game changer.

Whoever wins the quantum computing race may be able to create an ecosystem of specialized chips and applications around their standard. Leadership in quantum computing is, however, likely to change as often as the front car in a Formula 1 race. Although some limited capability may be developed and maintained for a while in secret, real achievements will have to undergo peer review to maximize the potential of breakthroughs in quantum computing. Nonetheless, many quantum industry experts and national security officials we talked to assume that there are secret quantum computing programs in government labs in China, the U.S., and Russia.

Quantum and The Magic Decoder Ring

What sparked governments' interest in quantum computing was fear, or hope, of breaking secret codes. As they have learned more about it, other possibilities have drawn their attention. If you could easily break encryption, cybersecurity would be in much worse shape than it is today. Encryption is not just a tool that governments use to transmit secret messages to spies and soldiers. Encryption is ubiquitous, working behind the scenes in our web browsers, emails, databases, ATMs, and a lot more. Without encryption, it would be almost impossible to defend against hacking successfully. So, should we fear that quantum computing research will endanger cybersecurity?

If you thought quantum physics is complicated, the mathematics behind modern encryption can also quickly leave you in the dust. Again, we are going to simplify. Most encryption codes are based on a mathematical process called factoring: By what whole numbers can another, larger number be divided? So, for the number 12, the factors are 1, 2, 3, 4, 6, and 12. You can do that kind of factoring in your head, but it's a lot harder when the number you are factoring is not just two digits (like the number 12) but, say, hundreds of digits.

Most encryption algorithms utilize factors (prime factors, to be precise) of very large numbers as their basis. The assumption is that, even with a modern supercomputer trying out all the permutations, it could not correctly guess the factors that are being used as the basis for a particular encryption code without thousands of years of run time. If quantum computers can be made to work, thousands of years' worth of conventional computing could be done in seconds and modern encryption could be cracked.

With that hope in mind, governments have been rumored for years to be collecting and storing other nations' encrypted messages that they now cannot crack. Someday, perhaps in the next few years, quantum computing might allow China, Russia, the U.K., or the U.S. to read messages that they intercepted years ago, what you might think of as reading other people's old mail or yesterday's news. That may prove interesting and maybe even useful in the field of counterintelligence, tracking down spies and their sources. If and when this happens, don't expect anyone to announce it. This is one aspect of the quantum computing race where no one is going to claim to be first across the finish line.

As for cracking encryption codes in use currently, remember that a functioning quantum computer, when it appears, will not be generally available any more than a supercomputer is today. No one would argue, however, that supercomputers are unimportant. Indeed, they are necessary for any number of important uses, including designing nuclear weapons. Quantum computers will be owned and operated only by governments and a few large companies. The governments that have them will be able to use them to revolutionize many aspects of science and technology, including cybersecurity. If you are not working in those governments or the few companies that will have a functioning quantum computer and you want to use one, you will have to access quantum machines in clouds operated by IBM, Google, Microsoft, and probably Rigetti. Sorry, but they are not going to let you rent time in their quantum cloud to decrypt Citibank's codes.

Moreover, cryptologists, the mathematicians who live in the abstract world of codes, have seen the threat from quantum computing coming for years now. They have created quantum-resistant coding algorithms, systems of encryption that are more complex, some of which use entirely different approaches than long number factoring. It is a safe assumption that major governments have been using quantum-resistant encryption methods for some time.

In fact, the U.S. government's National Institute for Standards (NIST) has been openly and publicly working with leading academic cryptologists to create a new quantum-resistant encryption standard that could be used by banks and other commercial and private-sector organizations. NIST is hoping to have a standard ready by 2024. Some people think that will be too late.

One of the new encryption methods being explored actually uses a form of quantum computing to transmit secure messages, using quantum to deal with quantum. Remember that at the quantum level, things change when you look at them? That quality may make it possible to transmit codes or even the messages themselves in a way that the recipient could be confident that the content was not cracked, observed, or copied (this is referred to as the no-cloning rule).

Companies, including Hewlett Packard, are trying to commercialize quantum key distribution (QKD), a way to send a "one-time pad," or single-use code, that both ends of a communication could use to encrypt and decrypt. Such symmetrical codes have in the past been risky because someone could intercept and copy the code book. With QKD, sending the pad as quantum photon-based messages eliminates that risk because by definition you know if someone has looked at a piece of quantum code. Unfortunately, thus far, the distance that QKD messages, which are made up of photons, can be transmitted is limited by the fact that the energy in a photon fades with time and distance.

In classical computing, messages made up of photons travel across the country on fiber-optic cables, but the photons are "boosted" or retransmitted repeatedly on their rapid journey. The method used to boost the photon signals on the internet backbone today observes and reproduces the photon, and would thus break the security of QKD. Solving that problem, being able to transmit quantum messages at a distance, is a high research priority, but not one to which experts are willing to assign a time frame. If someone succeeds at it, quantum computing, far from putting an end to encryption, might actually offer a highly secure method of communication.

In the meantime, banks and other commercial and private-sector organizations are going to have to shift from the encryption systems they use now to quantum-resistant systems. Whether that is two years away or ten is a matter of debate and conjecture, but there is a role for government to require that shift by a certain date through regulation and a new encryption standard.

Think of it as Y2K for encryption: a time when everyone is forced to update their software to ensure that a hacker with access to a quantum computer cannot someday become a problem. It is not a dire or immediate threat quite yet, but it will arrive sooner than most realize.

The Real Promise of Quantum Computing

So, assuming Chad Rigetti, his giant corporate competitors, or the Chinese can get a real quantum computer to operate as more than a science experiment, what will we do with it? Konstantinos Karagiannis of BT has been tracking how people are getting ready to use quantum computers by looking at what software they are writing and what quantum algorithms have been developed. "So far only two of the sixty quantum algorithms I know of are about encryption," he told us. Many of the nonencryption algorithms are for machine learning, which as we've seen has significant implications for cybersecurity.

Karagiannis thinks that "for AI to go to the next step it may need quantum computing to integrate all of those little AI programs" that are doing single tasks on a computer network. Chad Rigetti is excited about the possibility. "There is a very deep connection between machine learning and quantum computing. They could work together in a beautiful and elegant way."

What we discovered is that there is an enormous amount of academic work going on in anticipation of marrying quantum computing and machine learning. NASA, Stanford, and Google have come together to create QuAIL, the Quantum and AI Laboratory in Palo Alto. Even before there is a real operational quantum computer, teams at places such as MIT and the University of Toronto are busy writing machine learning applications in the new computer languages developed for quantum.

Now, think back to the previous chapter in which we said AI/ML was adding some nice single-function capabilities for network defense, but that no one had yet really done network orchestration and defense in real time without a human in the loop, using a Network Master AI/ML program. Instead, we suggested ML might already be in use as a tool for network attack today.

If, however, you were to combine a truly operational quantum computer with some specialized ML and orchestration applications for running and defending a classical computer network, it might just be possible to deal with the millions of actions that are simultaneously taking place on a network and its periphery, taking into account all of the data that is in storage about the network, factoring in information about what is happening in near real time elsewhere in cyberspace, and repairing or writing code on the fly. In short, you might be able to create the "one AI to rule them all" on a network. You might actually be able to defend a network successfully. Or attack one.

Here is where the so-called quantum arms race may be real. If an attack algorithm were written in new quantum code, taking advantage of an operational quantum computer's computational capacity, it might be possible to develop a tool that would collect everything that is known about a network, simulate it, and find the best way to attack it. Indeed, it could be possible to design a series of optimized attacks for a host of networks and then launch them more or less simultaneously, bringing a target nation or group of nations to a pre–industrial era condition in seconds or minutes.

Such a crippling attack is probably too difficult for teams of humans to execute today, but an operational quantum computer with bespoke, optimized ML/quantum programming might be able to do it. Former University of Southern California president C. L. Max Nikias offered the prediction that "whoever gets this technology first will be able to cripple traditional defenses and power grids and manipulate the global economy."

This may have been an overstatement, but given what we know of the tendencies of Russia, China, and the U.S. militaries and intelligence services, once they realize what an operational quantum computer could do, it probably will not take them long to start thinking like that. Will they create quantum-powered network defense first? Unlikely. Militaries think first of offensive weapons. It's in their DNA.

Assume for the sake of argument that a functional, operational 128-qubit quantum computer will be running by 2020, as Chad Rigetti predicts, and that dozens of ML and orchestration applications will be designed for it and running successfully by 2022. It should be possible by then to try a Network Master AI/ML system to defend a large, complicated network. Maybe that effort would, if funded properly, show progress by 2024, just five years from now.

In the meantime, people are putting processors in everything and connecting everything to networks at an amazing rate. Few of them are thinking about security, as we shall see in the next chapter.

Chapter 17

···········

5G AND IOT

Machines Too Dumb to Be Safe

> 5G will have an impact similar to the introduction of electricity or the car, affecting entire economies and benefiting entire societies.
>
> —STEVE MOLLENKOPF, CEO OF QUALCOMM,
> CES KEYNOTE, JANUARY 6, 2017

D o you live in a city in the United States? If so, sometime in 2019 or more likely in 2020 you may notice something new on your street. Or more accurately, several new things may appear. There may be a light gray box attached to the streetlight near you. Another such box will be on the lamppost just down the street. On the sidewalk there may be what looks like one of those Postal Service relay boxes where the letter carrier picks up the mail to be delivered on her route. The box will not, however, belong to the Postal Service. It will belong to a "phone company." When this happens, 5G will have arrived near you. So too will a new set of cyber risks. The fifth generation of mobile telephony technology (5G) will supercharge the Internet of Things (IoT), and neither will be secure.

If Verizon, AT&T, Sprint, and other carriers move ahead with their plans, they will initially spend a quarter trillion dollars dotting U.S. cities with these new 5G transmitters on poles and accompanying electrical transformers in what look like mailboxes. Globally it may cost as much as $5 trillion to install the 5G infrastructure. This is not going to be like when they shifted your mobile phone from 3G to 4G. You may not even remember when that happened because the change in your mobile phone's capabilities may have seemed slight. You will notice 5G.

You will actually know about 5G before it shows up on your doorstep. The "phone companies" will be spending millions on advertising, telling you about the 5G "revolution." While most ads about technology revolutions are, to be polite, hyperbole, when it comes to 5G the word may be justified. The fifth generation of mobile telephony technology, 5G, won't be twice as fast as the current 4G. It may be ten times as fast.

While 5G is much more capable in many ways than existing technology, on one important criterion it is actually inferior. 5G waves do not travel very far. That's why the boxes will be lower and closer to you and, therefore, you will see many more of them than the current, high-up 4G towers.

Those newly ubiquitous boxes will also be able to handle vastly more devices simultaneously. The international 5G standard calls for the ability to support one million devices in one square kilometer. Devices in your house or apartment, such as your TV, laptop, or nanny cam, might connect wirelessly directly to the 5G tower and, thereby, to the internet. The same thing may happen in your office building, where elevators, vending machines, surveillance cameras, printers, and copiers may all link directly. Just plug them in and they will be on the internet. You might be able to get rid of your wi-fi altogether, although that is a matter of debate among the experts.

One thing telecommunications experts agree on is that 5G will make it possible to connect many more devices, either directly or indirectly, to the internet and give all of those devices the ability to work much more rapidly. There will be no more latency, no more buffering, which will make possible more types of devices, including those that require reliable and instantaneous connectivity to the Internet of Things, such as autonomous vehicles.

For autonomous vehicles, otherwise known as driverless cars, to achieve their full potential, multiple sensors and devices on each vehicle will have to communicate instantly with nearby vehicles, sensors in the road, street signs, and traffic lights. To do all of that, the vehicles will need 5G communications, fast, unbuffered, and able to handle many devices in a small space. So, 5G is coming, fast, and so is a world of billions of devices talking to one another.

The 5G Security Debates

If you have already heard about 5G in the media, it has probably been in the context of a debate about security. The U.S. government somewhat belatedly noticed that a lot of new 5G equipment was going to be installed around the United States and the world and that the company most likely to be making the equipment was called Huawei. The Pentagon and the National Security Agency have never trusted that Chinese internet electronics company, thinking that its products might be laced with Chinese government backdoors and bugs. Huawei and its lawyers and lobbyists have vehemently denied the allegations.

Huawei has evolved from a maker of lower-quality knockoffs of U.S. technology (it originally made internet routers that looked identical to those made by the U.S. giant Cisco). It now has its own designs, which are high-quality products, and it sells them at a fraction of the price of U.S. and European competitors. In most of the world, earlier-generation U.S.-made internet routers have been replaced by Huawei's. That is not generally the case in the United States, where government pressure has kept large telecom companies buying from the more expensive U.S. or European vendors.

Before senior levels of the U.S. government seemed to notice, Huawei was wrapping up contracts to install 5G technology around the world. Alarmed, one Trump White House staffer, a U.S. Air Force general, publicly suggested that the U.S. government should operate the coming 5G network in America. The criticisms from the telephony carriers and Congress were instant and intense. The general was quickly off the White House staff, but the fear of Huawei owning the global 5G infrastructure grew. By 2019, the issue had become of such importance to the Trump administration that Secretary of State Mike Pompeo was flying around the world pressuring potential Huawei buyers, with mixed results. Some of America's close allies began announcing that they would ban Huawei from competing for the 5G build-out, but most of the world was still ordering from the Chinese.

All of this controversy may, however, be the wrong 5G security debate, or at least there may be a second 5G security issue that is equally important, but is not much discussed. That issue is about whether there should be security requirements for the 5G network, what they should be, and who should set them. This concern is not that companies, in addition to Huawei, may install backdoors and bugs. The fear is that hackers could.

The professional staff at the Federal Communications Commission was so concerned about the possibility of 5G being susceptible to hacking that they publicly published 132 questions to the communications industry about 5G security. They asked all about 5G security and authentication, encryption, physical security, DDoS attacks, patch management, and risk segmentation. Then they got to 5G and the Internet of Things.

The FCC professionals began by noting the obvious: "It is widely expected that 5G networks will be used to connect the myriad devices, sensors and other elements that will form the Internet of Things (IoT). The anticipated diversity and complexity of these networks, how they interconnect, and the sheer number of discrete elements they will comprise raise concerns about the effective management of cyber threats."

They went on to note that "some IoT devices will have limited security features." No kidding? "Could this have a negative effect on overall 5G network security?" Duh. "Are any lessons being learned from the October 2016 DDoS attacks?" You bet there are, and they are scary, as we will discuss in a minute.

Why did the professional staff experts at the FCC have to ask these questions publicly? They did so because the FCC commissioners, the people who decide on regulation, refuse to regulate the internet. The Republican appointees, encouraged by internet companies, have argued that they just can't regulate the internet even if it might need it, and can't regulate 5G security, because the law does not give them that authority. Nonsense.

Moreover, if the existing laws actually did not give the FCC the authority to regulate the internet, the FCC commissioners could ask the Congress for that power. They have not. Indeed, they have argued that it would stifle innovation and do any number of horrific things if anyone ever regulated anything related to the internet. So, here come 5G and the Internet of Things without any security regulations. Get ready. Strap in.

IoT: Down on the Farm

Even before autonomous vehicles begin running around on your street, they are driving about on some farms. Our favorite story about the IoT, one that demonstrates how it is creeping into every walk of life and simultaneously opening up vulnerabilities to global hackers, comes from down on the farm. If you have opened up your internal combustion engine car's hood lately to attempt do-it-yourself maintenance on the engine, you have been met with a sealed box that is relatively impervious to any owner's attempts to manipulate it. Well, it turns out the same is true on newer tractors, such as those from that staple of Americana, John Deere.

Newer tractors also come with satellite or wi-fi links, giving the driver precise location data and allowing for automated driving, fertilizing, and plowing. The link also allows data to flow back to John Deere, so the mothership will know when one of its green machines is about to break down in some way. It sounded like a good idea.

What apparently happened, however, was that many small problems with the tractor had to be addressed by a John Deere dealer's mobile repair team. Owners were left with their expensive, high-tech tractors sitting helplessly in fields waiting for the maintenance guys with the digital keys that opened up the engine and the digital diagnostic equipment that could be plugged into the vehicle. Of course, it cost money just to have the mobile repair truck show up and more if the problem needed any serious work. This is the part of the story where the Iowa farmer meets the Russian-speaking cyber criminal and the local problem goes global.

Somehow, no one is too sure how, irate farmers learned that hackers in Ukraine could help them "jailbreak" their tractors, meaning allow them to get around the factory-installed systems to prevent owners from getting at the innards, figuring out what the problem is, and repairing things themselves. For a small fee paid to a website in Ukraine, farmers were able to download a software tool to hack their own tractors. Wyatt, meet Ivan, and welcome to the global village, in which there are IoT devices arriving everywhere and hackers right behind them.

You Say IT and I Say OT, SCADA, Potato . . .

Part of the problem with understanding the IoT problem, what it is, and how to fix it is the terminology. As is often the case in technology, there are a lot of terms thrown around without precision or commonly accepted and widely understood definitions. In the case of IoT, there are a few adjacent technologies and terms that often get confused with it. They include:

IT and OT: Information technology and operations technology. The former is basically the internet and computer networks and devices designed to work using them. The latter is the world of industrial machine controls that preceded the internet and generally use an entirely different kind of software.

ICS and SCADA: These two types of software generally belong to the OT world. The former are industrial control systems, software from companies such as Siemens, Johnson Controls, and General Electric. ICS software runs factories and the machines in them. SCADA software can be thought of as a subset of programs that engage in supervisory controls and data acquisition. SCADA software often runs on little sensors that report data such as temperatures or voltages or pressure levels. Based on that data, some controls react automatically to avoid overloads and, uh, explosions.

The acronym SCADA is often used to describe the software that runs the power grid. It is also used to describe the controlling software on other networks such as railroad lines, pipelines, and petrochemical facilities.

The Stuxnet software attack on the Iranian nuclear centrifuges was an attack on an OT or ICS software created by Siemens. The attack's purpose was to make the controlling software cause devices to do irreparable self-harm. It worked for a while, reportedly destroying eight hundred centrifuges. In that case, the devices might not technically have been IoT because, as a defensive tactic, the Iranians had made sure that the plant was not in any way connected to the internet. The lesson to remember from that incident is that even when you think a device is not connected to the internet, it can be hit with a cyberattack.

Gimme That OT Religion

It may have been Stuxnet that gave religion to the OT and ICS world. For years the experts and operators who developed and wrote OT software wanted to have nothing to do with the internet and its inherent cyber threats. They were adamant that the threats and malicious actors in cyberspace could not get to them, and if they did, they would not be able to harm them. All of that has changed. John Livingston watched it change.

Livingston was a partner at the consulting firm McKinsey. After running the consultancy's offices in Singapore and South Africa, he took control in Chicago and ran the wireless and telecoms practice. John noticed the beginnings of the IoT and, upon deeper diligence, he noticed a resistance to putting sensors and analytics on industrial systems. "I can't put sensors on," he quoted clients as telling him, "because of cybersecurity." Industrial clients wanted to put sensors on networks, but knew that making that connection without being able to secure it was a recipe for disaster. So Livingston looked around and found a company called RK Neal in Kentucky. They were a small industrial-controls firm that had been making headway selling security software to electric power companies.

Planning to expand the firm's focus beyond the power companies, John quit McKinsey and signed on as CEO of a renamed company, now called Verve. The electric power industry's self-regulating body, NERC, had created cybersecurity standards for some parts of the power grid, and Verve had a software package that met the NERC compliance requirements. They knew the power grid and its vulnerabilities well. "But if you really want to shut off electric power, that's not who you attack," Livingston told us. "You

attack the gas pipelines. They are way less protected than the power grid."
So many power plants have shifted from coal to natural gas that if you cut
off the natural gas feed, you shut out the lights. The natural gas system is
"far more distributed with its compression stations, gasification, satellite
comms to wireless modems to PLCs." And how well secured are all those
devices? we asked. "Security just doesn't exist. They may have a password,
but that's it." What could possibly go wrong? Recall from chapter 10 that the
U.S. intelligence community's threat assessment of January 2019 said that
the Chinese government has the ability to disrupt the U.S. natural gas pipeline system.

Ten months before that public assessment, in March 2018, the gas industry had a wake-up call. The call came to Energy Services Group, not
exactly a household name. Yet, as is the case in so many of the industries that
we have examined, ESG is that company you never heard of that turns out to
be a crucial vendor to most of the big-name companies in the sector. When
ESG got hacked, things started to go wrong at the big gas pipeline companies
such as Duke Energy, Boardwalk Pipelines, and Energy Transfer Partners.
ESG provided the network they all used for buying and selling gas, billing
customers, and other essential activities. The pipeline companies disconnected from ESG to prevent the hack from spreading to their controls, an
admission that an internet-based attack could migrate into the controls for
the nation's pipelines.

A few months later, the city of Lawrence, Massachusetts, and the nearby
towns of North Andover and Andover, an hour northwest of Boston, went
up in flames. Almost simultaneously, hundreds of calls lit up the 911 emergency call centers. Houses were spontaneously combusting, everywhere. In
minutes the three fire departments had more houses burning down than
they had fire trucks. They called for help from cities and towns all over
eastern Massachusetts. Fire trucks raced up Interstate 495 in convoys es-
corted by the state police.

What they found looked like the area had been firebombed. There were
more than seventy structures, at as many locations, enveloped in flame,
their roofs blown off, walls collapsed. There had not just been fires. There
had first been explosions. Suspicion quickly focused on the natural gas sys-

tems in the homes and on the local provider, Columbia Gas. Police and fire personnel, fearful that there would be more explosions, ordered everyone out of all homes connected to Columbia Gas. Thousands of people had to find someplace else to spend the night as first responders inspected and cleared hundreds of homes. It would be many weeks, well into a chilly New England autumn, before most of the homes had heat again.

Among the hundreds of emergency responders who headed to Lawrence that September night in 2018 were the members of the go-team from the National Transportation Safety Board (NTSB). Famous for investigating airplane crashes around the world, and the far more frequent train derailments in the United States, the NTSB also has jurisdiction over pipelines. Their conclusion was that a contractor working for Columbia had created an overpressure situation, putting vastly too much gas into the system. No one thought that it was a hack, just a stupid mistake. In the OT and SCADA world, however, there were whispers. This time it wasn't a hack, but what would stop some bad guy from doing that intentionally and having the same result? Not much.

John Livingston was more discreet with us in describing the attitude of the gas industry. "The leadership is aware," he said cautiously, "but you have to convince the CEO and CFO or the board or nothing happens."

When it does happen, "it's eighteen to twenty-four months from getting religion to deploying solutions." That is if it is a straightforward deployment of security controls. "If the industrial control system ties in to the enterprise network," he said, referring to a company's internet-connected administrative computer systems, "it's a huge undertaking to fix it."

When Livingston's Verve team deploys to a firm, the first task they get asked to do is asset management. "Most people have no idea what they have" on their OT networks. It's hard to secure devices if you don't know you have them.

We don't mean to pick on the natural gas industry (okay, actually we do), but it is a good example of the old industries that have been running OT software on old metal devices for years and are now connecting their OT and IT networks. It turns out that letting OT and IT touch is like putting matter and antimatter together. It allows hackers to do things like they tried at a Saudi petrochemical facility, as John Livingston described it, "trying to kill people."

What's New? Ubiquitous Sensors— and They're Connected

If the world of old OT sensors and switches is not enough of a problem, what's new is the introduction and rapid growth of sensors that are intentionally designed to be connected to the internet. Your next refrigerator may be part of this trend. If so, welcome to the Internet of Things.

One fact we know about these IoT devices is that they seem to be multiplying rapidly. Gartner, the IT consultancy known for coming up with educated guesses that become generally accepted facts, estimated there were 8.4 billion IoT devices in 2017. That was a 31 percent increase over their estimate the prior year. Now their 2020 guess is 20.4 billion devices. In other words, a few years ago there was about one such device for every human being on Earth and in a few years there will be three such devices per human. If humans multiplied at that rate, the planet's ecosystem would quickly collapse. There is concern that the IoT devices, if manipulated malevolently, could produce a similar effect on networks.

What kind of device qualifies as part of the IoT? Any electronic device that has some sort of computer chip or computing ability and is connected to a network that is in turn connected to the internet is part of the IoT. The places they are used vary enormously and include heart pacemakers, self-driving cars, safety monitors on refineries and chemical plants, surveillance cameras, subway cars and airport trams, drones, switches on electric power substations, robotic welders on assembly lines, sensors in Coke vending machines, office building HVAC sensors and controls, self-diagnostic elevators, and on and on.

IoT devices are often basically just sensors with diagnostics that trigger software to do things like brake the car or train, order a human to come and refill the Coke machine, call a human to do preventive maintenance on a jet engine or an elevator, or give the human's heart a jolt. These devices often have very little software, storage space, or computing ability on them. Nonetheless, these IoT devices save a vast amount of money for the owners and operators of factories, office buildings, and grids of various kinds. What is not to like? We could start with: most of them are not secure, and many of them never can be.

What Harm Could a Little IoT Widget Do?

So what? Let's come back to the Saudi plant John Livingston mentioned. Sometime in 2018 a malicious actor hacked into the safety-monitoring system in a petrochemical plant in Saudi Arabia and shut off the IoT systems that were there to detect when pipes and vats are about to explode from overpressure or other errors. "The only thing that prevented an explosion was a mistake in the attackers' code," experts concluded after the fact. If there are IoT devices designed to detect impending explosions and shut things off, then hacking those devices is necessary if you want to create an explosion. It turned out that hacking those IoT devices in the Saudi facility was easy because, wait for it, they allegedly had no security designed in.

That is the problem with many IoT devices. You can get to them over the internet and you can shut them off, or in some cases turn them on even when you are not authorized to do so. Former Vice President Dick Cheney famously wanted his pacemaker or in-chest defibrillator modified so that it could not be activated remotely from the internet. In this case, Cheney's paranoia was justified. There have been studies that indicated potential problems with such devices. In 2017, the Food and Drug Administration, which regulates healthcare-related products, ordered Abbott Laboratories–St. Jude Medical to fix its pacemakers and implanted defibrillators because of "third-party control risk" of initiating shock or draining batteries.

Indeed the FDA is considering regulations that will require all medical devices to be "patchable," meaning that their software can be updated and repaired when necessary. They are also considering requiring a "bill of materials" for every device, listing the software and hardware involved and their provenance. (Does that IV drip device have some open-source software in it that might mean it is hackable?) For the FDA, this proactive attitude is a big turnaround, because for years they would not allow medical devices to accept security patches without prolonged, elaborate, and expensive testing. As a result, many medical devices were running ancient versions of Microsoft Windows software replete with known vulnerabilities. Many still are.

Other Bad Ways to Use the IoT

Because IoT devices have very little software on them and often have bespoke computer chips, there is seldom enough room on them to add security software such as identity and access management or endpoint protection. Thus, if you can maneuver your way on a network to get to the device (or if you just walk up to it in the real world), you can often give it a command and it will comply. The device usually has no way of knowing whether the command is authentic and comes from the network operations center of the company or whether it's malicious and from some GRU guy in Sverdlovsk.

The innocent, defenseless, not too bright IoT device can be used in interesting ways by hackers. First, the IoT device can be used as an access port into the corporate network. Walk up to the device, hook up your laptop or attach your thumb drive, and you might be able to run a hack into the company.

Second, you could use the IoT device to run a flood attack, or DDoS, pinging a website so often that no other traffic can get through. The target could be anywhere, or it could be on the same network as the device. The most famous instance of this kind of attack so far happened in October 2016 and involved baby monitors, a Latin American embassy in London, hundreds of major U.S. corporations (Amazon, PayPal, and Twitter among them), and a little-known company in an office park in New Hampshire.

Dyn, the company in New Hampshire, provides internet look-up and routing information (DNS) for a lot of big companies. It is another one of those companies, like ESG is to natural gas, that exist in every sector that no one has ever heard about but is actually essential (and could become an Achilles' heel) for well-known giants. Beginning at 7:00 A.M. on October 21, 2016, Dyn's servers were flooded by millions of pings, making it difficult for their customers to access the crucial Dyn DNS servers. The effect was to disrupt internet connectivity across North America.

The pings came from hundreds of thousands of IoT devices, including nanny cams, more sophisticated surveillance and security cameras, and a host of other devices. All of those devices had been affected by a malicious bot, a piece of software that guided itself around the world looking for unprotected IoT devices to infect and take over. The bot was given a name by the cybersecurity world. They called it Mirai.

Suspicions about who launched Mirai fell on the supporters in North America of the hacker Julian Assange, who has been linked to Russian intelligence and the hacking of the U.S. 2016 election. Word had been spreading that the United States was putting pressure on Ecuador to throw Assange out of their embassy in London, where he had taken refuge after arrest warrants were issued for him. Assange's organization eventually publicly called on his supporters to "stop taking down the U.S. internet. You proved your point." Apparently the hackers thought that if they disrupted the U.S. internet, the American government would relent in its efforts to arrest their hero. (Fourteen months later three men were indicted in the United States for cybercrimes using the Mirai botnet.)

What the Stuxnet attack, the hack of the Saudi petrochemical facility, and many other incidents demonstrate is that what sensors think is happening may not always be accurate and what control boards show is the condition may not always reflect reality. When simple artificial intelligence applications are given too much autonomy to act with too little verification of the readings they are employing, bad things can happen on the Internet of Things. They can happen without malicious activity, as may have been the case in the crashes of the 737 Max aircrafts (where a bad sensor reading may have caused an AI program to take control of the aircraft without telling the pilot), or they can be the result of hacking, as in the case of the two Ukrainian electrical power grid blackouts (where the control boards were hacked to indicate all was well, even after the GRU hackers had thrown the breakers on transformers all across the region).

You can: 1) seize control of unprotected IoT devices and use them to do damage (let gas pressure build up); 2) use the device to attack the network it's on; 3) use the device to launch attacks elsewhere; 4) store illicit data on the device (child pornography, stolen secrets, attack tools); or 5) employ any excess computing power on the device for purposes like Bitcoin mining.

Securing a Moving Train

If ever there were a case of painting a moving train, securing the IoT is one. The deployment of billions of devices is well under way and may be accelerating. Getting all of those devices to be secure will be impossible. As Lenin once asked, "What is to be done?" We suggest steps that would likely work only if they are part of a high-level government campaign to educate corporate leaders, device designers, and government regulators.

First, corporations or other network owners should ban any new IoT device from being connected unless it has been demonstrably proven to be secure.

Second, corporate leaders should initiate an inventory of what IoT devices have already been linked to their networks and disable the internet connections. That includes printers, photocopiers, and other office equipment that "phones home" to its manufacturer or maintenance provider. It was the food freezers at Target connecting to the HVAC service company that caused the 2013 hack that ended up getting the CEO and CIO fired.

Third, government regulators should have prevented the deployment of internet-connected devices that were insecure. They did not. Now, they must insist that no new IoT device be permitted to operate in a regulated environment until a third-party security assessment has determined the device poses no threat. Then, they need to use their regulatory powers to require all existing devices be retrofitted with security or replaced by newly designed devices created from the ground up with security in mind. For example:

- The U.S. Department of Transportation has made noises about issuing regulations requiring such assurances for driverless cars. At the same time, however, that department is, without much thought to security, requiring train operators to install new IoT sensors that could literally stop trains in their tracks (so-called positive train control systems).
- The FDA has said that new devices should be patchable, but what about all the old ones that are out there? They should issue regulations

that require all IoT medical devices to be secured or replaced by a
certain date.

- Federal Aviation Administration regulations maintain a high standard
for physical security and reliability of aircraft parts, but less so for the
huge volume of data that is downloaded from every aircraft and every
engine after each flight. The FAA should set a minimum standard for
what flight data is downloaded, how it is analyzed, how long it is stored
in a data lake, and what sort of ongoing AI review of the accumulated
data is conducted to search for indications of compromise.

- The Federal Energy Regulatory Commission should require any existing diagnostic or reporting devices anywhere on the power grid or
pipelines to be physically and virtually walled off from the "control
plane" of the grid and placed on a separate network. Physical and software firewalls can be placed between the IoT devices and the controls.
Physical diodes, devices that restrict data flows to one direction, can be
required. Future devices should not be allowed to connect to the network unless they have been certified as secure from malicious attack.

- Finally, government, academic, and industry experts should work
together to define new, more demanding security standards for IoT
devices and develop baseline procedures for continuous testing of those
devices. We suggest that standards include the device being able to
handle multifactor authentication, so that only authorized users can tell
it what to do. We would add having an endpoint agent on the device to
monitor for and prevent suspicious activity.

Until then, just be aware that a guy in Kiev can maybe kill your tractor,
a gal in Beijing can possibly see you on your camera and listen to you on
your personal device, while the folks in Moscow can probably blow up your
gas pipeline or set your house on fire. As the intrepid cable news reporters
always ask the disaster victims, "How does that make you feel?"

For now we have to accept that what cybersecurity people call the "attack surface" (the target deck that can be hacked) is growing enormously.
The opportunities for the offense are growing, again. The problem for the

defense is being made more difficult by the combination of insecure 5G and insecure IoT. For all the progress we are making in securing corporate and government networks, for all the promise of AI and quantum, the problem keeps expanding because neither government nor the IT industry will wait for a new technology to be secure before they deploy it.

:::::::::::::::::: **PART VI** ::::::::::::::::::

YOU AND THE WAY AHEAD

Chapter 18

•••••••••••

DERISKING OURSELVES

Personal Cybersecurity

> Passwords are like underwear. Don't let people see them, change
> them often, and don't share them with anyone.
>
> —ANONYMOUS

Thank you for your thoughts on defending the Pentagon in a cyber
war, but what about me?" the young woman in the audience asked us.
"How do I defend me?" At every lecture, every book signing, every
extended family dinner gathering, someone will ask that practical question.
Now that we've dealt with what corporations, governments, and the military
should do, let's talk about what you should be doing to protect yourself.

What Do You Value?

Just as we do when we are consulting for big corporations, we begin by asking you the question we ask the CEOs: What is important to you? The answer is not always obvious. You may think that your so-called personally
identifiable information (PII) is important. You wouldn't want strangers
to know your Social Security number, birth date, or telephone number. In

truth, they already do. Everybody's Social Security number has already been compromised. That's why we don't think any organization should use that number as a means to authenticate you. Even Medicare agrees. They just recently transitioned from using Social Security numbers for identifying patients.

PII has been stolen so many times now that the acceptance rate on the free credit-score monitoring service that you get offered after a data breach is around 15 percent. That means about 85 percent of people who have been told that their PII has been compromised do nothing. That is probably the appropriate response. Nonetheless, if you fear that someone is going to use your PII to take out a loan or get a credit card in your name, then you can go online to each of the major credit scoring agencies (including the notorious Equifax, which suffered a PII data breach of epic proportions in 2017) and "lock" your credit reporting. That way no one can access your score to process a loan without offering additional proof that they are, in fact, you.

So, if it's not your PII that you should worry about, what is it? Maybe it should be your passwords.

Most people now have dozens of online accounts: airlines, banks, email, insurance, social media, the DMV, etc. Keep a list of these accounts. Every time you have to use a password, add it to that list. In a month, we bet you'll be shocked at the number of accounts you have, and we also bet that most of your account credentials will be the same, or minor variations on a theme like your birthday or a loved one's birthday. In that case, you have a problem. If one website or app that you use gets hacked, and one will, the hacker will know your username (or email address) and password for that website. They will then use that username and password combination on a variety of large banking websites such as Bank of America, Wells Fargo, or Citibank. They will keep trying banks until they find yours. *Do not use the same password on more than one site.*

If your password is "password" or "123456" or some other brain-dead idea, you might as well stand on the corner and just pass out your money to the homeless. You would at least be doing some good in the process.

If your password is composed of six or fewer letters and/or numbers, it's also really easy for hackers to crack it using "brute-force" software. As its name would suggest, the brute-force method simply tries every combination of letters, numbers, and symbols until it gets the right combination, at a rate of millions of guesses per second. To confound such brute-force tools, longer passwords are better. You want a password of at least eight characters in length, but more is better. We like ten-character passwords that use a combination of lower- and uppercase letters, numbers, and those little symbols on the keyboard such as #, ^, *, and +. For an eight-character password that uses all of these different character types, there are 645,753,531,245,761 possible combinations. That's a lot of passwords for a hacker to guess.

You are thinking that you will not be able to remember all those different long, complex passwords. Of course you won't, unless you have some freakish photographic memory. You may think about writing them down on a yellow sticky and putting them under the mousepad by your computer. That's where we always look for them when we are at a new client site. Usually, we only have to visit a dozen cubicles before we find a password under a mousepad or in a desk drawer. Even at home, it's not a good idea to write them down on a piece of paper. You just never know who might find themselves looking through your desk.

Instead, we suggest you use a password manager. Apple has one built in to Macs and iPhones. Or you can pay a small fee and subscribe to one such as LastPass, Dashlane, or Zoho. Then you only have to remember the password you use for that service. It will remember the other twenty or thirty you use. Better yet, it will create long, complex, and unique passwords for each different account that you have. When you log in to a site with your phone or laptop, the password manager will automatically enter your password. These services synchronize on all of your devices, no matter how many laptops, desktops, or mobile phones you use.

To be doubly safe, use a password *and* something else, an additional factor. Lots of services now allow you to use two-factor authentication to access your account. This is true on Facebook, iTunes, Office 365, and most financial institutions. Usually, the second factor is a number that the website will send as a text message to your phone. You can also buy a USB thumb drive or other such device that you need to use in addition to your password to authenticate yourself. The problem with such a device is that, if you are like Rob Knake, you will immediately lose it and then you are really in trouble because you are locked out for good. While these solutions aren't airtight, they are probably better than the protection you have now.

Banks, Stocks, and Credit Cards

Everybody's credit-card account information gets stolen. It wasn't your fault. You didn't do anything wrong. *They* did, the people who run the brick-and-mortar store, the online store, the restaurant, or the hotel. There was a plague at gas stations and restaurants where hackers had emplaced physical scanners inside the credit-card readers, so that as the card reader was reading your card, they were too (newer cards with chips make this kind of attack harder to do). Many establishments, even if they are high-end ones, can offer poor cybersecurity.

Yes, it's inconvenient when you have to go to all of your service providers that deduct automatically from your credit card every month and tell them the new credit-card number. It is worth it to keep a list of all of those services, so when this happens to you (and it will), you can just sit down once for an hour or so and update all of the accounts.

Almost always the bank behind your credit card will make good. They will not charge you for the new TV that somebody bought at Walmart in Daytona Beach with your credit card. For unauthorized credit-card charges, you're only liable for up to fifty dollars of the losses. Credit-card fraud is now just considered a cost of doing business to your bank, but don't worry, they have already priced in their anticipated losses and they are still making a lot of money off of you.

When credit-card fraud started to get out of control years ago, banks all bought artificial-intelligence software that makes quick decisions in the background to determine whether or not it actually is you buying a TV at that Walmart in Florida. Fraudulent debit-card charges are a different story. You're liable for up to fifty dollars of the losses if you report the fraud within two (business) days, up to five hundred dollars if you report it more than two days after the theft, and up to the full amount of the fraudulent charge if you take more than sixty days to report it.

The banks' protections can be a pain when the AI gets it wrong. What if you do actually show up at that Florida Walmart and your card is declined at the checkout? Fortunately, most banks will allow you to talk to a human in advance of your traveling to someplace unusual (Really, you're actually going to Chad?) or before you buy a big-ticket item (Your first cruise in the Caribbean and you're spending ten grand?). You can often get the bank to agree not to process a charge outside of the country or over a certain dollar amount without you calling them in advance and giving them authorization, using a PIN or other proof.

The two best techniques to use if you are worried about someone getting your card information are: 1) only use a credit card, not a debit card, and 2) have a low spending limit on the credit line associated with the card, say, a thousand dollars a month (or more depending upon how profligate you want to be).

For all online banking and stock transactions, be sure that your financial institution will let you use two-factor authentication, as we discussed before. For transactions above a certain dollar value, ask them to have a human call you and ask you several security questions. Remember when you do set up security questions that the right answer is whatever you want it to be. If the question is "In what city were you born?" do not use the actual city where your mother gave birth to you. That is usually a matter of public record. Where were you born? Mos Eisley from *Star Wars*. What is your favorite sports team? Well, if everybody knows you are from Boston, do not answer that question with "The Red Sox." Try some nonexistent franchise like the Montreal Mavericks. Just remember your answer or put the answer in the notes section of your password manager.

Deception can often be helpful in security. You may want to actually spread false information about yourself. Create a fake birthday for your social media accounts. You don't have to tell a social media company what your birthday is, but go ahead and give them one anyway. Let all the world see it. Make sure it's fictional. The only downside is when all of your Facebook friends send you happy birthday messages in the wrong month, but when that happens, revel in your deception. It's working.

Security Settings

You can probably make your laptop or other device more secure than it is now. Your operating system is almost always in need of a security update. That is particularly true if you are running some old version, such as Windows 98, Windows XP, or Windows Vista. Get rid of them now. They cannot be fixed. Buy Windows 10. If you use a Mac, get the latest OS by clicking on the apple in the upper left, then About This Mac, then Software Update. It's free.

Turn on automatic software updates so you do not have to decide to do it every time. The same is true of your web browser. Chrome is the best web browser choice. Similarly, get rid of software with bad reputations for security, like Adobe Flash.

Should you use antivirus software? Yes. Download Sophos, McAfee, or Symantec. Whatever you use, turn on automatic updates. Even these antivirus companies can fail to protect you in time when a new virus enters the wild, so how do you avoid being infected to begin with? Email is one of the most common ways that computers become infected. You may receive phishing, or the more targeted spear-phishing, emails that attempt to trick you into thinking that they're from a legitimate source. Fraudsters will send out phishing emails to thousands (or even millions) of users at once, but increasingly we are seeing crafted phishing emails that are intended for a specific person. Phishing attempts may be fake password-reset emails "from" Microsoft, Google, Apple, or Facebook telling you that you need to log in to receive a message or that you need to open an attachment. Some of these emails are so expertly crafted that they are nearly indistinguishable from a genuine email from the company or person in question.

No matter how innocent or authentic an email appears, *do not* click any link or open any attachment contained within it without first checking the sender's email address, or hovering over the link with your mouse to make sure that it really does go to the website it claims to go to. If the email is not legitimate, just delete it. You can lose everything on your device by slipping up just once. (Remember the gullible employee, Dave, from chapter 4? Don't be Dave.)

When your device becomes compromised, the attacker can use your computer's power to participate in a flood attack on another network, or secretly steal your computational power to mine cryptocurrencies like Bitcoin. So, while they are not stealing data, files, or money from you, they are nonetheless hurting somebody somewhere with your computer. Without your knowing it, your machine is being used to do bad things.

Every Move You Make, Every Step You Take

It may or may not be a security risk, but it is more than a little creepy to think that somebody is watching you. Who wants a GRU officer in wintry Tula, during a boring shift posting Green Party propaganda on Facebook, amusing himself by seeing what's going on in your house?

You have cameras on your mobile device. You more than likely have a camera on your laptop, desktop, or both. Millions of Americans have installed security cameras inside their homes to keep an eye on hired help or pets. Many of these cameras now come with built-in microphones and speakers, so you can yell at the local youth to get off your lawn, or listen to hear your baby crying. Webcams and security cameras are notoriously insecure systems, so it is not difficult for hackers to gain access to those cameras and their microphones to watch and listen to you. It is even possible for these cameras to appear to be "off" when they really aren't.

There are countless cases of these devices being compromised. Some of this is due to poor engineering or software development on the part of the camera's manufacturer, which is by extension just a by-product of the low standards for cybersecurity in the Internet of Things world.

We do not know of a good way to be highly confident that your security cameras are secure, but if you're able to access them via a web browser without entering any username or password, you can probably assume that if somebody really had a reason for wanting to watch what your cameras are picking up, they could probably do so with very little work. If your cameras do use authentication, use the aforementioned best practices for choosing a password.

So, what can you do about this? To begin with, tape over the camera (or use a Post-it note) on your laptop or desktop until you want to use it for FaceTime or Skype, or use a sliding webcam cover, which can be found with ease on the internet (and is now ubiquitous in the cybersecurity world). Again, there is little probability that someone is sitting around watching what goes on in your household all day, but if you're worried regardless, turn the interior cameras off when you get home. Turn the computer off when you are not using it. If you are *really* paranoid and you have a device with a removable battery, take it out when you are not going to use it for a while.

On your mobile device, go into the controls or settings and find the part where you can decide which applications can use a cellular connection. It is there that you can also see which applications have decided that they should have access to your camera or microphone. Set them all to off. Instagram does not need access to your microphone all the time. No app does. Sure, some applications genuinely need access to these things, but you can always reinstate access when the app prompts you next time.

In fact, be aware of where you leave your mobile device when you are having private conversations or activities. You might want to put it in another room if you are worried about someone listening, which is especially true when you're traveling internationally. Some governments around the world have wide-reaching surveillance powers and would not hesitate to start spying on you through your smartphone the moment you step into the country. This is why many individuals in the cybersecurity community have cheap travel laptops that they use exclusively when they are out of the country.

What about Alexa, Siri, and friends? While their manufacturers give assurance after assurance that they are not recording all of your conversations or sending your data back to the mothership, it seems to be within the realm of possibility that someone could hack them to do just that. If you are paranoid, these household-assistant devices are really not a problem. No paranoid person would ever use one.

Back It Up

As someone who has had his White House emails paraded on national television, Dick Clarke is a little more careful than most people about what he writes, but anyone can slip up. There is also the potential for someone else's computer, with your email correspondence on it, being hacked. Yes, we have had that happen too.

As a general rule, if you do not want your comments ever to appear in the newspaper, a court case, or in a heated bedtime conversation with your partner, don't write them. If you have to write it, use Signal, Wickr, or some other encrypted messaging app. If you do elect to use one of these secure messaging apps, set it up so that it erases the messages after some short period of time. Otherwise, they can be read by anyone who unlocks your phone or the recipient's.

Why do you have five years' worth of emails on your iPhone and laptop anyway? Erase them, and just keep a couple months' worth of emails at a time. Oh, you're a digital pack rat and think that you may need to refer to them someday, or that your biographer will really enjoy using them for that great book about you? Well, if you insist on saving those *bon mots* for posterity, transfer them to a separate hard drive or thumb drive and erase them from your devices.

In fact, when you get that external hard drive, back up everything on your computer: emails, documents, and, most importantly, pictures. No one has hard copy pictures anymore, so when you lose your digital pictures, they may be lost forever. Back up everything at least once a month, as if you are paying your monthly bills, but make sure that you keep your external hard drive disconnected when it is not being used. If your backup is always connected, it can be hacked just as easily as your computer. If you are hit by a ransomware or wiperware attack, your backup might be as well. So keep it disconnected until your daily, weekly, or monthly session of backing up everything.

Yes, you can back up everything to the cloud, and more and more people are doing so. However, bear in mind that you are then at the mercy of the cloud provider's security and authentication practices, as well as the strength of your password. If you set it up properly and use a cloud service provider with a good track record of security, you will probably be okay, but there are inherent risks.

Overall, we think the best policy is to keep as few files as possible on your devices. Put everything in an external hard drive and a secure cloud drive, or, for the particularly paranoid, on a laptop that is never used to connect to the internet.

Losing Your Device

It is a real insight into how dependent we have all become on our mobile devices that, when we lose one, we feel powerless, and at our wits' end. There are some simple steps to ease the pain of the loss, but you have to take them in advance, as in right now.

First, use whole-disk encryption so that no one can open your device without a lengthy password or biometric authentication.

Second, as we said before, have everything backed up so you can quickly restore all of your data on your replacement device when you buy a new one.

Third, most devices now allow you to turn on a GPS tracker in advance so that you will know where the device is.

Fourth, configure your settings so that you can remotely wipe the device of all its data. For iPhone users, you can set this up so that you have to perform the wipe manually (though it will have to connect to the internet to receive the command), or so that the device wipes itself after a number of failed unlock attempts.

It can at times be prudent to give a very close friend access to some of your accounts. You can configure your cloud backups so that a friend can access them in the event that you are incapacitated. You can choose "trusted contacts" on Facebook that will receive security codes to help you recover access to your account in the event that you have forgotten your password. Some people are now attaching their various accounts' passwords to their last will, especially their investment or banking accounts. Morbid, we know, but you might want to make things easier for those who have to deal with that situation, whether sudden or expected. If you don't want to think about when you become "The Departed," then think what will happen when you have to access your parents' or partner's accounts after their demise. Have that talk now. Digital assets are sometimes as important as your physical assets, if not more so.

We know that all of this may have sent some of you running to find your computers so you can throw them out of the house (by the way, remove the hard drives first and physically destroy them), but that is not really necessary. For most people, the worst thing that happens when they are hacked is that they have to get new credit cards and tell all of their service providers the new card numbers. The bottom line is don't be so concerned about personal cyber risks that you fail to enjoy all the many wonderful things that the internet provides modern society just because there are threats lurking in the shadows.

Chapter 19

∎∎∎∎∎∎∎∎∎∎∎∎∎

EVERYTHING DONE
BUT THE CODING

The best time to plant a tree is twenty years ago. The second-best
time is now.

—FAKE CHINESE PROVERB

I n 2011, the Obama administration released its International Strategy for
Cyberspace. It was a solid document that built on work done in academia
and the think-tank community as well as by a group of experts from like-
minded countries that had been meeting to hash out how to handle conflict
in cyberspace for years. When four longtime experts in the field (Matt Devost, Jeff Moss, Neal Pollard, and Robert Stratton) looked at it, they came
to a simple conclusion: everything was done but "the coding." They wrote a
paper laying out their argument in "All Done Except the Coding: Implementing the International Strategy for Cyberspace." In essence, the strategy
was right. Now came the hard part of implementing it. They noted that the
document "rightfully commented on the need for innovative incentives for
the private sector to fulfill national security goals," but "the challenge, of
course, is how to achieve this."

The challenge then is, of course, the same challenge we face today. We know what the strategy is. What we need to do now is work to implement it. All that is left is the coding. That, unfortunately, is the hard part. For twenty years we have had the right strategy, questioned it, and returned to it. Yet for twenty years we have failed to implement it while searching in vain for an alternate that would get us out of doing the hard work. It's as if, after coming up with nuclear deterrence strategy in the Cold War, we never got around to building the nuclear triad. We need to summon the resources and political will to overcome this failure now.

When we teach, we often admonish our students that coming up with policy is the easy part. Implementing it is the hard part. We wish we could say that we have done the hard work already, but the thinking comes easier than the doing. We wish that government and business had taken the threat more seriously in its nascence and we had a stronger base on which to build a resilient cyber future. Yet we remain optimistic that this nation and those of like minds around the world can solve these problems.

We began this book by recalling the extensive damage that malicious activity in cyberspace has already done, the increasing militarization of network attacks, and the potential for far more significant activity. We do not mean to needlessly scare anybody, but things could get worse and the instability in cyberspace could spill over from war in the fifth domain to more traditional forms of combat in the other four. Because of the dependence of our society and economy on networks, severely damaging activity in cyberspace could still fundamentally change our way of life for extended periods of postattack recovery. It does not have to be this way.

We can fix things. We can do so with existing technologies and even using basically the same resilience strategy that several U.S. administrations have espoused but not implemented. In this book we have reiterated and elaborated upon that basic strategy with some new specifics, none of which are revolutionary approaches. Instead, we have looked for incentives, disincentives, nudges, and shoves to make the basic strategy of resilience work. That is not to say that implementing the ideas will be simple, straightforward, or without cost.

The resilience strategy seeks a continuous process to reduce risks and vulnerabilities, while creating systems that limit potential damage. We can reduce the threat of cyber warfare from something threatening our way of life to something akin to a major hurricane, a storm that can cause a localized dislocation for a short period of time.

Throughout this book, we have come back many times to the theme of working to shift the advantage from the attacker to the defender. This effort should be the overall goal of our national policy, and that of like-minded countries and companies. Ultimately, what we want is to be able to ignore cyberattacks. Instead of escalating, we want to be able to slough them off and continue on with our business.

No matter how secure our systems become, the forces that propel people to attack them will never cease. A future in which systems are harder to compromise, where the likelihood of attacks failing is higher, and where there are consequences for getting caught may drive many would-be attackers out of the field. It's possible to envision a future in which finding a zero-day vulnerability would require millions of dollars' worth of effort and yield only thousands of dollars in return. There may come a time when even the best-financed criminal groups can hammer on companies all day every day for years on end without receiving a dollar in return. Even if we can achieve these outcomes, even if most cyber criminals give up the game and decide to do something useful with their technical skills, there will still be those who seek to do us harm in cyberspace.

Thus, we must recognize what everyone in the field intuits, that there is no ultimate state, no resting place, no landing spot on the Sea of Tranquillity in which we can plant a flag. We must continually adapt and improve capabilities for individual companies and for the ecosystem as a whole. The goal is to achieve a state of ongoing improvement, where systems are continually being made more secure and the work of attacking these systems is harder, takes longer, and comes with greater risk of failure and punishment.

Above all else, we believe that what is necessary is a shift in mind-set. We need to accept that achieving cyber resilience is not a vague "shared responsibility." Instead, it requires the government to put the onus on owners and operators of networks and systems to make those assets resilient. Government has its roles, but the primary responsibility lies with the private sector. We need to stop pretending that the offense has an insurmountable advantage and to recognize that simple shifts in thinking like the kill chain and advances in technology such as endpoint detection and cloud computing have started to level the playing field.

Securing our countries, our businesses, and ourselves in cyberspace is far from hopeless. We have the strategy. We have the tools. Now we just need to do the hard work. What is missing is national consensus, will, and priority-setting. We as a nation have choices when it comes to how we live in the age of cyberspace: significantly reducing risks now, muddling through, or dealing with this set of issues later at great cost. Avoiding a decision is, in itself, a decision, and a dangerous one.

Glossary

·········

Advanced Persistent Threat (APT): A term to describe the most capable offensive cyber actors, often nation-states, that are able to maintain long-term campaigns against even the most hardened targets.

Authentication: A procedure that verifies a user is who he or she claims to be.

Backdoor: A pathway to maintain access to a computer system or network whose existence is known only to a small number of individuals. A backdoor can be implanted in software intentionally by its developers for debugging purposes or under the compulsion of a government, or can be created by a threat actor that has successfully exploited a vulnerability in the system or software.

Border Gateway Protocol (BGP): An internet protocol that is used to make decisions regarding the routing of information among major ISPs (also called Tier 1 information service providers) such as Verizon, AT&T, China Telecom, British Telecom, Deutsche Telekom, and Japan Telecom. BGP tables posted by those providers list to which corporations and institutions they connect and for whom traffic should be routed to them. BGP is an insecure system subject to manipulation.

Botnet: A network of devices that have been co-opted by a malicious actor and can be used to execute large-scale operations in a coordinated fashion, such as distributed denial-of-service (DDoS) attacks. Devices that belong to a botnet generally "phone home" to a command-and-control server many times each day to receive instructions.

Chief Information Officer (CIO): The most senior information technology executive in an organization, a position that has become more and more commonplace since the 1980s. The CIO generally reports to the CEO, but may instead report to the COO.

Chief Information Security Officer (CISO): The most senior cybersecurity executive in an organization. The CISO should report to either the chief risk officer or CEO and is usually responsible for managing security technologies and ensuring compliance with the applicable cyber regulatory regimes.

Cloud: Computing infrastructure usually managed and maintained by a third party. Use of the cloud permits organizations to purchase only the data storage and computational power that they need at any given time. Cloud service providers exploit economies of scale to minimize the cost of their services, and use of the cloud also allows their customers to avoid expending capital on their own computing infrastructure.

Cyber Command: A unified military command within the U.S. Department of Defense tasked with managing and coordinating the U.S. military's offensive and defensive cyber operations. The U.S. Cyber Command was created in 2009 and consists of personnel from the Army, Navy, Air Force, and Marine Corps branches of the U.S. armed forces.

Cybersecurity and Infrastructure Security Agency (CISA): A unit in the U.S. Department of Homeland Security created in late 2018 out of the National Protection and Programs Directorate (NPPD) to assist the private sector and civilian U.S. government agencies with their cybersecurity. CISA also has some responsibility for the physical security of key infrastructure components unrelated to information technology.

Cyber War Risk Insurance Act (CWRIA): A proposal made in this book for a Cyber War Risk Insurance Act modeled along the lines of an existing government program to backstop commercial insurance in the event of a major terrorist attack.

Data Lake: A virtual repository in which current and perhaps past data is stored. The information contained within a data lake can be queried and is often useful for business intelligence or analytical purposes.

Defense Advanced Research Projects Agency (DARPA): A U.S. Defense Department office that funds university and laboratory investigations and experiments into new concepts, and known, inter alia, for funding the research that led to the creation of the internet.

Defense Industrial Base (DIB): Those privately owned and operated corporations that manufacture weapons and supporting systems utilized by the armed forces.

Direct-Recording Electronic (DRE): A term used to describe a class of electronic voting machines that do not create a paper trail to permit auditing of votes cast.

Distributed Denial-of-Service (DDoS) Attack: An offensive cyber operation in which a network is paralyzed by an inundation of requests by a large number of devices. DDoS attacks are generally executed by a botnet consisting of tens of thousands of machines, which allows threat actors to overwhelm websites or networks, making them unusable.

Domain Name System (DNS): A system underpinning the internet that converts domain names into numerical IP addresses needed for routing. DNS exists as a distributed directory, whereby low-level DNS servers contain only routing information for small organizations, and the highest-level DNS servers contain routing information for major websites, services, and top-level domains such as .com, .net, or .org.

D-Trip: Nickname of the Democratic Congressional Campaign Committee (DCCC), an organization of the Democratic Party devoted to the election of members to the lower house of the U.S. Congress.

Encryption: The scrambling of information so that it is unreadable to those who do not have the encryption key needed to unscramble it. Encrypting traffic prevents those who intercept it from being able to read it. Most encryption today is achieved by using public-key encryption, whose strength resides in the fact that one must determine the prime factors of a very large number in order to break the code. Even employing all computational resources on Earth, modern encryption now cannot be broken on a time scale meaningful to human life.

Endpoint: A device connected to a network, typically a desktop or laptop computer. Endpoint security software monitors activity of the device for unusual or prohibited activity. EDR software (endpoint detection and response) is typically an agent installed on the device.

Exploit: A method by which an actor can take advantage of a vulnerability in a piece of software, hardware, or a computing system. Exploits can take the form of a short script, intricately developed software, or a sequence of commands. They are generally used to gain unauthorized persistence on a network, or escalate administrative privileges for the threat actor to enable them to carry out espionage or other forms of cybercrime.

Financial Action Task Force (FATF): An international organization of nation-state governments created to combat international money laundering through the creation of banking and legal standards.

GRU: The Main Directorate of the General Staff of the Armed Forces of the Russian Federation. The GRU is a Russian military-intelligence and special-operations service, whose head reports to the Ministry of Defense. The GRU has been responsible for a number of high-profile cyber activities, most notably the hacking and disinformation campaign related to the 2016 U.S. presidential election.

Honeypots: Files on a network designed to attract hackers so that their activities and techniques can be observed. Such files are usually populated with data that looks real, but is actually fake.

Identity and Access Management (IAM): A class of software used to authenticate network users in order to prevent unauthorized access to data or services. Modern identity and access management products often integrate with user directory databases to manage permissions, and utilize multifactor authentication for an extra layer of security.

Industrial Control System (ICS): A blanket term used to describe a collection of programmable logic controllers (PLCs), supervisory control and data acquisition (SCADA) systems, and various other control devices used to manage industrial processes. Industrial control systems interpret data from sensors with command functions and translate these inputs into actions that manipulate devices such as valves, regulators, actuators, relays, or switches.

Information Sharing and Analysis Center (ISAC): A consortium of companies in a particular industry created for the purpose of sharing data about computer security threats and security best practices.

Information Technology (IT): Hardware and software that create, store, retrieve, transmit, and manipulate data.

Intercontinental Ballistic Missile (ICBM): A land-based, guided missile capable of traveling in excess of five thousand kilometers to deploy and detonate one or more nuclear weapons on an enemy target(s).

Internet of Things (IoT): The expanding network of devices that are internet connected. This includes, but is not limited to, devices such as "smart" appliances, networked health-care equipment, and infrastructure monitoring electronics. In the context of cybersecurity, Internet of Things devices are notoriously insecure, and when used in an enterprise or otherwise sensitive setting, can present a significant security risk to an organization.

Islamic State in Syria (ISIS): A name widely used to denote a terrorist organization that calls itself simply Islamic State, and that Arab governments call Daesh. The group occupied and controlled major cities during the 2013–2017 period in Libya, Syria, and Iraq, and had cells elsewhere, including in Yemen and Afghanistan. As of 2019, it continues to exist in underground cells and in remote areas in the Middle East.

Machine Learning (ML): The employment of algorithms to progressively train software models to complete a specific task more effectively. Machine learning is often used to identify spam email, classify images, or, in the case of cybersecurity, detect malicious network traffic.

Malware: Software that causes computers or networks to behave in an unintended manner. Examples of malware include ransomware, Trojans, viruses, keyloggers, and worms.

Managed Security Service Provider (MSSP): A company to which other firms outsource some security of their network.

Multifactor Authentication (MFA): An authentication process that employs more than one authenticating factor to grant a user access to a device, application, network, or database. Multifactor authentication usually requires that users provide something they know, something they have, and something they are. Examples of these factors are passwords (which satisfy the knowledge requirement), one-time log-in codes sent to a user's phone (which satisfy the possession requirement), and fingerprints (which satisfy the inherence requirement). Modern identity and access management software uses multifactor authentication to prevent threat actors from maliciously gaining authenticated access to a network.

National Institute of Standards and Technology (NIST): An agency within the U.S. Department of Commerce known for creating generally accepted norms and procedures (standards), formerly called the Bureau of Weights and Measures.

North American Electric Reliability Council (NERC): An association of electric power generation and distribution companies that issues standards and self-regulatory guidelines for the power industry in the United States and Canada. NERC seeks to preempt and prevent significant government regulation, which, in the United States, would be issued by the Federal Energy Regulatory Commission (FERC).

Operations Technology (OT): Hardware and software designed to facilitate manufacturing processes and infrastructure operations.

P5+1: The five permanent members of the United Nations Security Council (China, France, Russia, the United Kingdom, and the United States) and Germany were the nations that negotiated the nuclear development restrictions agreement with Iran.

Patch: A software update pushed over the internet by the software developer, usually to correct a mistake in code, including errors that may create the possibility of misuse of the software.

People's Liberation Army (PLA): The armed forces of the People's Republic of China.

Personally Identifiable Information (PII): Information about an individual that can be used either on its own or in conjunction with information from other sources to identify the individual. Examples of PII are Social Security numbers, addresses, dates of birth, passport numbers, and more.

Presidential Decision Directive (PDD): A formal policy statement signed by the President of the United States, articulating decisions on a set of national security issues. Traditionally, presidents from the Democratic Party use acronyms beginning with P for this purpose and those from the Republican Party use similar acronyms beginning with N, as in NSPM 13 for National Security Policy Memorandum 13. Bush-era documents are National Security presidential directives and Homeland Security presidential directives. Obama-era documents are presidential policy directives (PPDs).

Privileged Access Management (PAM): See "Identity and Access Management." PAM software protects extremely sensitive data and involves more extensive proof of identity to access that data.

Quantum Computing: Computation that exploits quantum-mechanical phenomena such as superposition performed on particles called qubits. Classical computing operates digitally with bits that are in either an on or off state, 1 or 0. Qubits can be in many states simultaneously, allowing greater computational power.

Ransomware: A form of malware that encrypts critical system files or user data and holds it for ransom, often instructing the user to send a payment in cryptocurrency to the malware author before the encryption key will be released.

ReallyU: A system proposed in this book to verify an identity online or in person using a federated multifactor system created by consortiums of private companies and government agencies.

RSA: The RSA Corporation, now a division of Dell, is a cybersecurity and encryption vendor, which created one of the first public key-encryption systems. Also used to describe a series of annual conferences and exhibitions on cybersecurity. The acronym is derived from the cofounders' names: Rivest, Shamir, and Adleman.

Schengen Accord: A 1985 treaty signed by five of the then ten member states of the European Economic Community that abolished internal border checks, and is the basis for the free movement of EU citizens within the EU. The original agreement was superseded by the Schengen Convention in 1990, which adopted a common visa policy. The Schengen rules were incorporated into EU law in 1999.

Secure Development Life Cycle (SDLC): A set of procedures first developed by Microsoft to ensure that software was developed and then maintained in a secure manner.

Secure Segmented Diverse-Source Microgrid (SSDM): A proposal made in this book to create a system to generate electricity locally, including using alternative energy sources. The SSDM would not be connected to regional or national networks.

Security Operations Center (SOC): A physical location in a corporation where computer security specialists monitor the company's network for signs of intrusion or other threats.

Software as a Service (SaaS): A model in which a customer buys a subscription to use a piece of software for a finite period, contrasted with the license model in which the customer buys and then owns a copy of the software. For SaaS software models, the software may reside online rather than on the customers' own machines.

Stuxnet: The popular name of software allegedly designed and utilized by the United States to destroy certain physical objects, specifically nuclear enrichment centrifuges at Natanz, Iran.

Supervisory Control and Data Acquisition (SCADA): Software for networks of devices that control systems of machines such as valves, pumps, generators, and transformers. SCADA software collects information about the condition and activities of the system, and can use this data to execute commands.

Tabletop Exercise (TTX): Usually a meeting around a large conference table utilizing a fictional scenario, meant to simulate a meeting that would occur if a real event or series of events happened, often called a crisis management event. TTXs are used to train personnel on their crisis roles and responsibilities and to identify gaps in an organization's preparedness or security.

Tailored Access Operations (TAO): An office within the U.S. National Security Agency assigned the task of penetrating foreign information technology networks and targets of special significance or difficulty. TAO was reorganized and merged into Computer Network Operations in 2017.

Threat Actor: An entity that regularly engages in unauthorized penetration of computer networks to access and exfiltrate information or to engage in destructive activities on the network.

Two-Factor Authentication (2FA): A means of proving user identity in order to be granted access to a device, application, network, or database. Two-factor authentication usually requires that users provide something they know, and prove possession of something they have. Examples of these factors are passwords (which satisfy the knowledge requirement) and one-time log-in codes sent to a user's phone (which satisfy the possession requirement). Multi-factor authentication (MFA) sometimes takes this a step further and may include a biometric identification procedure such as a thumbprint, an iris scan, or facial recognition.

Virtual Private Network (VPN): An encrypted pathway or "tunnel" over the internet usually from a remote site, such as one's home, to an organization's primary network. VPNs are thought to be a secure means of accessing corporate databases and applications from off-site and may involve a corporate gateway that examines the security status of the remote computer before granting access.

Wiper: Sometimes rendered "wipr," it is a software attack tool that erases all data found on a device or network in such a manner that the erased data is not recoverable. Wiperware may lurk on a network for days, waiting to be included in a network backup so that when the backup is mounted after an attack, the wiperware will activate and erase that too.

Year Two Thousand (Y2K): Refers to an international effort prior to January 1, 2000, to modify computer software in order to avoid an expected malfunction on that date. There was a belief that failure to modify such software in time would result in widespread failure of software-controlled devices and machinery at 12:01 A.M. of 01/01/2000.

Zero-day vulnerability: A software attack tool that has never been used before and for which, therefore, no defense currently exists. A zero-day attack tool is an exploit that utilizes a previously unused vulnerability in software or hardware. *Zero Days* is also the name of a 2016 documentary film about Stuxnet, directed by Alex Gibney.

Acknowledgments and Disclosures

As we note in the text, the cyber workforce is stretched thin. We observed this firsthand as we tried to schedule time with many of the people who appear in or have otherwise influenced what we write. Meetings were often canceled as incidents popped up or news headlines unfolded. Thus, we are grateful to those who took time to share their insights and experience with us.

In one sense, this book was about a year in development from when our first editor at Penguin Press, Warren Bass, green-lit the project to when we finalized the manuscript with the highly capable Emily Cunningham (we thank them both). In another sense, it was about ten years in the making.

In the decade since we wrote *Cyber War*, we have continued to learn and debate the topic with countless professionals in the field. Too many people have shaped our thinking to list them all here, but we are grateful to the bipartisan community of policy makers who care deeply about this issue and the large pool of practitioners and technologists who have patiently (and sometimes not so patiently) explained to us much of the technical minutiae of how cyberspace works.

Among the many people who helped us with advice, research, or granted us interviews are Ed Amoroso, Konstantinos Karagiannis, Wil Oxford, Bob

Brennan, Jim Gable, Seth Lloyd, Bob Ackerman, Peiter Zatko, Terry Mc-Auliffe, Eric Rosenbach, Chad Rigetti, Chris Weedbrook, Ray Rothrock, Chris Coleman, Simon Rosenberg, John Livingston, Laura Rosenberger, Corey Schou, Phil Dunkelberger, Joe Weiss, Connor Pate, Erin Michelle Perri, Aaron Ach, Aaron Rinehart, Casey Rosenthal, Dan Guido, Adam Shostack, Michael Sechrist, Todd Inskeep, Bill Rose, Bill Phelps, Evan Wolff, John Woods, Phil Venables, Rohan Amin, Jason Healey, Chris Day, Norm Laudermilch, Malcolm Harkins, Dmitri Alperovitch, Dustin Hillard, Fred Wilmot, Bryan Hurd, Jim Routh, Keith Alexander, Gary Gagnon, Jeremy Grant, Ori Eisen, Dave Aitel, Andy Ozment, Neal Jenkins, Sameer Bhalotra, Sounil Yu, Frank DiGiovanni, Evan Dornbush, Larry Zelvin, and Alex Niejelow.

Rob Knake fully acknowledges that many of his views on what the nation needs to do to secure itself were formed in the crucible of the Obama-era cyber office at the National Security Council. Thus, they borrow from the insights (in no particular order) of Howard Schmidt, Miriam Perlberg, Sameer Bhalotra, David Edelman, Peter Lord, Andrew Scott, Robert Novy, Jennifer Silk, Andy Ozment, Tom Donahue, Ryan Gillis, Chris Finan, Eric Greenwald, Ari Schwartz, Aaron Cooper, Naomi Lefkovitz, Zach Nunn, Megan Stifel, Alex Niejelow, Samara Moore, Nathaniel Gleicher, Michael Daniel, Dan Prieto, and Earl Crane.

The crew at Good Harbor Security Risk Management has been a steady source of ideas, comments, research, and encouragement. This book would not have been possible without the diligent work of Tyler Pedigo and Chris Kotyk, researching and editing. Thanks also to Good Harbor president Emilian Papadopoulos, as well as Evan Sills, Jake Gilden, Paul Kumst, and Reda Baig.

Rob Knake would like to thank Jim Lindsay and Adam Segal at the Council on Foreign Relations, and Stephen Flynn and Phil Anderson at Northeastern University's Global Resilience Institute for supporting his work on this book. Matt Cohen and Lorand Lasaki at the Council on Foreign Relations and Akash Patel, Nate Toll, Justin Haner, Rebecca Leeper, Duo Hong, and Emmanuel Ortega at Northeastern University all provided valuable research support.

We also wish to thank those who helped and advised and would rather not be named. They know who they are and that we are grateful.

Because we both are active as cyber consultants and cyber investment advisers, we have also drawn on our day jobs for ideas. Lest anyone think that we have a conflict of interest from any past or current affiliation, in the spirit of full disclosure we note the following relationships: Dick Clarke is an adviser to the Paladin Capital Group, one of the leading cybersecurity venture-capital firms in the United States. He either has been or is now a member of the corporate board of directors or the advisory board of the following cyber-related companies: Akamai, Bit9 + Carbon Black, Multi-Plan, PGP, TruSTAR, Red 5, Veracode, Nok Nok Labs, Wickr, HawkEye 360, BlueCat Networks, and Versive. He has also consulted for a large number of firms, among them the following cyber-product companies: Symantec, Microsoft, RSA, McAfee, and SRA. He has small personal investments in several publicly traded cyber-related companies, including Apple.

As pertaining to companies mentioned in this book, Rob Knake advises Oracle Corporation, of which the Dyn Corporation is a subsidiary and Immensive, Inc. He has been an adviser to Cylance and has done consulting work for Microsoft, Northrop Grumman, and Booz Allen Hamilton. He has also consulted at the Department of Homeland Security as well as having been an employee there.

As required by law and security agreements signed by both authors as a condition of their employment in the White House in past administrations, the text of this book was reviewed by National Security Council staff to prevent any unauthorized disclosure of classified information.

Notes

■■■■■■■

Chapter 1: The Back of the Beast

5 **Venture capital investment in cybersecurity:** Gertrude Chavez-Dreyfuss, "Venture Capital Funding of Cybersecurity Firms Hit Record High in 2018: Report," Reuters, January 17, 2019, www.reuters.com/article/us-usa-cyber -investment/venture-capital-funding-of-cybersecurity-firms-hit-record -high-in-2018-report-idUSKCN1PB163.

5 **Cyber insurance was long:** "Aon: U.S. Cyber Insurance Premiums Rise 37%, to $1.84B," *Claims Journal*, July 11, 2018, www.claimsjournal.com/news/national /2018/07/11/285644.htm.

6 **It is a positive attribute of cyberspace:** For a discussion on the malleability of cyberspace as a man-made domain, see Dorothy Denning, "Rethinking the Cyber Domain and Deterrence," *Joint Force Quarterly* 77 (April 2015), ndupress .ndu.edu/portals/68/documents/jfq/jfq-77/jfq-77_8-15_denning.pdf, and Joseph S. Nye Jr., "Cyber Power," Belfer Center, Harvard Kennedy School, Harvard University, May 2010, www.belfercenter.org/sites/default/files/files/publication /cyber-power.pdf.

8 **By some estimates, the digital economy:** "How Big Is the Digital Economy?," Bureau of Economic Analysis, U.S. Department of Commerce, www.bea.gov /sites/default/files/2018-04/infographic-how-big-is-the-digital-economy.pdf.

8 **McKinsey estimates that:** James Manyika, "Digital Economy: Trends, Opportunities and Challenges," McKinsey Global Institute Research, May 2016,

www.ntia.doc.gov/files/ntia/publications/james_manyika_digital_economy
_deba_may_16_v4.pdf.

10 **Presidential Decision Directive 63:** Presidential Decision Directive/NSC-
63, Critical Infrastructure Protection, May 22, 1998, fas.org/irp/offdocs/pdd/pdd
-63.htm.

12 **Late in the Obama administration:** "Stewardship of IANA Functions Tran-
sitions to Global Internet Community as Contract with U.S. Government Ends,"
ICANN, October 1, 2016, www.icann.org/news/announcement-2016-10-01-en.

13 **The best strategies can be summed up:** We borrowed this idea from Jason
Healey at Columbia University, who attributes it to former National Security
Adviser Brent Scowcroft.

13 **It's the right idea:** Jason Healey called for a "defense-dominant" strategy in a
2017 Atlantic Council report. Again, we like the approach but think the label
is wrong. See Jason Healey, "A Nonstate Strategy for Saving Cyberspace," Atlantic Council Strategy Papers, January 2017, www.atlanticcouncil.org/images
/publications/AC_StrategyPapers_No8_Saving_Cyberspace_WEB.pdf.

14 **the word "resilience":** See, for example, Executive Order 13636 from the
Obama administration, which stated: "It is the policy of the United States to
enhance the security and resilience of the Nation's critical infrastructure...."
"Executive Order—Improving Critical Infrastructure Cybersecurity," White
House, February 12, 2013, obamawhitehouse.archives.gov/the-press-office
/2013/02/12/executive-order-improving-critical-infrastructure-cybersecurity.
See also the Trump administration's National Cyber Strategy, which made
"foster[ing] a vibrant and resilient digital economy" one of its pillars; White
House, September 2018, www.whitehouse.gov/wp-content/uploads/2018/09
/National-Cyber-Strategy.pdf.

14 **an ill-defined and vague concept:** There is a danger with an idea as vague
and open-ended as cyber resilience. If the concept just means accepting that
losses will occur and recovering from them quickly, then it becomes part of the
defeatist attitude in the field. Using a narrow definition, Equifax, which lost
every single one of its hundred-million-plus records of individuals' credit reports, was perfectly resilient. The incident never stopped the company from
collecting more data or from selling it. A year after the breach, the company's
stock had recovered all its losses. While anyone who bought Equifax on the
way down and sold it before third-quarter results came in would have something to celebrate, everyone else impacted by the data breach would have
tarred and feathered any executive at the company who claimed that they were
resilient.

14 **For resilience to be a useful concept:** In his book *Antifragile,* Nassim Taleb
suggested that "antifragility" was the next evolution beyond resilience, that we
want to form businesses and societies that are, in the words of Max Cleland,

"strong at the broken places." Antifragility is the right concept. But it was poor branding. Where the concept of *The Black Swan*, Taleb's previous book, became widely used in business schools and boardrooms, antifragility never did. It's unfortunate because it is the right concept.

15 **Rodin defines resilience as:** Judith Rodin, *The Resilience Dividend: Being Strong in a World Where Things Go Wrong* (New York: PublicAffairs, 2014), 3.

Chapter 2: EternalBlue, Eternal War

17 **patients were sent away:** Damien Gayle, Alexandra Topping, Ian Sample, Sarah Marsh, and Vikram Dodd, "NHS seeks to recover from global cyber-attack as security concerns resurface," *Guardian,* May 13, 2017, www.theguardian.com/society/2017/may/12/hospitals-across-england-hit-by-large-scale-cyber-attack.

18 **National Security Agency's EternalBlue weapon:** Security Response Team, "Petya ransomware outbreak: Here's what you need to know," Symantec Blogs/Threat Intelligence, October 24, 2017, www.symantec.com/blogs/threat-intelligence/petya-ransomware-wiper.

19 **damages cost them almost $900 million:** Andy Greenberg, "The Untold Story of NotPetya, the Most Devastating Cyberattack in History," *Wired*, August 22, 2018, www.wired.com/story/notpetya-cyberattack-ukraine-russia-code-crashed-the-world.

19 **NotPetya was an operation:** Ellen Nakashima, "Russian Military Was Behind 'NotPetya' Cyberattack in Ukraine, CIA Concludes," *Washington Post,* January 12, 2018, wapo.st/2AV5FxW.

21 **cyber tools without his personal approval:** David E. Sanger, "Trump Loosens Secretive Restraints on Ordering Cyberattacks," *New York Times*, September 20, 2018, www.nytimes.com/2018/09/20/us/politics/trump-cyberattacks-orders.html.

21 **removed those restrictions in 2018:** Dustin Volz, "White House Confirms It Has Relaxed Rules on U.S. Use of Cyberweapons," *Wall Street Journal*, September 20, 2018, www.wsj.com/articles/white-house-confirms-it-has-relaxed-rules-on-u-s-use-of-cyber-weapons-1537476729.

22 **One of those recommendations:** Recommendation 30 of the NSA Review Group reads, "We recommend that the National Security Council staff should manage an interagency process to review on a regular basis the activities of the U.S. Government regarding attacks that exploit a previously unknown vulnerability in a computer application or system. These are often called 'Zero Day' attacks because developers have had zero days to address and patch the vulnerability. U.S. policy should generally move to ensure that Zero Days are quickly blocked, so that the underlying vulnerabilities are patched on U.S. Government

and other networks. In rare instances, U.S. policy may briefly authorize using a Zero Day for high priority intelligence collection, following senior, inter-agency review involving all appropriate departments." See "Liberty and Security in a Changing World," Report and Recommendations of the President's Review Group on Intelligence and Communications Technologies, December 12, 2013.

22 **issue a patch for the problem:** Ellen Nakashima and Craig Timberg, "NSA officials worried about the day its potent hacking tool would get loose. Then it did.," *Washington Post*, May 16, 2017, www.washingtonpost.com/business /technology/nsa-officials-worried-about-the-day-its-potent-hacking-tool -would-get-loose-then-it-did/2017/05/16/50670b16-3978-11e7-a058 -ddbb23c75d82_story.html.

22 **walking out of NSA facilities:** Josh Gerstein, "Judge Won't Release Ex-NSA Contractor Accused of Hoarding Classified Data," *Politico*, October 21, 2016, www .politico.com/story/2016/10/hal-harold-martin-nsa-classified-data-230168.

23 **Kaspersky denies that this is what happened:** Shane Harris and Gordon Lubold, "Russian Hackers Stole NSA Data on U.S. Cyber Defense," *Wall Street Journal*, October 5, 2017, www.wsj.com/articles/russian-hackers-stole-nsa-data -on-u-s-cyber-defense-1507222108.

23 **Israel's military intelligence Unit 8200:** Alex Hern and Peter Beaumont, "Israel hack uncovered Russian spies' use of Kaspersky in 2015, report says," *Guardian*, October 11, 2017, www.theguardian.com/technology/2017/oct/11/israel -hack-uncovered-russian-spies-use-kaspersky-lab-2015-report-us-software- federal-government.

24 **no one in the U.S. government:** Brad Smith, "The Need for Urgent Collect-ive Action to Keep People Safe Online: Lessons from Last Week's Cyberat-tack," *Microsoft Blog*, May 14, 2017, blogs.microsoft.com/on-the-issues/2017/05 /14/need-urgent-collective-action-keep-people-safe-online-lessons-last -weeks-cyberattack.

24 **in the Vault 7 documents:** Semantic Security Response, "Longhorn: Tools used by cyberespionage group linked to Vault 7," Symantec Official Blog, April 10, 2017, www.symantec.com/connect/blogs/longhorn-tools-used-cyberespionage -group-linked-vault-7.

24 **groups known as APT 3 and APT 10:** Andrew Griffin, "Wikileaks Files Detail CIA 'Umbrage' Project, Which Would Allow Spies to Pin Attacks on Other Countries," *Independent*, March 8, 2017, www.independent.co.uk/life -style/gadgets-and-tech/news/wikileaks-files-cia-umbrage-hacker-secret -spies-explained-countries-donald-trump-russia-a7618661.html.

25 **most "reckless and indiscriminate":** This quote is attributed to British De-fense Secretary Gavin Williamson, said at a meeting with U.S. Defense Sec-retary Jim Mattis and other defense ministers in Brussels in 2018.

25 **shut down a French television network:** Joseph Menn and Leigh Thomas, "France Probes Russian Lead in TV5Monde Hacking: Sources," *Reuters*, June 10, 2015, reut.rs/1IGfCBo.

26 **"the warning lights are blinking red":** On July 13, 2018, DNI Coats made these statements at a Hudson Institute event regarding cyber threats posed by Russia.

27 **shut down by an Iranian attack:** David Sanger, "US Indicts 7 Iranians in Cyberattacks on Banks and a Dam," *New York Times*, March 24, 2016, www .nytimes.com/2016/03/25/world/middleeast/us-indicts-iranians-in-cyberattacks -on-banks-and-a-dam.html.

27 **lethal chemical leak in the future:** Clifford Krauss and Nicole Perlroth, "A Cyberattack in Saudi Arabia Had a Deadly Goal. Experts Fear Another Try.," *New York Times*, March 15, 2018, www.nytimes.com/2018/03/15/technology /saudi-arabia-hacks-cyberattacks.html.

27 **disrupt other nation's cyber activities:** Robert Chesney, "The 2018 DOD Cyber Strategy: Understanding 'Defense Forward' in Light of the NDAA and PPD-20 Changes," *Lawfare*, September 25, 2018, www.lawfareblog.com/2018 -dod-cyber-strategy-understanding-defense-forward-light-ndaa-and-ppd -20-changes.

Chapter 3: Two Kinds of Companies?

33 **"If we have data":** Nick Theodore, "'We Have Data, Let's Look at Data,'" Virtual Store Trials, June 7, 2017, https://casestudies.storetrials.com/we-have -data-lets-look-at-data-e8a06e2e3331.

34 **Very quickly, CrowdStrike observed:** Joseph Menn, "China Tried to Hack U.S. Firms Even After Cyber Pact: CrowdStrike," *Reuters*, October 19, 2015, www .reuters.com/article/us-usa-china-cybersecurity-idUSKCN0SD0AT20151020.

34 **Alperovitch wrote on the company blog:** Dmitri Alperovitch, "The Latest on Chinese-affiliated Intrusions into Commercial Companies," CrowdStrike, October 19, 2015, www.crowdstrike.com/blog/the-latest-on-chinese-affiliated -intrusions-into-commercial-companies.

36 **significant opponent of Obama-era rules:** Rob Knake and Aitel have a long-running feud over the VEP process. It's complicated. For a more thorough discussion, see Ari Schwartz and Rob Knake, "Government's Role in Vulner-ability Disclosure," Cyber Security Project, Belfer Center, Harvard Kennedy School, Harvard University, June 2016, www.belfercenter.org/sites/default /files/legacy/files/vulnerability-disclosure-web-final3.pdf; Dave Aitel and Matt Tait, "Everything You Know About the Vulnerability Equities Process Is Wrong," *LawFare*, August 18, 2016, www.lawfareblog.com/everything-you-know-about -vulnerability-equities-process-wrong.

37 **Only months after** *Cyber War* **was published:** For a thorough discussion of Stuxnet, see Kim Zetter, *Countdown to Zero Day: Stuxnet and the Launch of the World's First Digital Weapon* (New York: Crown, 2014); for the movie version, see Alex Gibney's 2016 documentary *Zero Days.*

39 **there are seventy-seven Chinese APT groups alone:** APT Groups and Operations is a publicly available Google Sheet maintained by Florian Roth, the CTO at Nextron Systems, a German cybersecurity company. The database can be accessed at docs.google.com/spreadsheets/d/1H9_xaxQHpWaa4O _Son4Gx0YOIzlcBWMsdvePFX68EKU/edit#gid=361554658.

40 **the Department of Health and Human Services:** The Department of Health and Human Services Breach Portal is available at ocrportal.hhs.gov/ocr/breach /breach_report.jsf.

40 **When Inskeep and other researchers:** Inskeep's presentation of this data at the 2018 RSA Conference can be accessed at www.rsaconference.com/events /us18/agenda/sessions/10891-evidence-based-security-the-new-top-five -controls. Knake advised Booz Allen Hamilton on this project.

43 **analysis of public information on cybersecurity incidents:** This analysis was performed by Akash Patel at Northeastern University's Global Resilience Institute, based on data from www.privacyrights.org, www.databreaches.net, www.idtheftcenter.org, ocrportal.hhs.gov, www.krebsonsecurity.com, www .law360.com, and the state attorneys general websites for California, Montana, New Jersey, and New Hampshire.

43 **It is difficult to square the fact that in 2013:** Ellen Nakashima, "U.S. Notified 3,000 Companies in 2013 About Cyberattacks," *Washington Post,* March 24, 2014, www.washingtonpost.com/world/national-security/2014/03/24/74aff686 -aed9-11e3-96dc-d6ea14c099f9_story.html

43 **Keith Alexander, the former director of the NSA:** See Alexander's speech at the American Enterprise Institute, Washington, D.C., July 9, 2012, www.youtube .com/watch?v=JOFk44yy6IQ.

44 **"Basically, you are either dealing with Mossad":** James Mickens, "This World of Ours," Usenix.org, January 2014, www.usenix.org/system/files/1401_08-12 _mickens.pdf.

45 **National Institute of Standards and Technology (NIST, pronounced like "mist"):** The NIST Cybersecurity Framework is available free to the public at www.nist.gov/cyberframework.

45 **known as the 800 series:** NIST Special Publication 800-series General Information, May 21, 2018, www.nist.gov/itl/nist-special-publication-800-series -general-information.

45 **When Inskeep looked at last year's report:** "2017 Data Breach Investigations Report," 10th ed., Verizon, www.ictsecuritymagazine.com/wp-content/uploads /2017-Data-Breach-Investigations-Report.pdf.

Chapter 4: The Kill Chain

49 **"Intelligence-Driven Computer Network Defense":** Eric Hutchins, Michael Cloppert, and Rohan Amin, "Intelligence-Driven Computer Network Defense Informed by Analysis of Adversary Campaigns and Intrusion Kill Chains," Lockheed Martin Corporation, 2011, www.lockheedmartin.com/content/dam /lockheed-martin/rms/documents/cyber/LM-White-Paper-Intel-Driven -Defense.pdf.

58 **He dubbed the chart:** The ATT&CK Matrix is conveniently located at https://attack.mitre.org (there is no ampersand in the web address).

Chapter 5: The Tech Stack

63 **"not built to be used":** Pete Johnson, "#gluecon 2013 Day 2 Recap," June 7, 2013, *Nerd Guru* (blog), https://nerdguru.wordpress.com.

66 **The matrix tries to capture everything:** Yu's presentation of the Cyber Defense Matrix at the 2016 RSA Conference can be found at www.rsaconference .com/writable/presentations/file_upload/pdil-w02f_understanding_the _security_vendor_landscape...-final.pdf.

69 **"Solving Cybersecurity in the Next Five Years":** Yu's presentation at the 2017 RSA Conference can be found at www.youtube.com/watch?v=NckLpAEwkJE.

70 **a concept borrowed from the military:** For a thorough discussion of the OODA loop, see Daniel Ford, *Vision So Noble: John Boyd, the OODA Loop, and America's War on Terror* (n.p.: CreateSpace Independent Publishing Platform, 2010).

72 **DevOps, short for "development and operations":** For a kind and gentle explanation of DevOps (in novel form) see Gene Kim, Kevin Behr, and George Spafford, *The Phoenix Project: A Novel About IT, DevOps, and Helping Your Business Win* (Glenside, Penn.: IT Revolution Press, 2013).

73 **According to data from Spamhaus:** The "Spamhaus Botnet Threat Report 2017" put Amazon at number two on its list, behind the French hosting provider OVH. See www.spamhaus.org/news/article/772/spamhaus-botnet-threat -report-2017; rolling data from Spamhaus provided at www.spamhaus.org /statistics/networks showed Amazon as the number four worst spammer on January 15, 2019.

74 **how to defeat an APT actor:** Rob Joyce's presentation on "Disrupting Nation State Hackers" at USENIX Enigma 2016 conference, January 17, 2016, can be accessed at www.youtube.com/watch?v=bDJb8WOJYdA.

75 **Amoroso, a member of the task force:** "Building a Defensible Cyberspace," Report of the New York Cyber Taskforce, Columbia School of International and Public Affairs, November 2, 2017, sipa.columbia.edu/sites/default/files/3668 _SIPA%20Defensible%20Cyberspace-WEB.PDF.

76 **dubbed Spectre and Meltdown:** For a fuller discussion of Meltdown and Spectre, see Josh Fruhlinger, "Spectre and Meltdown Explained: What They Are, How They Work, What's at Risk," CSO Online, January 15, 2018, www.csoonline .com/article/3247868/vulnerabilities/spectre-and-meltdown-explained-what -they-are-how-they-work-whats-at-risk.html.

77 **Researchers at CrowdStrike uncovered:** See Jason Geffner, "VENOM: Virtualized Environment Neglected Operations Manipulation," CrowdStrike, May 21, 2015, venom.crowdstrike.com.

78 **Mudge Zatko was the de facto leader:** For a fuller treatment, see Dennis Fisher, " 'We Got to Be Cool About This': An Oral History of the LØpht," Duo .com, March 6, 2018, duo.com/decipher/an-oral-history-of-the-l0pht.

79 **Taking a sample of:** Mudge Zatko's PowerPoint presentation of this research at CanSecWest 2013 can be found at cansecwest.com/slides/2013/CanSecWest -Final-Mudge_v1-no-notes.pptx.

81 **By formally defining and verifying:** There are a lot of problems still to be worked out in informal methods. For a thorough discussion, see Kathleen Fisher, "Using Formal Methods to Eliminate Exploitable Bugs," 24th USENIX Security Symposium, August 13, 2015, www.usenix.org/conference/usenixsecurity15 /technical-sessions/presentation/fisher.

Chapter 6: Cyber Resilience: The Best Bad Idea We've Got

85 **The websites of U.S. banks such as JPMorgan:** *United States of America v. Ahmad Fathi,* United States District Court, Southern District of New York, March 24, 2016, www.justice.gov/opa/file/834996/download; Rob Knake has also written about these attacks in "Obama's Cyberdoctrine," *Foreign Affairs,* May 6, 2016, www .foreignaffairs.com/articles/united-states/2016-05-06/obamas-cyberdoctrine.

86 **"We'd like them to act":** Siobhan Gorman and Danny Yadron, "Banks Seek U.S. Help on Iran Cyberattacks," *Wall Street Journal,* January 16, 2013, www.wsj .com/articles/SB10001424127887324734904578244302923178548.

88 **That study, released in 1997:** "Critical Foundations: Protecting America's Infrastructures," Report of the President's Commission on Critical Infrastructure Protection, October 1997, fas.org/sgp/library/pccip.pdf.

89 **President Bush rescinded PDD 63:** Homeland Security Presidential Directive HSPD 7, December 17, 2003, www.energy.gov/oe/downloads/homeland -security-presidential-directive-hspd-7-december-17-2003.

89 **When a bipartisan group chaired by Jim Lewis:** "Securing Cyberspace for the 44th Presidency," report of the CSIS Commission on Cybersecurity for the 44th Presidency, Center for Strategic and International Studies, December 2008, csis-prod.s3.amazonaws.com/s3fs-public/legacy_files/files/media/csis /pubs/081208_securingcyberspace_44.pdf.

89 **Once President Obama came into office:** "Cyberspace Policy Review: Assuring a Trusted and Resilient Information and Communications Infrastructure," White House, May 29, 2009, fas.org/irp/eprint/cyber-review.pdf.

91 **With unusual candor:** Financial data and information on its technology workforce is drawn from JPMorgan's 2017 annual report, www.jpmorganchase .com/corporate/investor-relations/document/annualreport-2017.pdf; data on JPMorgan's cybersecurity spending is from "JPMorgan Chase Competitive Strategy Teardown: How The Bank Stacks Up On Fintech & Innovation," *CBInsights,* January 11, 2018, www.cbinsights.com/research/jpmorgan-chase -competitive-strategy-teardown-expert-intelligence.

92 **As Daniel explained:** Michael J. Daniel's presentation at the 2013 RSA Conference, "007 or DDOS: What Is Real-World Cyber Policy?," https://obama whitehouse.archives.gov/sites/default/files/docs/2013-02-28_final_rsa _speech.pdf.

94 **writing in the** *Financial Times*: Keith Alexander, "A Transatlantic Alliance Is Crucial in an Era of Cyberwarfare," *Financial Times,* September 4, 2018, www .ft.com/content/c01a7f94-af81-11e8-87e0-d84e0d934341.

95 **Alan Charles Raul, the former vice chairman:** Alan Charles Raul, "Cyber-defense Is a Government Responsibility," *Wall Street Journal,* January 5, 2015, www.wsj.com/articles/alan-charles-raul-cyberdefense-is-a-government -responsibility-1420502942.

95 **privacy impact assessments:** "Privacy Impact Assessments,"August 24, 2015, www.dhs.gov/privacy-documents-national-protection-and-programs-direc torate-nppd.

96 **Comprehensive National Cybersecurity Initiative:** "The Comprehensive National Cybersecurity Initiative," https://obamawhitehouse.archives.gov/issues /foreign-policy/cybersecurity/national-initiative.

96 **Enhanced Cybersecurity Services:** More information can be found at www .dhs.gov/enhanced-cybersecurity-services.

96 **This technical reality:** Joel Hruska, "UK Introduces Law to Ban Civilian Encryption, But Government Policies Recommend Its Use," ExtremeTech. com,November4,2015,www.extremetech.com/extreme/217478-uk-introduces -law-to-ban-civilian-encryption-but-government-policies-recommend -its-use.

97 **Nobody paid much attention until:** Corey Bennett, "John Bolton, Cyber Warrior," *Politico,* April 1, 2018, www.politico.com/story/2018/04/01/john-bolton -cyber-hawk-russia-451937.

99 **the Active Cyber Defense Certainty Act:** www.congress.gov/bill/115th -congress/house-bill/4036/text.

100 **In his classic** *The Causes of War*: Stephen Van Evera, *The Causes of War: Power and the Roots of Conflict* (Ithaca, N.Y.: Cornell University Press, 1999).

100 **Allan Friedman and Peter Singer argue:** Allan Friedman and Peter Singer, "Cult of the Cyber Offensive," *Foreign Policy,* January 15, 2014, www.foreignpolicy.com/2014/01/15/cult-of-the-cyber-offensive.

101 **When a group of Wall Street security executives:** "Building a Defensible Cyberspace," New York Cyber Task Force, Columbia School of International and Public Affairs, November 2, 2017, http://sipa.columbia.edu/sites/default/files/3668_SIPA%20Defensible%20Cyberspace-WEB.PDF.

Chapter 7: Nudges and Shoves

109 **the White House delivered to Congress:** "Fact Sheet: Cybersecurity Legislative Proposal," White House, May 12, 2011, obamawhitehouse.archives.gov/the-press-office/2011/05/12/fact-sheet-cybersecurity-legislative-proposal.

110 **The CSIS commission report:** "Securing Cyberspace for the 44th Presidency," Report of the CSIS Commission on Cybersecurity for the 44th Presidency, Center for Strategic and International Studies, December 2008, https://csis-prod.s3.amazonaws.com/s3fs-public/legacy_files/files/media/csis/pubs/081208_securingcyberspace_44.pdf.

111 **She pulled out a copy of a book:** Richard Thaler and Cass Sunstein, *Nudge: Improving Decisions About Health, Wealth, and Happiness* (New York: Penguin, 2009).

113 **Twenty years ago, when President Clinton:** "Defending America's Cyberspace: National Plan for Information Systems Protection," White House, 2000, https://fas.org/irp/offdocs/pdd/CIP-plan.pdf.

113 **Surprisingly, the Department:** U.S. Department of Homeland Security Cybersecurity Strategy, May 15, 2018, www.dhs.gov/sites/default/files/publications/DHS-Cybersecurity-Strategy_1.pdf.

115 **Regulation E of the Electronic Funds Transfer Act:** Robert K. Knake, "No, the FDIC Doesn't Insure Your Bank Account Against Cybercrime (and Why That Is OK)," Council on Foreign Relations, December 2, 2015, www.cfr.org/blog/no-fdic-doesnt-insure-your-bank-account-against-cybercrime-and-why-ok.

116 **The Ponemon Institute:** "2017 Cost of Data Breach Study," Ponemon Institute, June 2017, info.resilientsystems.com/hubfs/IBM_Resilient_Branded_Content/White_Papers/2017_Global_CODB_Report_Final.pdf.

116 **Oil tankers operating in U.S. waters:** Robert K. Knake, "To Prevent Another Equifax Breach, Treat Data Leaks Like Oil Spills," Council on Foreign Relations, September 8, 2017, www.cfr.org/blog/prevent-another-equifax-breach-treat-data-leaks-oil-spills.

117 **California has required since 2012:** "California Attorney General Concludes That Failing to Implement the Center for Internet Security's (CIS) Critical

Security Controls 'Constitutes a Lack of Reasonable Security,'" Center for Internet Security, February 22, 2016, www.prnewswire.com/news-releases/california -attorney-general-concludes-that-failing-to-implement-the-center-for-internet -securitys-cis-critical-security-controls-constitutes-a-lack-of-reasonable -security-300223659.html.

117 **In September 2018, Governor Jerry Brown:** Adi Robertson, "California Just Became the First State with an Internet of Things Cybersecurity Law," The Verge, September 28, 2018, www.theverge.com/2018/9/28/17874768/california -iot-smart-device-cybersecurity-bill-sb-327-signed-law.

117 **Ohio enacted legislation in 2018:** Michael Kassner, "Ohio Law Creates Cybersecurity 'Safe Harbor' for Businesses," TechRepublic, January 3, 2019, www.techrepublic.com/article/ohio-law-creates-cybersecurity-safe-harbor -for-businesses.

117 **New York's Department of Financial Services:** Nate Lord, "What Is the NYDFS Cybersecurity Regulation? A Cybersecurity Compliance Requirement for Financial Institutions," Digital Guardian, January 3, 2019, digitalguardian .com/blog/what-nydfs-cybersecurity-regulation-new-cybersecurity-compliance -requirement-financial.

120 **According to Chris Demchak:** Chris C. Demchak and Yuval Shavitt, "China's Maxim—Leave No Access Point Unexploited: The Hidden Story of China Telecom's BGP Hijacking," *Military Cyber Affairs* 3, no. 1, article 7 (2018), doi .org/10.5038/2378-0789.3.1.1050.

120 **regularly redirecting internet traffic:** Justin Sherman, "Hijacking the Internet Is Far Too Easy," *Slate*, November 16, 2018, slate.com/technology/2018/11 /bgp-hijacking-russia-china-protocols-redirect-internet-traffic.html.

121 **Zurich, the big Swiss insurance company:** Steve Evans, "Mondelez's Not-Petya Cyber Attack Claim Disputed by Zurich," Reinsurance News, December 17, 2018, www.reinsurancene.ws/mondelezs-notpetya-cyber-attack-claim-disputed -by-zurich-report.

126 **According to the Royal Canadian Mounted Police:** "Ransomware: Recognize, Reject, and Report It!," Royal Canadian Mounted Police, Scams and Frauds, accessed on January 15, 2019, www.rcmp-grc.gc.ca/scams-fraudes/ransomware -rancongiciels-eng.htm#fn1.

126 **The two Iranians wrote:** "SamSam Subjects," wanted poster, Federal Bureau of Investigation, accessed on January 15, 2019, www.fbi.gov/wanted/cyber/samsam -subjects.

126 **declined to pay the fifty-thousand-dollar demand:** Chris Teale, "Atlanta Mayor Says Cyberattack Came as 'Surprise' to City, Residents," Smart Cities Dive, May 11, 2018, www.smartcitiesdive.com/news/atlanta-cyberattack-surprise -Keisha-Lance-Bottoms/523323.

Chapter 8: Is It Really You?

129 **"rely less and less on passwords"**: Munir Kotadia, "Gates Predicts Death of the Password," CNET, February 25, 2004, www.cnet.com/news/gates-predicts-death-of-the-password.

130 **President Bush signed:** Homeland Security Presidential Directive 12: Policy for a Common Identification Standard for Federal Employees and Contractors, White House, August 27, 2004, www.dhs.gov/homeland-security-presidential-directive-12.

134 **So can anyone else with that information:** "Key IRS Identity Theft Indicators Continue Dramatic Decline in 2017; Security Summit Marks 2017 Progress Against Identity Theft," Internal Revenue Service, February 8, 2018, www.irs.gov/newsroom/key-irs-identity-theft-indicators-continue-dramatic-decline-in-2017-security-summit-marks-2017-progress-against-identity-theft.

134 **One of the first initiatives:** "National Strategy for Trusted Identities in Cyberspace," White House, April 2011, www.hsdl.org/?view&did=7010.

136 **Grant has helped bring together:** See Better Identity Coalition, About Us, www.betteridentity.org.

Chapter 9: Fixing the People Problem

152 **fifty thousand new cybersecurity practitioners:** "Report on Securing and Growing the Digital Economy," Commission on Enhancing National Cybersecurity" December 1, 2016, obamawhitehouse.archives.gov/sites/default/files/docs/cybersecurity_report.pdf.

Chapter 10: Power Grids and Power Plays

156 **Bush's 2003 National Strategy to Secure Cyberspace:** "The National Strategy to Secure Cyberspace," White House, February 2003, www.us-cert.gov/sites/default/files/publications/cyberspace_strategy.pdf.

157 **an internet worm:** "Final Report on the August 14, 2003 Blackout in the United States and Canada: Causes and Recommendations," U.S.-Canada Power System Outage Task Force, U.S. Department of Energy, April 2004, www.energy.gov/sites/prod/files/oeprod/DocumentsandMedia/BlackoutFinal-Web.pdf.

157 **a generator was attacked:** Emanuel Bernabeu and Farid Katiraei, "Aurora Vulnerability: Issues and Solutions," Quanta Technology and Dominion, July 24, 2011, www.smartgrid.gov/files/Aurora_Vulnerability_Issues_Solution_Hardware_Mitigation_De_201102.pdf.

157 **Russian hackers plunged much of Ukraine:** Jim Finkle, "US Firm Blames Russian 'Sandworm' Hackers for Ukraine Outage," Reuters, January 7, 2016, reut.rs/1OebtCB.

157 **Bruce Willis's *Live Free or Die Hard*:** In the movie, Bruce Willis squared off against a villainous ex-government cybersecurity expert that Manohla Dargis thought was inspired by Clarke. Manohla Dargis, "Pick Your Poison: Fists or Fireballs," *New York Times*, June 27, 2007, www.nytimes.com/2007/06/27/movies /27hard.html.

158 **lower the threshold of incident reporting:** "FERC Requires Expanded Cybersecurity Incident Reporting," Federal Energy Regulatory Commission, July 19, 2018, www.ferc.gov/media/news-releases/2018/2018-3/07-19-18-E -1.asp.

165 **DoD Missile Defense Agency:** "Historical Funding for MDA FY85-17," U.S. Department of Defense Missile Defense Agency, accessed January 8, 2019, mda .mil/global/documents/pdf/FY17_histfunds.pdf.

165 **Congress approved $11.5 billion:** Mike Stone, "U.S. Missile Defense Agency Budget Boosted to $11.5 Billion," Reuters, March 22, 2018, reut.rs/2GdhC8R.

166 **upwards of $140 billion:** Jeff Daniels, "Competition to Replace US Nuclear Missiles Is Down to 2 Companies, but Uncertainties Remain," CNBC, August 22, 2017, cnb.cx/2xaP8oY.

Chapter 12: The Military, Domains, and Dominance

182 **cyber operations to the Pentagon:** Ellen Nakashima, "White House authorizes 'offensive cyber operations' to deter foreign adversaries," *Washington Post*, September 20, 2018, www.washingtonpost.com/world/national-security/trump -authorizes-offensive-cyber-operations-to-deter-foreign-adversaries-bolton -says/2018/09/20/b5880578-bd0b-11e8-b7d2-0773aa1e33da_story.html.

182 **President Obama had reined in cyber operations:** David E. Sanger, "Pentagon Puts Cyberwarriors on the Offensive, Increasing Risk of Conflict," *New York Times*, June 17, 2018, www.nytimes.com/2018/06/17/us/politics/cyber -command-trump.html.

184 **five stated objectives:** "1. Ensuring the Joint Force can achieve its missions in a contested cyberspace environment; 2. Strengthening the Joint Force by conducting cyberspace operations that enhance U.S. military advantages; 3. Defending U.S. critical infrastructure from malicious cyber activity that alone, or as part of a campaign, could cause a significant cyber incident; 4. Securing DoD information and systems against malicious cyber activity, including DoD information on non-DoD-owned networks; and 5. Expanding DoD cyber cooperation with interagency, industry, and international partners." See "Summary: Department of Defense Cyber Strategy 2018," U.S. Department of

Defense, September 2018, media.defense.gov/2018/Sep/18/2002041658/-1/-1
/1/CYBER_STRATEGY_SUMMARY_FINAL.PDF.

188 **Iran did penetrate:** Julian E. Barnes and Siobhan Gorman, "U.S. Says Iran
Hacked Navy Computers," *Wall Street Journal,* September 27, 2013, www.wsj
.com/articles/us-says-iran-hacked-navy-computers-1380314771.

188 **successfully used wiper hacks:** Lily Hay Newman, "The Iran Hacks Cybersecurity Experts Feared May Be Here," *Wired,* December 18, 2018, www.wired
.com/story/iran-hacks-nuclear-deal-shamoon-charming-kitten.

189 **issued a scathing report:** "Weapon Systems Cybersecurity," Report to the
Committee on Armed Services, U.S. Senate, GAO-19-128, Government Accountability Office, October 2018, www.gao.gov/assets/700/694913.pdf.

189 **USS *Freedom*-class combatants are vulnerable to hacking:** Andrea Shalal-
Esa, "Cyber vulnerabilities found in Navy's newest warship: official," Reuters,
April 23, 2013, www.reuters.com/article/us-usa-cybersecurity-ship/cyber
-vulnerabilities-found-in-navys-newest-warship-official-idUSBRE93N02X
20130424.

189 **Naval Undersea Warfare Center in Rhode Island:** Gordon Lubold and
Dustin Volz, "Navy, Industry Partners are 'Under Cyber Siege' by Chinese
Hackers, Review Asserts," *Wall Street Journal,* March 12, 2019, www.wsj.com
/articles/navy-industry-partners-are-under-cyber-siege-review-asserts
-11552415553.

190 **Windows XP operating system:** Jeremy Hsu, "Why the Military Can't Quit
Windows XP," *Slate,* June 4, 2018, slate.com/technology/2018/06/why-the
-military-cant-quit-windows-xp.html.

190 **Among the weapons systems compromised:** Caitlin Dewey, "The US Weapons Systems That Experts Say Were Hacked by the Chinese," *Washington Post,*
May 28, 2013, wapo.st/18qIQBk.

193 **he was "largely disappointed":** Ash Carter, "A Lasting Defeat: The Campaign
to Destroy ISIS," Belfer Center, Harvard Kennedy School, Harvard University,
October 2017, www.belfercenter.org/publication/lasting-defeat-campaign
-destroy-isis.

193 **operations without his personal approval:** David E. Sanger, "Trump Loosens Secretive Restraints on Ordering Cyberattacks," New York Times, September 20, 2018, www.nytimes.com/2018/09/20/us/politics/trump-cyberattacks
-orders.html.

194 **The CIA and the NSA did:** James Bamford, "NSA Snooping Was Only the
Beginning. Meet the Spy Chief Leading Us into Cyberwar," *Wired,* June 12,
2013, www.wired.com/2013/06/general-keith-alexander-cyberwar.

194 **authorized a contingency plan:** David E. Sanger and Mark Mazzetti, "U.S.
Had Cyberattack Plan If Iran Nuclear Dispute Led to Conflict," *New York Times,*

February 16, 2016, www.nytimes.com/2016/02/17/world/middleeast/us-had
-cyberattack-planned-if-iran-nuclear-negotiations-failed.html.

195 **They were not given that authority until 2018:** Robert Chesney, "The
2018 DOD Cyber Strategy: Understanding 'Defense Forward' in Light of
the NDAA and PPD-20 Changes," Lawfare, September 25, 2018, www.lawfareblog
.com/2018-dod-cyber-strategy-understanding-defense-forward-light-ndaa
-and-ppd-20-changes.

195 **In the 2018 Department of Defense Cyber Strategy:** "Department of Defense Cyber Strategy Summary," Department of Defense, 2018, https://media
.defense.gov/2018/Sep/18/2002041658/-1/-1/1/CYBER_STRATEGY
_SUMMARY_FINAL.PDF.

195 **North Korean ballistic missile tests:** David E. Sanger and William J. Broad,
"Trump Inherits a Secret Cyberwar Against North Korean Missiles," *New York
Times,* March 4, 2017, www.nytimes.com/2017/03/04/world/asia/north-korea
-missile-program-sabotage.html.

196 **authority to the Department of Defense:** Dakota S. Rudesill, "Trump's Secret
Order on Pulling the Cyber Trigger," *Lawfare,* August 29 2018, www.lawfareblog
.com/trumps-secret-order-pulling-cyber-trigger.

Chapter 13: A Schengen Accord for the Internet

205 **"Cyberspace is not borderless":** Author interview with Michael Daniel, 2019.

205 **Eric Schmidt thinks the internet:** Lora Kolodny, "Former Google CEO Predicts the Internet Will Split in Two—And One Part Will Be Led by China,"
CNBC, September 20, 2018, www.cnbc.com/2018/09/20/eric-schmidt-ex
-google-ceo-predicts-internet-split-china.html.

205 **the *New York Times* editorial board:** Editorial Board, "There May Soon Be
Three Internets. America's Won't Necessarily Be the Best," *New York Times,*
October 15, 2018, www.nytimes.com/2018/10/15/opinion/internet-google
-china-balkanization.html.

205 **"open, interoperable, secure, and reliable":** "International Strategy for Cyberspace: Prosperity, Security, and Openness in a Networked World," White House,
May 2011, https://obamawhitehouse.archives.gov/sites/default/files/rss_viewer
/international_strategy_for_cyberspace.pdf.

206 **While Russia announced plans:** Tracy Staedter, "Why Russia Is Building Its
Own Internet," IEEE Spectrum, January 17, 2018, spectrum.ieee.org/tech-talk
/telecom/internet/could-russia-really-build-its-own-alternate-internet.

206 **as of the spring of 2019:** Catalin Cimpanu, "Russia to disconnect from the
internet as part of a planned test," ZDNet, February 11, 2019, www.zdnet.com
/article/russia-to-disconnect-from-the-internet-as-part-of-a-planned-test.

209 **When Yahoo told France:** For an excellent discussion on this topic, see Tim Wu and Jack Goldsmith, *Who Controls the Internet? Illusions of a Borderless World* (New York: Oxford University Press, 2006).

210 **UN's Group of Governmental Experts:** Elaine Korzak, "UN GGE on Cybersecurity: The End of an Era?," *The Diplomat*, July 31, 2017, https://thediplomat .com/2017/07/un-gge-on-cybersecurity-have-china-and-russia-just-made -cyberspace-less-safe.

211 **"offered the best chance for the UK":** Asa Bennett, "Did Britain really vote Brexit to cut immigration?," *Telegraph*, June 29, 2016, www.telegraph.co.uk/news /2016/06/29/did-britain-really-vote-brexit-to-cut-immigration.

213 **The attempt to jettison NAFTA:** For an overview of these provisions, see Anupam Chander, "The Coming North American Digital Trade Zone," Council on Foreign Relations, October 9, 2018, www.cfr.org/blog/coming-north -american-digital-trade-zone.

213 **As Michael Geist:** Michael Geist, "How the USMCA falls short on digital trade, data protection and privacy," *Washington Post*, October 3, 2018, www .washingtonpost.com/news/global-opinions/wp/2018/10/03/how-the-usmca -falls-short-on-digital-trade-data-protection-and-privacy.

214 **The CLOUD Act, passed:** For a solid overview of the Cloud Act see Jennifer Daskal and Peter Swire, "Why the Cloud Act Is Good for Privacy and Human Rights," *Lawfare*, March 14, 2018, www.lawfareblog.com/why-cloud-act-good -privacy-and-human-rights.

Chapter 14: Democracy's Shield

219 **"Brush your teeth":** Andy Greenberg, "Hacked or Not, Audit This Election (And All Future Ones)," *Wired*, November 23, 2016, www.wired.com/2016/11 /hacked-not-audit-election-rest.

219 **Chen revealed his findings:** Adrian Chen, "The Agency," *New York Times*, June 2, 2015, www.nytimes.com/2015/06/07/magazine/the-agency.html.

220 **what the Internet Research Agency was doing:** Ellen Nakashima, "US Cyber Command Operation Disrupted Internet Access of Russian Troll Factory on Day of 2018 Midterms," *Washington Post*, February 27, 2019, www.washingtonpost .com/world/national-security/us-cyber-command-operation-disrupted -internet-access-of-russian-troll-factory-on-day-of-2018-midterms/2019/02 /26/1827fc9e-36d6-11e9-af5b-b51b7ff322e9_story.html.

221 **"Their [U.S. adversaries'] dream":** Alex Stamos, "The Battle for the Soul of the Internet," National Security and Technology Congressional Briefing Series, Washington, D.C., November 15, 2018.

224 **an action plan for defending against hybrid war:** Jamie Fly, Laura Rosenberger, and David Salvo, "The ASD Policy Blueprint for Countering Authori-

tarian Interference in Democracies," German Marshall Fund of the United States, June 26, 2018, www.gmfus.org/publications/asd-policy-blueprint-countering -authoritarian-interference-democracies.

226 **went on to write a playbook:** "Cybersecurity Campaign Playbook," Belfer Center, Harvard Kennedy School, Harvard University, November 2017, www .belfercenter.org/publication/cybersecurity-campaign-playbook.

227 **would give up and go home:** Michael Powell and Peter Slevin, "Several Factors Contributed to 'Lost' Voters in Ohio," *Washington Post,* December 15, 2004, www.washingtonpost.com/wp-dyn/articles/A64737-2004Dec14.html.

228 **Russians attempted to break into:** Cynthia McFadden, William M. Arkin, and Kevin Monahan, "Russians Penetrated U.S. Voter Systems, Top U.S. Official Says," NBC News, February 7, 2018, www.nbcnews.com/politics/elections /russians-penetrated-u-s-voter-systems-says-top-u-s-n845721.

228 **"state IT officials":** Stamos, "The Battle for the Soul of the Internet."

233 **the American people do not:** Ellen Nakashima, "U.S. cyber force credited with helping stop Russia from undermining midterms," *Washington Post,* February 14, 2019, www.washingtonpost.com/world/national-security/us-cyber-force -credited-with-helping-stop-russia-from-undermining-midterms/2019/02/14 /ceef46ae-3086-11e9-813a-0ab2f17e305b_story.html.

Chapter 15: Real and Artificial Intelligence

239 **"Whoever becomes the leader":** Vladimir Putin made these remarks at National Knowledge Day while speaking to students in the Yaroslavl region of the Russian Federation in September 2017, https://ruptly.tv/#/videos/20170901-032.

242 **the birthplace of AI:** James Moor, "The Dartmouth College Artificial Intelligence Conference: The Next Fifty Years," *AI Magazine* 27, no. 4 (December 2006): 87–89.

249 **bans autonomous weapons:** "Autonomy in Weapon Systems," Department of Defense Directive Number 3000.09, U.S. Department of Defense, May 8, 2017, www.esd.whs.mil/Portals/54/Documents/DD/issuances/dodd/300009p.pdf.

250 **"generative adversarial network" to fool other software:** Omid Poursaeed et al., "Generative Adversarial Perturbations," *CVPR* (2018), vision.cornell.edu /se3/wp-content/uploads/2018/03/2387.pdf.

250 **AI attack program called DeepLocker:** Marc Ph. Stoecklin, with Jiyong Jang and Dhilung Kirat, "DeepLocker: How AI Can Power a Stealthy New Breed of Malware," IBM.com, August 8, 2018, securityintelligence.com/deep locker-how-ai-can-power-a-stealthy-new-breed-of-malware.

Chapter 16: A Quantum of Solace for Security

255 **the famous double-slit experiment:** "The Quantum Experiment That Broke Reality," *Space Time*, PBS Digital Studios, July 27, 2016, youtu.be/p-MNSLsjjdo.

256 **Chinese scientists created two entangled photons:** Juan Yin et al., "Satellite-Based Entanglement Distribution over 1200 Kilometers," *Science* 356, no. 6343 (June 2017): 1140–44.

259 **The Chinese government has what:** Stephen Chen, "China Building World's Biggest Quantum Research Facility," *South China Morning Post,* September 11, 2017, www.scmp.com/news/china/society/article/2110563/china-building-worlds -biggest-quantum-research-facility.

261 **quantum-resistant encryption standard:** "Post-Quantum Cryptography," National Institute of Standards and Technology, CSRM.NIST.com, accessed January 4, 2019, csrc.nist.gov/projects/post-quantum-cryptography.

Chapter 17: 5G and IoT

266 **quarter trillion dollars:** Hillol Roy, "Tackling the Cost of a 5G Build," Accenture, August 3, 2018, www.accenture.com/us-en/insights/strategy/5G -network-build.

268 **publicly published 132 questions:** "Promoting Unlicensed Use of the 6 Ghz Band," Notice of Proposed Rulemaking, Federal Communications Commission, October 2, 2018, https://docs.fcc.gov/public/attachments/DOC-354364A1.pdf.

268 **"It is widely expected that 5G networks":** Federal Communications Commission, "Fifth Generation Wireless Network and Device Security," *Federal Register* 82, no.13 (January 23, 2017): 7825–30, www.govinfo.gov/content/pkg /FR-2017-01-23/pdf/2017-01325.pdf.

269 **farmers learned that hackers:** Jason Koebler, "Why American Farmers Are Hacking Their Tractors with Ukrainian Firmware," *Motherboard,* March 21, 2017, motherboard.vice.com/en_us/article/xykkkd/why-american-farmers-are -hacking-their-tractors-with-ukrainian-firmware.

275 **in a petrochemical plant in Saudi Arabia:** David E. Sanger, "Hack of Saudi Petrochemical Plant Was Coordinated from Russian Institute," *New York Times,* October 23, 2018, www.nytimes.com/2018/10/23/us/politics/russian -hackers-saudi-chemical-plant.html.

275 **"third-party control risk":** Warning letter to Abbott Laboratories from the Food and Drug Administration, April 12, 2017, www.fda.gov/iceci/enforce mentactions/warningletters/2017/ucm552687.htm.

278 **issuing regulations requiring such assurances:** Colin Dwyer, "Department of Transportation Rolls Out New Guidelines for Self-Driving Cars," National Public Radio, September 12, 2017, www.npr.org/sections/the-two-way/2017/09

/12/550533833/department-of-transportation-rolls-out-new-guidelines-for
-self-driving-cars.

Chapter 18: Derisking Ourselves

285 **We like ten-character passwords:** "How to Choose a Password," Office of
Information Security, University of Cincinnati, accessed January 6, 2019,
www.uc.edu/infosec/password/choosepassword.html.
286 **Fraudulent debit-card charges:** "Lost or Stolen Credit, ATM, and Debit
Cards," Consumer Information, Federal Trade Commission, August 2012, www
.consumer.ftc.gov/articles/0213-lost-or-stolen-credit-atm-and-debit-cards.

Chapter 19: Everything Done but the Coding

295 **released its International Strategy for Cyberspace:** "International Strategy
for Cyberspace," White House, May 2011, obamawhitehouse.archives.gov/sites
/default/files/rss_viewer/international_strategy_for_cyberspace.pdf.
295 **a simple conclusion:** Matthew G. Devost, Jeff Moss, Neal A. Pollard, and
Robert J. Stratton III, "All Done Except the Coding: Implementing the International Strategy for Cyberspace," *Georgetown Journal of International Affairs*
(2011), 197–208, www.jstor.org/stable/43133830?seq=1#page_scan_tab_contents.

Index

.....